Intuitive Thinking
as a Spiritual Path

A Philosophy of Freedom

Why is it so difficult
to accept criticism? Why
can't we see travail as
an opportunity for growth?

If we know + feel anxiety
why can't we control it +
understand consequences?

How do we develop
trust in the universe? In
the spiritual beings? Can we
live in the uncertainty to there
a spiritual world + if we don't
know how can we trust?

CLASSICS IN ANTHROPOSOPHY

The Spiritual Guidance of the Individual and Humanity

Theosophy

How To Know Higher Worlds

INTUITIVE THINKING
AS A SPIRITUAL PATH

RUDOLF STEINER

A Philosophy of Freedom

Translated by MICHAEL LIPSON

ANTHROPOSOPHIC PRESS

This volume is a translation of *Die Philosophie der Freiheit* (Vol. 4 in the Bibliographic Survey, 1961) published by Rudolf Steiner Verlag, Dornach, Switzerland. The previous translation of this text in English was published as *The Philosophy of Spiritual Activity* by Anthroposophic Press, Hudson, N.Y., 1986.

Published by Anthroposophic Press, Inc.
RR 4, Box 94 A-1, Hudson, N.Y. 12534

Library of Congress Cataloging-in-Publication Data

Steiner, Rudolf, 1861–1925.
    [Philosophie der Freiheit. English]
    Intuitive thinking as a spiritual path : philosophy of freedom /
  Rudolf Steiner ; translated by Michael Lipson.
      p. cm.—(Classics in anthroposophy)
      Includes index.
      ISBN 0-88010-385-X (pbk.)
      1. Anthroposophy. I. Title. II. Series.
    BP595.S894P4613   1995   95-7753
    299'.935—dc20   CIP

Cover painting and design: Barbara Richey

10 9 8 7 6 5 4 3 2 1

Printed in the United States of America

CONTENTS

Translator's Introduction   *vii*

Introduction by Gertrude Reif Hughes   *xiii*

Preface to the Revised Edition, 1918   *1*

PART I : THEORY
The Knowledge of Freedom

1. Conscious Human Action   *5*

2. The Fundamental Urge for Knowledge   *18*

3. Thinking in the Service of Understanding
   the World   *27*

4. The World as Percept   *49*

5. Knowing the World   *73*

6. Human Individuality   *97*

7. Are There Limits to Cognition?   *104*

PART II : PRACTICE
The Reality of Freedom

  8. The Factors of Life   *127*

  9. The Idea of Freedom   *135*

10. Freedom-Philosophy and Monism   *163*

11. World Purpose and Life Purpose
    (Human Destiny)   *173*

12. Moral Imagination
    (Darwinism and Ethics)   *180*

13. The Value of Life
    (Pessimism and Optimism)   *194*

14. Individuality and Genus   *225*

FINAL QUESTIONS
The Consequences of Monism   *231*

Appendices (1918)   *243*

Bibliography   *259*
Index   *263*

Michael Lipson

The real heartbreak of translation does not come from the distance between German and English, but from the gap between spiritual and word-bound consciousness. It was Steiner's life-long sacrifice to engage in *this* translation, the constriction of spirit into speech. Whether the language he had to use was philosophical, theosophical, or any other, he remained painfully aware of the impossibility of his task.[1]

In each year of his life after 1900, Steiner continued to recommend this book (formerly called simply *The Philosophy of Freedom*) as well as his other epistemological works to his students.[2] He insisted that his later "occult" communications presupposed, as a first step to

---

1. Georg Kühlewind, *Working with Anthroposophy* (Hudson, NY: The Anthroposophic Press, 1992). See Rudolf Steiner, *Der Tod als Lebenswandlung*, GA 182, Lecture of 16 October 1918, Zurich.
2. Otto Palmer, *Rudolf Steiner on his book The Philosophy of Freedom* (Spring Valley, NY: The Anthroposophic Press, 1975).

understanding them, the radical change in *thinking* consciousness for which this book can serve as a partial training manual. A transformation of consciousness appropriate to our age begins with the intensification of thinking as we know it in ordinary mental life; it moves beyond, but never denies, the achievements of Western philosophy.

Yet Steiner was capable of calling the book a "stammering"—not in false modesty, but to acknowledge that what we say about higher kinds of cognition is inevitably partial and easily susceptible to distortion. A book like *Intuitive Thinking as a Spiritual Path* can incite or goad us into inner practices, but it does not even attempt to deliver a fixed content for us to possess. Further, as Steiner emphasized in one lecture, "I surely know that this *Philosophy of Freedom* bears all the pockmarks of the children's diseases that afflicted the life of thinking as it developed in the course of the nineteenth century."[3]   It therefore has both intrinsic, and cultural / historical, grounds for a certain incompleteness.

It is an incompleteness we, the readers, are called upon to remedy. For Steiner approached the problem of spiritual expression in a supremely tactical way. Instead of establishing a fixed terminology to give his meaning a specious uniformity, he took the opposite course. Without fanfare, he used ordinary words, like "thinking," "feeling," and "willing," to denote processes of cosmic proportions. Without indicating his shifts, he used such

---

3. Rudolf Steiner, Lecture of December 19, 1919 (GA 333).

words now in the humblest, now in the most exalted sense. And he was content to use several different words, at different times, to express similar meanings. The cumulative effect of these maneuvers is to encourage the reader to develop an especially active style of reading: "How does he mean this?" is a question we should often find ourselves asking. At the end of Chapter 7, Steiner gives explicit prominence to the question of vocabulary, and puts us on notice that he will use language with a rare sense of license. He thus anticipates the constructivists and hermeneuts of our own day, by setting the responsibility for the effects of the book on us, his readers.

The current translation attempts to make the text as contemporary in sound and style as possible while preserving accuracy. This effort owes much to the editorial assistance of Christopher Bamford and Andrew Cooper, as well as an enormous debt to all previous translations, especially that of Michael Wilson.[4] Many happy formulations have been simply lifted from that book, because I could not match, much less improve them. Interested readers should also refer to Wilson's helpful notes on some of the words that present difficulties of translation and interpretation. Among these are *Geist*, here most often rendered as "spirit"; *Vorstellung/Vorstellen*, here most often "mental picture/mental picturing"; *Erkennen*, here "cognition" or "cognizing"; *Wollen*, "wishing," "wanting," "willing"; *Begriff,* "concept"; and *Wahrnehmung*, "percept." These especially thorny words, like others, are given variously

---

4. London: Rudolf Steiner Press, 1963.

in English depending on the meaning they take in each passage. Of these, only "cognizing" for *Erkennen* represents a real break with previous translations. I use "cognition" and "cognizing," despite their Latinate, alienated quality, because they convey the mind's active grasp of specific meanings in a way that "knowledge" or "knowing" do not. The act of "cognizing," rather than the relatively passive "knowing," fits better to a text Steiner originally hoped would bear the English title, *The Philosophy of Spiritual Activity*.[5]

By suggesting an alternate title in English, Steiner again proved himself flexible regarding terminology. We have taken this as permission to retranslate the title and we have called it, this time, *Intuitive Thinking as a Spiritual Path: A Philosophy of Freedom*. The new title emphasizes the unique focus of Steiner's work, among all the spiritual movements of our time, on the development of thinking consciousness into something altogether different from its manifestation in ordinary mental life. The thinking appropriate to an understanding of the perceptual world necessarily includes a development in how we perceive, and so we could also have used some such title as *Intuitive Thinking and Perceiving as a Spiritual Path*, if it were not both awkward and hard to understand. It is clear from Steiner's emphasis on the two "directions" from which experience comes to meet us that both thinking and perceiving are susceptible of infinite exercise and development.

---

5. Cf. Wilson, p.xiv.

Despite terminological fluidity, Steiner was exact in his use of the words *wahr* (true) and *wirklich* (real). Truth, as a feeling, applies to our sense of the world of thinking; the real, as a feeling, applies to our sense of the world of perception. Cognition of the kind Steiner points to in this book brings us to a new world of "true reality" that involves both the evidentiary clarity of thought (truth) and perception (the real). I have therefore tried to translate these terms consistently, even when it does some violence to English usage, to underscore the precise duality Steiner indicates and overcomes.

I have also tried to preserve Steiner's implicature. He had many ways of hinting, rather than declaring— subtly alerting us to knowable, if elusive, sources of the known world. One technique was his frequent use of the outmoded "that which" (*dasjenige, was*) construction (as in, "that which we can form mental pictures about.") [6] I have resisted the linguistic pressure to collapse such constructions and dry out their suggestiveness. They bear a lineal and substantive relation to the great "that which" of I John 1:1, "That which was from the beginning, which we have heard, which we have seen with our eyes, which we have looked upon, and our hands have handled, of the Word of life ...."

---

6. Cf. *Dokumente zur Philosophie der Freiheit* (Dornach, Switzerland: Rudolf Steiner Verlag, 1994) pp. 40 and 90 *et passim*, where Steiner's 1918 revisions to the text emphasize the importance of just this construction.

We should recall that Steiner's goal was to stimulate the exercise of a thinking independent not only from words, but from the physical body and brain.[7] In keeping with this goal, we are well justified in re-translating *Intuitive Thinking as a Spiritual Path* into English from time to time, both to reflect evolving understandings of the book and to liberate ourselves from a nominalistic equation of words with concepts. In this way, we have an advantage over German-language readers, who are tempted to imagine their version of the text as final. By approaching Steiner through inadequate and changing English terms, we are the more likely to face the inadequacy of all terms, and leap to his meaning.

---

7.   Rudolf Steiner, GA 163, Lecture of August 30, 1915.

Gertrude Reif Hughes

Rudolf Steiner's study of human freedom is really a study of human ways of knowing. Steiner made knowledge a key to freedom and individual responsibility, because he discovered that the processes of cognition, which he usually just called "thinking," share an essential quality with the essence of selfhood or individuality: each could, in some sense, know itself. Accordingly, his "philosophy" of freedom is actually a meditation on human capacities to know and on individuality as a basis for socially responsible action. These three elements—freedom, thinking, and individuality—interweave in Steiner's work like three strands of a single braid, uniting through their dynamic cooperations the subtle interconnections of a complex and powerful vision.

Steiner's argument may sound technical, as though one needs to be particularly competent in epistemology or the history of philosophy to follow him. In fact, expert knowledge may be a hindrance. His book is designed to stimulate more than to instruct. If it is read responsively but without the distractions of either assent or dissent, it arouses confidence in the possibility of human free will and a desire to work toward developing it.

Steiner is interested in freedom as a creative force. Instead of focusing on the various legal, biological, or cultural conditions that foster or inhibit freedom, he presents it as a potential for human beings to realize more and more fully in their personal and interpersonal lives. Every chapter of his book calls us to become free by recognizing and developing the spiritual nature of our human cognitive powers.

In his preface to the revised edition of 1918, published on the book's twenty-fifth anniversary, Steiner emphasized the centrality of thinking, apparently because early readers had missed its significance. If you want to investigate the limits that biological or social conditions place upon human freedom and responsibility, he recommended, first try to settle a prior question: Can absolute limits be set to human knowledge? He showed that such limits make no epistemological sense because, in the very act of identifying something as unknowable, our thinking renders it known. Enormous consequences for human freedom follow. If there is no theoretical limit to what humans can know, then we cannot authorize our actions by claiming that some unassailable dogma allows them. Demonstrably the authority for any human action must derive from what human beings can, at least in principle, understand for themselves. Nothing need be taken on faith.

Readers sometimes find it daunting to have to consider such matters closely. Steiner, however, was not just devising an elegant argument against determinism, he was sounding a challenge to live responsibly with urgent questions about the conduct of life. He wanted to awaken in his readers a disposition to act both independently and constructively. His book speaks to us if we seek the basis for human freedom in an understanding of human thinking and knowing so that our moral decisions can be based on knowledge, not just on belief.

Thinking has a bad reputation with many people, perhaps especially with those who incline toward a spiritual path. Steiner's emphasis on it sets him apart from other writers who concern themselves with soul life. Compared to the warmth of feeling and the visibility of action, thinking seems cold and remote. "No other activity of the human soul is as easily misunderstood as thinking," he says in his 1918 addition to Chapter 8, "The Factors of Life." He uncovers the reason for this misconception by contrasting "essential thinking" with merely remembered thinking. Usually only our remembered thinking is evident to us; we notice only what we've already thought, not what processes are occurring right now as we think those thoughts.

When we merely remember our thinking, we remember it as much less vital than our emotions and desires. But "whoever turns toward *essential* thinking finds within it both feeling and will" in their deepest reality. As distinct from merely remembered thinking, "essential thinking" consists of the unique property that Steiner discovered: thinking can notice itself. Simple to say, the phenomenon is hard to experience because it is so comparatively subtle and because we are not disposed to pay attention to it.

When we do notice our thinking—not our thoughts but the processes that produce our thoughts—what do we notice it *with*? The very same activity that we call thinking. "Essential thinking" is an exceptional case of knowing in the same way that the pronoun, "I," is an exceptional case of pronoun reference. Just as "I" always refers to the sayer of "I" and to no one else, so, in the special case when thinking notices itself instead of anything else, observer and observed are identical. Hidden in this obvious yet elusive property of thinking lies a long list of powerful implications for personal and social life: that thinking is essentially intuitive, that it is neither subjective nor objective, that we as individuals can undertake to cultivate its intuitive nature and so develop moral insight, and that our moral insights, though individually achieved, can serve rather than alienate our fellow human beings. To appreciate what these interconnected implications mean for the practice of freedom, it is helpful to turn first to the other strand in the threefold braid, individuality.

Like thinking, individualism has a bad reputation, particularly among socially concerned people. Once prized and still valued for its entrepreneurial power, individualism is now also widely regarded as the cause of sexual, racial, and economic injustices. How, then, can individualism enhance freedom, and what does either of them have to do with thinking or cognition? Answers to both questions evolve from Steiner's view that human beings can practice an "ethical individualism" as he sometimes called it.

When Steiner speaks of "ethical individualism" he means that it is communitarian rather than antisocial. Instead of conceiving individuals and society at one another's expense, Steiner notes that social arrangements are produced by individuals for the benefit of individuality. Codes of law and morality do not exist independently of human beings, to be restrictively imposed upon us. We ourselves create the codes and we ourselves can change them. "States and societies exist because they turn out to be the necessary consequence of individual life. ... [T]he social order is formed so that it can then react favorably on the individual," who is "the source of all morality."

Of course, individualism may provoke conflict, but it can also create a matrix for mutual understanding. Instead of competing with you selfishly, I can use my selfhood to recognize yours. When human beings manage to respond to individuality rather than to type, they are most likely to achieve social harmony. When we view one another generically we cannot hope to understand one another. The real opposite of individual is not "society" but "genus" or type. Steiner devotes an entire chapter, "Individuality and Genus," to this point. To illustrate, he uses misunderstandings and inequities based on gender:

> We are most obstinate in judging according to type when it is a question of a person's sex. Man almost always sees in woman, and woman in man, too much of the general character of the other sex and too little of what is individual.

Generalizing or generic thinking erases individuality. When sex is constituted as a genus, individuals of either sex tend to become invisible *as individuals*. This is particularly true of women, at least when they are considered to be the second sex and men the first, as is usually the case. Steiner continues:

> The activity of a man in life is determined by his individual capacities and inclinations; that of the woman is supposed to be determined exclusively by the fact that she is, precisely, a woman. Woman is supposed to be the slave of the generic, of what is universally womanish.

The opposition between the individual and the generic also produces a useful way to counter the standard fear that individualism creates anarchy. When I perform a criminal act, Steiner says, I do so not from what is individual in me but from shared instincts and urges that I have accepted uncritically without deciding consciously whether they are appropriate for me:

> Through my instincts, my drives, I am the kind of person of whom there are twelve to the dozen; I am an individual by means of the particular form of the idea by which, within the dozen, I designate myself as *I*.

Far from being in conflict with freedom, individualism as Steiner presents it is the expression of freedom. In this more profound sense, a free society requires of its members not less individualism but more.

But individualism will express freedom, and freedom will accommodate all individualities, only if motives can be brought to a certain level. Steiner's discussion of motives brings his findings about thinking to new heights of individual responsibility and liberty. At this high point of Steiner's increasingly powerful exposition, the activity of thinking—in the form of an intuitive understanding of motive—takes on its full significance as the starting point for a path of spiritual development.

The argument, which centers around the scope and nature of intuition, goes like this: To identify a motive for action that can be freely chosen by a particular individual in a specific situation requires a particular kind of cognition, the ability to intuit. Intuition knows without arguments, demonstrations, or other discursive means. For Steiner, the intuitive is not the instinctual or dimly felt but that which is directly knowable, without mediation. In a classic description, he calls it "the conscious experience, within what is purely spiritual, of a purely spiritual content." Then he links intuition to the activity of thinking: "The essence of thinking can be grasped only through intuition."

In other words, thinking and intuition overlap because of a simple but subtle fact that Steiner discovered about the "essence of thinking"—that thinking can "know" itself intuitively. Because it knows itself intuitively—that is, without the intervention of anything other than itself—thinking, like all other intuitions, qualifies as an essentially spiritual experience. Other intuitions may be beyond our ordinary powers, but by learning to notice our own thinking activity, not just its results, we become aware that thinking itself constitutes the very cognitive experience, intuition, that Steiner describes as "conscious experience, within what is purely spiritual, of a purely spiritual content"—something qualitatively different from a mere addition to our store of informative ideas, something essentially spiritual.

In its intuitive essence, thinking is a universal human capacity. Its intuitive (that is, spiritual) essence exists as a potential. It awaits our attention. When, with the help of Steiner's book, we recognize that thinking is an essentially spiritual activity, we discover that it can school us. In that sense—Steiner's sense—thinking is a spiritual path. We set out on it when we start learning to concentrate at will and begin to feel both need and desire for this willed focus. If we can free our attention from its habitual modes and associations, and if we can focus it at will as we ourselves decide, then we can have, without entering a trance or invoking mystical aids, a conscious experience of a spiritual content. Steiner sometimes called it *pure thinking*—will-filled or body-free thinking—and he presented it in a style designed to stimulate it in his readers.

Steiner stressed that thinking is not to be viewed as merely personal or subjective, even though it usually feels like a private experience. He firmly refutes the widely held, unexamined assumption (not to say dogma) that thinking must be subjective: "Thinking is *beyond* subject and object. It forms both of these concepts, just as it does all others." Developed in one's own unique way by each individual who undertakes to do so, the thinking capacity can become reliable intuition, allowing one to find the motivation for what one "must" do and to choose it freely. In such choices, individuality and cognition unite to produce freedom, freely undertaken actions that are both fully individual and socially constructive.

No outside authority, however benign or exalted, can motivate a free deed. Steiner emphatically rejects obedience. It is not an appropriate motivating force for free individuals. If my moral decisions merely conform to social norms and ethical codes, I am just "a higher form of robot." Instead of trying to obey, I should strive "to see why any given principle should work as a motive." Even the most highminded obedience is not free unless I have first decided for myself why this code should govern me at this moment. General standards, no matter how admirable, can perhaps help one develop an inclination toward responsible actions, but they cannot authorize free deeds. Habit, inertia, and obedience are all anathema to free action. It can come only from individually discovered motivation that is prompted by warm confidence in the rightness of the deed itself, not by a desire for its outcome, not even by a concern for its beneficiary.

According to Steiner's lofty yet practicable ideal, conduct worthy to be called "free" has to be motivated by a particular person's own intuitions as to what she or he should do in any particular case. A free being asks, What can I myself do and how do I know what it is right for me to do in this particular situation? If it is cultivated, the essentially intuitive nature of thinking can bring answers. At this level of insight and morality, what motivates is not duty but something like love, a warmly interested yet unselfish desire that cannot be coerced but can arise in us as an intuited intention. "Free beings are those who can *will* what they themselves hold to be right."

Steiner designed all his books to discourage passive collecting of information and to encourage instead conscious pondering and questioning, particularly of hitherto unexamined notions. Like Steiner's other writings, *Intuitive Thinking as a Spiritual Path* offers a mode of inquiry rather than a set of creeds, pieties, or doctrines. His style makes us practice a more active thinking so that we can become aware of its power, vitality, and essentially spiritual nature. His work stimulates our soul's own activity, stirring our latent powers and strengthening them so that we may eventually become able to think his insights ourselves.

We need to awaken to the functioning presence of spiritual realities in our lives. They are much more subtle, less sensational, more delicate, less crude, than we may expect. Consequently they are easy to overlook. One hundred years ago, at the close of the nineteenth century, Steiner gave to the twentieth and twenty-first centuries a new understanding of an ordinary human capacity—thinking. He showed that it is essentially a spiritual activity. At the close of the twentieth century, we can become more receptive to the existence of this commonly held, if ordinarily dormant, human ability by developing it. If we don't use it, we will lose it. *Intuitive Thinking* shows how and why to begin.

Middletown, Connecticut, 1995

Preface to the Revised Edition, 1918

Everything discussed in this book is organized around two [1]
root questions of the human soul. *First*, can we understand
human nature in such a way that this understanding serves
as the basis for everything else we may meet in the way of
experience or science? (For we have the sense that what
we meet in this way cannot sustain *itself*, because doubt
and critical thinking can drive it into the realm of uncertainty.) *Second*, can we human beings, as willing entities,
ascribe freedom to ourselves, or is this freedom a mere illusion that arises because we do not see the threads of necessity upon which our willing, like any other natural
event, depends? This is no artificial question. It proceeds
naturally from a certain mood of soul. We even feel that
the soul would be less than it should be if it never earnestly
came face to face with these two possibilities: freedom or
necessity of the will. The purpose of this book is to show

*NOTE: As an aid to readers wishing to follow the text in German, the
numbers that appear in the margins indicate Rudolf Steiner's original
paragraphing in the German edition.*

that our inner experiences of the second question depend upon how we view the first. I try to present a view of the human being that can support all other knowledge. I also attempt to show how this view fully justifies the idea of freedom of the will, provided that one finds the region of the soul where free will can develop.

[2]   Once achieved, this view can become part of the very life of the soul itself. But no theoretical answer is given that, once acquired, is simply carried as a conviction preserved by memory. Such an answer would have to be an illusion, according to the style of thought underlying this book. Therefore no such finished, closed-off answer is provided here; rather, reference is made to a region of soul experience in which, through the soul's inner activity, the question answers itself in a living way, always anew, whenever a human being needs it. Once we have found the region of the soul where these questions unfold, really perceiving this region gives all that we need to answer these riddles of life. Thereafter, we can journey further through the depths and breadths of this life of riddles, as need and fate provide. Indeed, with this region of soul experience, we seem to have located an insight that finds justification and validity through its own life, and through the relationship of this life to the whole life of the human soul.

[3]   This is how I thought about the content of this book when I wrote it out twenty-five years ago. Today as well, I must characterize the book's key thoughts in the same way. At that time, I limited myself to saying no *more* than is connected *in the strictest sense* to the two root questions described above. If anyone is surprised to find

nothing here about the world of spiritual experience described in my later writings, it should be borne in mind that I did not want at that time to discuss the results of spiritual research; rather, my purpose was first to lay the foundations on which such results can rest. This "philosophy of freedom" does not contain specific results of that kind, any more than it contains specific results from natural science. But what it does contain will be indispensable, in my opinion, to anyone striving for certainty in such knowledge. What the book says might also be acceptable to many who, for whatever reasons of their own, want nothing to do with the results of spiritual-scientific research. Those who are drawn to these results may also find significant my attempt to demonstrate how an unprejudiced consideration of simply the two questions characterized above, which are fundamental for *all* cognition, leads to the view that human beings live within an actual spiritual world. In this book, I try to validate cognition of the spiritual realm *before* one enters spiritual experience. Hence there is no need to cast furtive glances toward the experiences that I put forward later on, as long as one is able or willing to enter into the style of the discussion itself.

Thus this book seems to me quite separate from my actual spiritual-scientific writings. On the other hand, it also seems to be connected with them in the most intimate way, so that now, after twenty-five years, I can republish the text essentially unaltered. I have, however, made additions of some length to a number of chapters. Misinterpretations of what I had said made such extensive

[4]

additions seem necessary. The only passages I have re-written are those in which, a quarter century ago, I expressed myself poorly. (Only people of ill will would take these changes as proof that I have changed my fundamental conviction).

[5]   The book has now been out of print for many years. I feel that the same things need to be said today as twenty-five years ago; nevertheless, I hesitated long over the completion of this new edition. I asked myself again and again whether I ought, in this or that passage, to confront the numerous philosophical views that have come to light since the appearance of the first edition. In recent years, involvement in purely spiritual-scientific researches prevented me from doing this in the way I would wish. Yet I have convinced myself, after the most thorough survey I could make of current philosophical work, that such discussion does not belong here, tempting as it might be in itself. What seemed necessary to say about the latest philosophical tendencies, from the point of view taken in *Intuitive Thinking as a Spiritual Path: A Philosophy of Freedom*, can be found in the second volume of my *Riddles of Philosophy*.*[1]

April, 1918

Rudolf Steiner

---

*All footnotes are the publisher's notes, unless they are identified as the author's notes.

1. *The Riddles of Philosophy* (Spring Valley, NY: Anthroposophic Press, 1973).

PART I : THEORY

The Knowledge of Freedom

CHAPTER 1

CONSCIOUS HUMAN ACTION

Is a human being spiritually *free,* or subject to the iron [1]
necessity of purely natural law? Few questions have ex-
cited so much ingenuity. The idea of the freedom of human will has found both sanguine supporters and stiff-
necked opponents in plenty. There are those who, in their
moral zeal, cast aspersions on the intellect of anyone
who can deny so obvious a *fact* as freedom. They are opposed by others who see the acme of unscientific thinking in the belief that the lawfulness of nature fails to
apply to the area of human action and thinking. One and
the same thing is explained equally often as the most pre-
cious possession of humankind and as its worst illusion.
Infinite subtlety has been expended to explain how human freedom is consistent with the workings of nature of
which, after all, human beings are also a part. No less effort has gone into the attempt from the other side to explain how such a delusion could ever have arisen. All but
the most superficial thinkers feel that we have to do here
with one of the most important questions of life, religion,

conduct, and science. And it is among the sad signs of the superficiality of contemporary thinking that a book intending to coin a "new belief" from the results of recent scientific research—David Friedrich Strauss's *The Old and New Belief*—contains nothing on this question but the words:

> We need not here go into the question of the freedom of human will. The supposed freedom of indifferent choice has been recognized as an empty phantom by every philosophy worthy of the name, while the moral valuation of human conduct and character remains untouched by the question.[1]

I cite this passage, not because I think the book from which it derives has any special significance, but because it seems to me to express the opinion which the majority of our thinking contemporaries have been able to achieve on this question. Today, everyone who can claim to have outgrown scientific kindergarten appears to know that freedom cannot consist in choosing arbitrarily between two possible actions. There is always, so it is claimed, a quite specific *reason* why a person performs one specific action from among several possibilities.

[2]   This seems obvious. Nevertheless, present-day opponents of freedom direct their principal attacks only

---

1. D.F. Strauss (1808–1874), *Der alte und der neue Glaube* (1872). A German theologian and philosopher, David Friedrich Strauss developed a Hegelian theory of Biblical interpretation. He caused a storm with his historical-critical *Life of Jesus*, in which he called the Gospels "a historical myth."

against freedom of choice. After all, Herbert Spencer, whose views daily gain wider acceptance, says:

> That anyone could desire or not desire arbitrarily, which is the real proposition concealed in the dogma of free will, is refuted as much through the analysis of consciousness as through the content of the preceding chapter [on psychology].[2]

Others also proceed from the same point of view when they combat the concept of free will. Their arguments can all be found in germinal form as early as Spinoza. What he presented with clarity and simplicity against the idea of freedom has since been repeated countless times, only generally sheathed in the most sophistic theoretical doctrines, so that it becomes difficult to recognize the simple course of thought on which everything depends. In a letter of October or November, 1674, Spinoza writes:

> Thus, I call a thing *free* that exists and acts out of the pure necessity of its nature; and I call it *compelled*, if its existence and activity are determined in a precise and fixed manner by something else. Thus God, for example, though necessary, is free,

---

2.   Herbert Spencer (1820–1903)*, The Principles of Psychology* (1855). German edition Dr. B. Vetter, Stuttgart, 1882. Spencer was an English philosopher, friend of Huxley, Tyndall, George Eliot, and John Stuart Mill. He attempted a comprehensive, systematic (materialist/dualist) account of all cosmic phenomena, including mental and moral principles."The spirit in our present civilization is the spirit which John Stuart Mill and Herbert Spencer have already worked into their philosophies." Rudolf Steiner, *A Modern Art of Education* (London: Rudolf Steiner Press, 1981).

because he exists only out of the necessity of his nature. Similarly, God knows himself and everything else freely, because it follows from the necessity of his nature alone that he should know everything. You see, then, that I locate freedom not in free decision, but in free necessity.

[3]   Let us, however, descend to created things, which are all determined to exist and to act in fixed and precise ways by outside causes. To see this more clearly, let us imagine a very simple case. A stone, for example, receives a certain momentum from an external cause that comes into contact with it, so that later, when the impact of the external cause has ceased, it necessarily continues to move. This persistence of the stone is compelled, and not necessary, because it had to be established by the impact of an external cause. What applies here to the stone, applies to everything else, no matter how complex and multifaceted; everything is necessarily determined by an outside cause to exist and to act in a fixed and precise manner.

[4]   *Now please assume that the stone, as it moves, thinks and knows that it is trying, as much as it can, to continue in motion. This stone, which is only conscious of its effort and by no means indifferent, will believe that it is quite free and that it continues in its motion not because of an external cause but only because it wills to do so. But this is that human freedom that all claim to possess and that only consists in people being aware of their*

desires, but not knowing the causes by which they are determined. Thus the child believes that it freely desires the milk; the angry boy, that he freely demands revenge; and the coward flight. Again, drunkards believe it is a free decision to say what, when sober again, they will wish that they had not said, and since this prejudice is inborn in all humans, it is not easy to free oneself from it. For, although experience teaches us sufficiently that people are least able to moderate their desires and that, moved by contradictory passions, they see what is better and do what is worse, yet they still consider themselves free, and this because they desire some things less intensely and because some desires can be easily inhibited through the recollection of something else that is familiar.[3]

Because this view is expressed clearly and definitely, it is easy to discover the fundamental error in it. Just as a stone necessarily carries out a specific movement in response to an impact, human beings are supposed to carry   *[5]*

---

3. Baruch Spinoza (1632–1677). Marrano-Dutch philosopher of Jewish-Portuguese parentage. Expelled from the Synagogue, he supported himself by grinding lenses and devoted himself to philosophy, especially Cartesianism, deriving a kind of "rational pantheism" from it. See Rudolf Steiner, *The Riddles of Philosophy.* "Spinozism is a world conception that seeks the *ground* of all world events in God, and derives all process according to external necessary laws from this ground, just as mathematical truths are derived from axioms (p.161)." Spinoza was important to Goethe and to German Romantic idealism generally. See Yirmiyahu Yovel, *Spinoza and Other Heretics* (Princeton: Princeton University Press, 1989).

out an action by a similar necessity if impelled to it by any reason. Human beings imagine themselves to be the free originators of their actions only because they are aware of these actions. In so doing, however, they overlook the causes driving them, which they must obey unerringly. The error in this train of thought is easy to find. Spinoza and all who think like him overlook the human capacity to be aware not only of one's actions, but also of the causes by which one's actions are guided.

No one will dispute that a child is *unfree* when it desires milk, as is a drunkard who says things and later regrets them. Both know nothing of the causes, active in the depths of their organism, that exercise irresistible control over them. But is it justifiable to lump together actions of this kind with those in which humans are conscious not only of their actions but also of the reasons that motivate them? Are the actions of human beings really all of a single kind? Should the acts of a warrior on the battlefield, a scientist in the laboratory, a diplomat involved in complex negotiations, be set scientifically on the same level as that of a child when it desires milk? It is certainly true that the solution to a problem is best sought where it is simplest. But the lack of a capacity to discriminate has often brought about endless confusion. And there is, after all, a profound difference between knowing and not knowing why I do something. This seems self-evident. Yet the opponents of freedom never ask whether a motive that I know, and see through, compels me in the same sense as the organic process that causes a child to cry for milk.

Eduard von Hartmann, in his *Phenomenology of Moral* *[6]*
Consciousness, claims that human willing depends on
two main factors: motive and character.[4] If we consider
all human beings as the same, or at least see their differences as negligible, then their will appears to be determined from *without*, namely by the circumstances they
encounter. But if we consider that different human beings
make an idea or mental picture into a motive only when
their character is such that the idea in question gives rise
to a desire, then human beings appear to be determined
from *within* and not from *without*. But because we must
ourselves make an idea that impinges from without into a
motive of action in accordance with our character, we
imagine that we are free, that is, independent of external
motivation. But, according to Eduard von Hartmann, the
truth is that

> even though we ourselves first raise ideas into
> motives, yet we do this not arbitrarily, but accord-
> ing to the necessity of our characterological organi-
> zation; *that is, we are anything but free.*

Here, too, no consideration is given to the difference
between motives that I allow to affect me only after having permeated them with my consciousness, and those
that I follow without having a clear knowledge of them.

---

4. Eduard von Hartmann (1842–1906), *Die Phänomenologie des sittlichen Bewusstseins* [Phenomenology of Moral Consciousness] (1879).
Von Hartmann combined the views of Kant, Hegel, and Schopenhauer
into a doctrine of evolutionary history based on the conflict of unconscious will with unconscious reason. He was a major figure of the time
and influenced many subsequent thinkers, including C. G. Jung.

[7]   This leads immediately to the standpoint from which the matter will be considered here. *Can* the question of the freedom of our will be posed narrowly by itself? And, if not, with what other questions must it necessarily be linked?

[8]   If there is a difference between a conscious motive and an unconscious drive, then the conscious motive will bring with it an action that must be judged differently from an action done out of blind impulse. Our first question will concern this difference. The position we must take on freedom itself will depend on the result of this inquiry.

[9]   What does it mean to have *knowledge* of the motives of one's actions? This question has been given too little attention, because we always tear in two the inseparable whole that is the human being. We distinguish between the doer and the knower, but we have nothing to say about the one who matters most: the one who acts out of knowledge.

[10]   People say that human beings are free when they obey reason alone and not animal desires. Or they say that freedom means being able to determine one's life and actions according to purposes and decisions.

[11]   Nothing is gained by such claims. For the question is precisely whether reason, purposes, and decisions exercise control over human beings in the same way as animal desires. If a reasonable decision arises in me of itself, with the same necessity as hunger and thirst, then I can but obey its compulsion, and my freedom is an illusion.

[12]   Another turn of phrase puts it thus: to be free does not mean being able to will whatever one wills, but being able to do what one wills. In his *Atomistics of the Will*, the

poet-philosopher Robert Hamerling expresses this idea incisively:

Human beings can certainly do what they will— but they cannot will what they will, since their willing is determined by *motives.* They cannot will what they will? Let us look at these words more closely. Do they contain any reasonable meaning? Must freedom of the will then consist in being able to will something without having grounds, without a motive? But what does willing mean other than *having grounds* to do or attempt this rather than that? To will something, without grounds, without motive, would mean willing something *without willing it.* The concept of motivation is inseparably linked to the concept of the will. Without a determining motive, the will is an empty *capacity*: it only becomes active and real through the motive. Thus it is quite correct that the human will is not 'free,' inasmuch as its direction is always determined by the strongest motive. But it is absurd, in contrast to this 'unfreedom,' to speak of a conceivable 'freedom' of the will that involves being able to will what one does *not* will.[5]

---

5. Robert Hamerling (1830-1889) *Atomistik des Willens* (Volume 2, p. 213 ff.) Hamerling was an Austrian poet, philosopher, dramatist, and schoolteacher in Vienna, Graz, and Trieste. He was an acquaintance of Rudolf Steiner. See "Robert Hamerling, Poet and Thinker" in *The Presence of the Dead* (Hudson, NY: Anthroposophic Press, 1990). See also *Rudolf Steiner, An Autobiography* and *Karmic Relationships,* vol. II (London: Rudolf Steiner Press, 1974).

[13]   Even here, only motives in general are discussed, without considering the difference between conscious and unconscious motives. If a motive acts upon me, and I am forced to follow it because it proves to be the "strongest" of its kind, then the thought of freedom ceases to have any meaning. Why should it matter to me whether I can do something or not, if I am *forced* by the motive to do it? The first question is not whether I can or cannot do something once the motive has operated upon me, but whether there exist only motives of the kind that operate with compelling necessity. If *I have to* will something, then I may even be utterly indifferent as to whether I can actually do it. If, because of my character and the circumstances prevailing in my environment, a motive were forced upon me that my thinking showed me was unreasonable, then I would even have to be glad if I could not do what I will.

[14]   It is not a question of whether I can execute a decision once it is made, but of *how the decision arises within me.*

[15]   What distinguishes humans from all other organic beings rests on rational thinking. Activity we have in common with other organisms. Seeking analogies for human action in the animal kingdom does not help to clarify the concept of freedom. Modern natural science loves such analogies. And when science succeeds in finding among animals something similar to human action, it believes it has touched on the most important question of the science of humanity. Paul Rée's book, *The Illusion of Free Will* offers one example of the misunderstandings to which this opinion leads. On page 5, Rée states, with regard to freedom,

It is easy to explain why it appears to us as if the movement of the stone is necessary while the donkey's will is not. The causes that move the stone are, after all, external and visible. But the causes by which the donkey desires are internal and invisible: between us and the site of their activity there lies the donkey's skull.... One does not see the causal determination and therefore imagines that it is not present. The will, we say, while it is the cause of the donkey's turning around, is itself undetermined; it is an absolute beginning.[6]

Here, too, is an utter disregard for human actions in which the human being has an awareness of the reasons for the action, for Rée explains, "between us and the site of their activity there lies the donkey's skull." We can see from these words alone that Rée has no inkling that there exist actions (not a donkey's, but a human's) for which there lies, between us and the action, the motive *that has become conscious*. He proves this again a few pages later when he says: "We are not aware of the *causes* by which our will is determined, and so we imagine that it is not causally determined at all." But enough of examples *[16]* proving that many fight against freedom without at all knowing what freedom is.

Obviously, my action cannot be *free* if I, as the actor, *[17]* do not know why I carry it out. But what about an action

---

6. Paul Rée (1849–1901), *Die Illusion der Willensfreiheit*. Rée was a friend of Friedrich Nietzsche and Lou Andréas Salome and an influential "alternative" thinker of the time.

for which the reasons are known? This leads us to ask: what is the origin and the significance of thinking? For without understanding the soul's activity of *thinking*, no concept of the knowledge of anything, including an action, is possible. When we understand what thinking means in general, it will be easy to clarify the role that thinking plays in human action. As Hegel rightly says, "Thinking turns the soul, with which beasts too are gifted, into spirit." [7]Therefore thinking will also give to human action its characteristic stamp.

[18]   This is by no means to claim that all our actions flow only from the sober deliberations of our reason. I am far from calling *human*, in the highest sense, only those actions that proceed from abstract judgment alone. But as soon as our actions lift themselves above the satisfaction of purely animal desires, our motives are always permeated by thoughts. Love, pity, patriotism are springs of action that cannot be reduced to cold rational concepts. People say that the heart, the sensibility, comes into its own in such matters. No doubt. But heart and sensibility do not create the motives of action. They presuppose

7. Georg Wilhelm Friedrich Hegel (1770–1831), *Enzyklopädie der philosophischen Wissenschaften* (1817, second edition 1827). The quotation is from the Preface. See also Rudolf Steiner, *The Riddles of Philosophy.* For instance, "[Hegel] wanted to express clearly and poignantly that he regarded *thinking* that is conscious of itself as the highest human activity, as the force through which alone a human being can gain a position with respect to ultimate questions.... Hegel is a personality who lives completely in the element of thought." (p. 169).

them and then receive them into their own realm. Pity appears in my heart when *the mental image* of a person who arouses pity in me enters my consciousness. The way to the heart goes through the head.

Love is no exception here. If it is not a mere expression of the sexual drive, then love is based on mental pictures that we form of the beloved. And the more idealistic these mental pictures are, the more blessed is the love. Here, too, thought is the father of feeling. People say that love makes us blind to the beloved's flaws. But we can also turn this around and claim that love opens our eyes to the beloved's strengths. Many pass by these good qualities without noticing them. One person sees them and, just for this reason, love awakens in the soul. What else has this person done but make a mental picture of what a hundred others have ignored? Love is not theirs because they lack the *mental picture*.

We can approach the matter however we like: it only *[19]* grows clearer that the question regarding the nature of human actions presupposes another, that of the origin of thinking. I shall therefore turn to this question next.

CHAPTER 2

THE FUNDAMENTAL URGE
FOR KNOWLEDGE

> Two souls, alas, dwell within my breast,
> Each wants to separate from the other;
> One, in hearty lovelust,
> Clings to earth with clutching organs;
> The other lifts itself mightily from the dust
> To high ancestral regions.
>
> Goethe, *Faust* I, 1112

[1]   With these words, Goethe characterizes a trait deeply based in human nature. As human beings, we are not organized in a fully integrated, unified way. We always demand more than the world freely offers. Nature gives us needs, and the satisfaction of some of these she leaves to our own activity. The gifts allotted to us are abundant, but even more abundant is our desire. We seem born for dissatisfaction. The urge to know is only a special case of this dissatisfaction. We look at a tree twice. The first time, we see its branches at rest, the second time in motion. We are unsatisfied with this observation. Why, we ask, does the tree present itself to us now at rest, now in motion? Every glance at nature engenders a host of questions within us.

We receive a new problem with each phenomenon that greets us. Every experience becomes a riddle. We see a creature similar to the mother animal emerging from the egg, and we ask the reason for this similarity. We observe a living creature's growth and development to a certain degree of perfection, and we seek the conditions of this experience. Nowhere are we content with what nature displays before our senses. We look everywhere for what we call an *explanation* of the facts.

That which we seek in things, over and above what is given to us immediately, splits our entire being into two parts. We become aware of standing in opposition to the world, as independent beings. The universe appears to us as two opposites: *I* and *world*. [2]

We set up this barrier between ourselves and the world as soon as consciousness lights up within us. But we never lose the feeling that we do belong to the world, that a link exists that connects us to it, that we are creatures not *outside*, but within, the universe. [3]

This feeling engenders an effort to bridge the opposition. And, in the final analysis, the whole spiritual striving of humankind consists in bridging this opposition. The history of spiritual life is a continual searching for the unity between the I and the world. Religion, art, and science share this as their goal. The *religious believer* seeks the solution to the world-riddle posed by the I, which is unsatisfied by the merely phenomenal world, in the revelation meted out by God. *Artists* try to incorporate the ideas of their I in various materials to reconcile what lives within them to the outer world. They, too, feel unsatisfied with [4] the merely phenomenal world and seek to build into it the something more that their I, going above and beyond the world of phenomena, contains. *Thinkers* seek the laws of phenomena, striving to penetrate in thinking what they experience through observation. Only when we have made the *world content* into our *thought content* do we rediscover the connection from which we have sundered ourselves. We shall see later that this goal is reached only when the tasks of scientific research are understood much more profoundly than often occurs.

The whole relation between the I and the world that I have portrayed here meets us on the stage of history in the contrast between a unitary worldview, or *monism*, and a two-world theory, or *dualism*. Dualism directs its gaze solely to the separation that human consciousness effects between the I and the world. Its whole effort is a futile struggle to reconcile these opposites, which it may call *spirit* and *matter*, *subject* and *object*, or *thinking* and *phenomenon*. It feels that a bridge between the two worlds must exist, but it is incapable of finding it. When human beings experience themselves as "I," they can do no other than think of this "I" as being on the side of *spirit*. When to this I they then oppose the world, they ascribe to the latter the perceptual world given to the senses: the *material* world. In this way, human beings locate themselves within the opposition of spirit and matter. They do so all the more because their own bodies belong to the material world. The "I" thus belongs to the spiritual, as a part of it; while *material* things and processes, which are perceived by the senses, belong to the "world." All the riddles, therefore, that have to do with spirit and matter must be rediscovered by human beings in the fundamental riddle of their own essential being. *Monism* directs its gaze exclusively to unity, and seeks to deny or erase the opposites, present though these are. Neither monism nor dualism is satisfactory, for neither does justice to the facts. *Dualism* sees spirit (I) and matter (world) as two fundamentally different entities, and therefore it cannot understand how the two can affect one another. How could spirit know what is going on in matter, if matter's specific nature is altogether foreign to spirit? Or, given these conditions, how could spirit affect matter so that intentions translate into deeds? The most ingenious and absurd hypotheses have been proposed to answer these questions. Yet, to the present day, things are hardly better with monism which, until now, has attempted three solutions: either it denies spirit and becomes materialism; or it denies matter, seeking salvation through spiritualism; or else it claims that matter and spirit are inseparably united even in the simplest entity, so that it should come as no surprise if these two forms of existence, which after all are never apart, appear together in human beings.

Materialism can never offer a satisfactory explanation *[5]* of the world. For every attempt at an explanation must begin with one's forming *thoughts* about phenomena. Thus, materialism starts with the *thought* of matter or of material processes. In so doing, it already has two different kinds of facts on hand: the material world and thoughts about it. Materialism attempts to understand the latter by seeing them as a purely material process. It believes that thinking occurs in the brain in the same way as digestion occurs in the animal organism. Just as it ascribes mechanical and organic effects to matter, materialism also assigns to matter the capacity, under certain circumstances, to think. But it forgets that all it has done is to shift the problem to another location. Materialists ascribe the capacity to think to matter rather than to themselves. And this brings them back to the starting point. How does matter manage to think about its own existence? Why does it not simply go on existing, perfectly content with itself? Materialism turns aside from the specific subject, our own I, and arrives at an unspecific, hazy configuration: matter. Here the same riddle comes up again. The materialist view can only displace the problem, not solve it.

[6]   And what of the spiritualist view? Pure *spiritualists* deny matter any independent existence and conceive of it only as a product of spirit. If they apply this view to the riddle of their own human existence, they are driven into a corner. Over against the I, which may be placed on the side of spirit, there suddenly appears the sensory world. No *spiritual* point of entry into it seems open; it has to be perceived and experienced by the I through material processes. As long as it tries to explain itself solely as a spiritual entity, the "I" cannot find such material processes within itself. What it works out for itself spiritually never contains the sense world. It is as if the "I" has to admit that the world remains closed to it unless it puts itself into an unspiritual relationship to the world. Similarly, when we decide to act, we must translate our intentions into reality with the help of material stuff and

forces. We are thus referred back to the outer world. The most extreme spiritualist, or perhaps the thinker who, through his absolute idealism, presents himself as an extreme spiritualist, is Johann Gottlieb Fichte.[1] Fichte attempted to derive the whole world structure from the "I." What he in fact succeeded in creating was a magnificent *thought picture* of the world, but one without any experiential content. Just as it is impossible for the materialist to declare spirit out of existence, so the spiritualist cannot disavow the external material world.

When we direct our cognition to the "I," we initially *[7]* perceive the activity of this "I" in the development of a world of ideas unfolded through thought. Because of this, those with a spiritualist worldview sometimes feel themselves tempted, in regard to their own human essence, to acknowledge nothing of the spirit except this world of ideas. In such cases, spiritualism becomes one-sided idealism. It does not arrive at the point of seeking a *spiritual* world *through* a world of ideas. It sees the spiritual world in the idea-world itself. Its world view is forced to remain fixed, as if spellbound, within the activity of the "I" itself.

---

1. Fichte (1762–1814). A disciple of Kant, Fichte went on to develop his own powerful system of transcendental idealism. His influence reached from the Romantic philosophy of Novalis and Coleridge to Rudolf Steiner. Steiner returned again and again to Fichte, beginning with his Inaugural Dissertation, "The Fundamentals of a Theory of Cognition with Special Reference to Fichte's Scientific Teaching" (1891), published as *Truth and Science [Knowledge]* (1892). See *Autobiography* and, for instance, *The Riddle of Man* (Spring Valley: Mercury Press, 1990).

[8]   A curious variant of idealism is the view of Friedrich Albert Lange, as represented in his widely read *History of Materialism*.[2] Lange takes the position that materialism is quite right when it explains all world phenomena, including our thinking, as products of purely material processes, while, conversely, matter and its processes are themselves a product of thinking.

> The senses give us *effects* of things, not faithful pictures, let alone the things themselves. But these mere effects include the senses along with the brain and the molecular vibrations within it.

That is, our thinking is produced by material processes, and these are produced by the thinking of the "I." Lange's philosophy is thus nothing but the conceptual version of the story of the brave Münchhausen, who holds himself up in the air by his own pigtail.[3]

[9]   A third form of monism sees both essences, matter and spirit, as already united in the simplest entity (the atom). But here too, nothing is achieved except that the question, which actually originates in our consciousness, is

---

2. F. A. Lange (1828–1875) was Professor at Marburg where he established a long-lasting tradition of Neo-Kantianism. Lange introduced Darwinism and philosophy of history into Germany. See also Rudolf Steiner, *The Riddles of Philosophy*, pp. 323–330.

3. Baron Münchhausen (1720–1797) was a German soldier who served with distinction in the Russian campaign against the Turks. A noted raconteur, famed for exploits and adventures, his name became associated with absurdly exaggerated stories. A collection of such Münchhausen tales was published in London in 1785 by Rudolph Erich Raspe (1737–1794), himself a scholar and adventurer.

displaced to a different arena. If it is an indivisible unity, how does a unitary entity manage to express itself in a twofold way?

In regard to all these points of view, we must emphasize [10] that the fundamental and primal opposition confronts us first in our own consciousness. It is we who separate ourselves from the native ground of nature and place ourselves as "I" in opposition to the "world." Goethe gives this its classical expression in his essay, "Nature," even if his style initially appears quite unscientific: "We live in her (Nature's) midst and are strangers to her. She speaks with us continually, yet does not betray her secret to us." But Goethe also knows the reverse aspect: "All humans are within her and she in them."[4]

It is true that we have estranged ourselves from nature; [11] but it is just as true that we feel we are in her and belong to her. It can only be her activity that lives in us.

We must find the way back to her again. A simple re- [12] flection can show us the way. To be sure, we have torn ourselves away from nature, but we must still have taken something with us into our own being. We must seek out this natural being within ourselves, and then we shall also rediscover the connection to her. Dualism fails to do this. It considers the inner human as a spiritual being, quite foreign to nature, and then seeks to attach this being to nature. No wonder that it cannot find the connecting link. We can only find nature outside us if we first know her *within* us. What is akin to her within us will be our guide.

---

4. Goethe, *Fragment über die Nature*, Fragment on Nature.

Our way is thus mapped out for us. We do not wish to speculate about the interaction of nature and spirit. We wish to descend into the depths of our own being, to find there those elements that we have saved in our flight out of nature.

[13]   The investigation of our own being must bring us the solution to the riddle. We must come to a point where we can say to ourselves: Here I am no longer merely "I." There is something here that is more than "I."

[14]   I am aware that some who have read to this point will not find my explanations correspond to "the present state of science." I can only reply that up to now I have been concerned not with scientific results but rather with a simple description of what we all experience in our own consciousnesses. Diverse statements about attempts to reconcile consciousness with the world also entered the stream of argument, but only to clarify the actual facts. For this reason, too, I attach no value to using the individual expressions, such as "I," "spirit," "world," "nature," and so forth, in the precise way that is usual in psychology and philosophy. Everyday consciousness is unfamiliar with the sharp distinctions of science, and up to this point, my intention has been to survey the facts of everyday life. What concerns me is not how science until now has interpreted consciousness but rather how consciousness experiences itself hour by hour.

CHAPTER 3

THINKING IN THE SERVICE
OF UNDERSTANDING
THE WORLD

When I observe how a billiard ball, once struck, transfers   *[1]*
its movement to another, I remain completely without influence over the course of this process. The direction of
motion and the velocity of the second ball are determined
by the direction and velocity of the first. As long as I remain a mere observer, I can say something about the
movement of the second ball *only after* it has actually be-
gun. But the situation is different when I begin to think
about the content of my observation. The purpose of my
thinking is to form concepts about the process I observe. I
connect the concept of an elastic sphere with certain other
concepts of mechanics and take into consideration the particular circumstances prevailing in the given case. Thus, to
the process that plays itself out without my participation I
seek to add a second process, which goes on in the conceptual sphere. This sphere depends on me, as is evident in my
being able to content myself with observation, renouncing
any search for concepts, if I have no need of them. But if
this need is present, then I am satisfied only when I have

brought concepts such as "sphere," "elasticity," "movement," "impact," "velocity," etc. into a certain connection with each other. To this interconnection of concepts the observed process then stands in a particular relation. Certainly the process that I observe completes itself independently of me. Just as certainly, however, the conceptual process cannot play itself out without my participation.

[2]   Whether my activity is really an expression of my independent essence, or whether contemporary physiologists are right in saying that I cannot think as I wish, but rather *have to* think as the thoughts and thought-connections currently in my consciousness determine[1]—this will be the subject of later discussion. For the time being, we wish merely to establish that, with regard to the objects and processes given us without our participation, we feel compelled continually to seek concepts and conceptual connections that stand in a certain relationship to those objects and processes. For the moment, we shall leave aside the question of whether this activity is really *our* activity, or whether we carry it out in accord with unalterable

---

1. Compare Theodor Ziehen, *Principles of Physiological Psychology*, Jena, 1893. (Author's note)
 Ziehen (1862–1950) was a German psychiatrist, physiologist, and psychologist. Cf. Rudolf Steiner, *Anthroposophy and Science* (Spring Valley: Mercury Press, 1991): " Ziehen undertook to explain mental life in such a way that he replaced it by brain activity. His explanation is essentially the following: he contemplates mental life; he then considers the brain and nervous system anatomically and physiologically (to the extent that present empirical research permits) and shows which processes, in his opinion are present in the brain for a particular mental activity (including memory)." (pp 81ff).

necessity. Certainly, it is unquestionable that it initially appears as our own. We know perfectly well that the corresponding concepts are not given with the objects. That I am myself the active one may depend upon an illusion; nevertheless, that is how immediate observation portrays the matter. Therefore the question is: what do we gain by finding the conceptual counterpart to an event?

There is a profound difference, for me, between the *[3]* way in which the parts of an event relate to one another before and after the discovery of the corresponding concepts. Mere observation can follow the parts of a given event in succession, but their connection remains obscure until concepts are brought in to help. I see the first billiard ball move toward the second in a certain direction and with a certain velocity; I must wait to see what will happen upon impact and, even then, I can only follow what happens with my eyes. Let us suppose that, at the moment of impact, someone conceals from me the area where the process goes on. As a mere observer, I am then without knowledge of what happens next. The situation is different if, before the process is concealed from me, I discover the concepts corresponding to the constellation of relationships. In that case, I can report what happens even if I can no longer observe it. By itself, a process or object that is merely observed suggests nothing about its connection to other processes or objects. The connection only becomes evident if observation is linked to thinking.

Insofar as we are conscious of it, *observation* and *[4]* *thinking* are the two points of departure for all human spiritual striving. The workings of both common human understanding and the most complicated scientific investigations rest on these two pillars of our spirit. Philosophers have proceeded from various primal oppositions—such as idea and reality, subject and object, appearance and thing-in-itself, I and Not-I, idea and will, concept and matter, force and substance, conscious and unconscious—but it can easily be shown that the contrast between *observation* and *thinking* precedes all of these as the most important antithesis for human beings.

[5]   No matter what principle we wish to establish, we must either show that we have observed it somewhere or we must express it in the form of a clear thought that anyone can rethink. When philosophers begin to speak about their first principles, they must put things in conceptual form and therefore they must make use of thinking. Thus, indirectly, they admit that their activity presupposes thinking. Nothing is being said yet about whether thinking or something else is the chief element of world evolution. But it is clear from the start that, without thinking, philosophers can gain no knowledge of such an element. Thinking might play a minor role in the origin of world phenomena, but in the origin of a view of those phenomena, it surely plays a major role.

[6]   As for observation, we need it because of the way we are organized. Our thinking about a horse and the object horse are two things that arise separately for us. And the object is accessible to us only through observation. Merely staring at a horse does not enable us to produce the concept *horse*, and neither will mere thinking bring forth the corresponding object.

Chronologically, observation even precedes thinking.   *[7]*
For we can become aware of thinking, too, only through
observation. At the beginning of this chapter, when we
showed how thinking lights up in the face of an event and
goes beyond what it finds given without its assistance,
this was essentially the description of an observation. It
is through observation that we first become aware of anything entering the circle of our experience. The content of
sensations, perceptions, views, feelings, acts of will,
dream and fantasy constructions, representations, concepts and ideas, illusions and hallucinations—the content
of all of these is given to us through *observation.*

Thinking differs essentially, as an object of observa-   *[8]*
tion, from all other things. The observation of a table or
a tree occurs for me as soon as the objects enter the horizon of my experience. But I do not observe my thinking
about the objects at the same time as I observe them. I
observe the table, and I carry out my thinking about the
table, but I do not observe that thinking in the same moment as my observation of the table. If I want to observe,
along with the table, my thinking about the table, I must
first take up a standpoint outside my own activity. While
observation of objects and processes, and thinking about
them, are both everyday situations that fill my ongoing
life, *the observation of thinking* is a kind of exceptional
state. We must take this fact properly into account if we
are to determine the relationship of thinking to all other
contents of observation. We must be clear that, when we
observe thinking, we are applying to thinking a proce-
dure that is normal when we consider all the rest of our

world-content but that is not normally applied to thinking itself.

[9]   Someone could object that what I have noted here about thinking applies equally to feeling and other spiritual activities. The feeling of pleasure, for example, is also kindled by an object, and I observe the object, but not the feeling of pleasure. This objection is based on an error. Pleasure does not at all stand in the same relation to its object as the concept formed by thinking does. I am definitely aware that the concept of a thing is formed by my activity, while pleasure is created in me by an object in the same way as, for example, a falling stone causes a change in an object on which it falls. For observation, pleasure is given in exactly the same way as the process that occasions it. The same is not true of concepts. I can ask why a specific process creates the feeling of pleasure in me. But I certainly cannot ask why a process creates a specific number of concepts in me. To do so would simply be meaningless. Thinking about a process has nothing to do with an effect on me. I learn nothing at all about myself by knowing the concepts corresponding to the observed change that a hurled stone causes in a pane of glass. But I learn a great deal about my personality if I know the feeling that a specific process awakens within me. If I say of an observed object, "This is a rose," then I express nothing at all about myself. But if I say of the rose, "It gives me a feeling of pleasure," then I have characterized not only the rose but also myself in relationship to the rose.

[10]   As objects of observation, then, thinking and feeling cannot be equated. The same conclusion could easily be

derived for the other activities of the human spirit. Unlike thinking, these can be grouped with other observed objects and processes. It is part of the peculiar nature of thinking that it is an activity directed only to the observed object, and not to the thinker. This is clear from how we express our thoughts about a thing, compared to how we express our feelings or acts of will. If I see an object and recognize it as a table, I do not generally say "I am thinking about a table," but rather "This is a table." Yet I could certainly say, "I am pleased with the table." In the first case, I am not concerned with communicating that I have entered into a relationship with the table; but in the second case it is precisely this relationship that is significant. Furthermore, with the statement, "I am thinking about a table," I have already entered into the exceptional state mentioned above, in which I make into an object of observation something that is always contained within my spiritual activity but not as an observed object.

This is the characteristic nature of thinking. The thinker [11] forgets thinking while doing it. What concerns the thinker is not thinking, but the observed object of thinking.

Hence the first observation that we make about think- [12] ing is that it is the unobserved element in our normal spiritual life.

It is because thinking is based on our own activity that [13] we do not observe it in everyday spiritual life. What I do not produce myself enters my observational field as an object. I see it as something that arose without me. It confronts me; and I must accept it as the prerequisite for my process of thinking. While thinking about the object, I am occupied with it and my gaze is turned toward it. My attention is directed not toward my activity, but toward the object of this activity. In other words, when I think, I do not look at my thinking, which I myself am producing, but at the object of thinking, which I am not producing.

[14]   I am in the same situation even if I allow the exceptional state of affairs to occur and think about my thinking itself. I can never observe my present thinking; only after I have thought can I take the experiences I have had during my thinking process as the object of my thinking. If I wanted to observe my present thinking, I would have to split myself into two personalities, one that thinks and one that looks on during this thinking, which I cannot do. I can observe my present thinking only in two separate acts. The thinking to be observed is never the one currently active, but a different one. For this purpose, it does not matter whether I make observations about my own earlier thinking, follow the thought process of another person, or, as with the movement of billiard balls, suppose an imaginary thought process.

[15]   These two are therefore incompatible: active production and contemplative confrontation. The first book of Moses already recognizes this. In the Book of Genesis, God produces the world in the first six days of creation; only once it is there is it possible to contemplate it: "And God looked at everything he had made, and behold, it was very good." The same holds true of our thinking. It must first be there if we are to observe it.

[16]   It is impossible for us to observe thinking as it occurs at each moment for the same reason that we can know our

thinking more immediately and intimately than any other process in the world. Precisely because we ourselves produce our thinking, we know the characteristics of its course and how it occurs. What can be found only indirectly in other spheres of observation—the appropriate connections and the relationship of individual objects— we know in a completely immediate way in thinking. Without going beyond the phenomena, I cannot know why thunder follows lightning for my observation. But I know immediately, from the content of the two concepts, why my *thinking* links the *concept* of thunder with that of lightning. Naturally it is not a question of whether I have correct concepts of lightning and thunder. The connection between those that I do have is clear, by means of the very concepts themselves.

This transparent clarity we experience in relation to the thinking process is completely independent of our knowledge of the physiological bases of thinking. I am speaking here of thinking as given by observation of our spiritual activity. I am not concerned with how one material process in the brain occasions or influences another when I carry out an operation in thought. What I observe about thinking is not the process in my brain linking the concepts of lightning and thunder, but rather the process enabling me to bring the two concepts into a specific relationship. Observation tells me that nothing guides me in combining my thoughts except the content of my thoughts. I am not guided by the material processes in my brain. In a less materialistic age than our own, this observation would of course be completely superfluous. But today—when there

[17]

are people who believe that once we know what matter is we will also know how matter thinks—it must still be stated that one can talk about thinking without immediately running into brain physiology. Most people today find it hard to grasp the concept of thinking in its purity. Whoever immediately counters the view of thinking developed here with the statement of Cabanis that "the brain secretes thoughts as the liver does gall or the salivary ducts saliva" simply does not know what I am talking about.[2] Such a person wants to find thinking through a mere process of observation—wants to proceed with thinking in the same way as we proceed with other objects of the world content. But thinking cannot be found in this way, because precisely as an object of world content thinking eludes normal observation, as I have shown. Those who cannot overcome materialism lack the capacity to induce in themselves the exceptional state that brings into consciousness what remains unconscious during all other spiritual activity. Just as one cannot discuss color with the blind, so one cannot discuss thinking with those who lack the good will to place themselves in this position. But at least they should not imagine that we take physiological processes to be thinking. They cannot explain thinking because they simply do not see it.

---

2. Pierre-Jean-Georges Cabanis (1757–1808). A French physician and philosopher, Professor of Hygiene (1794) and legal medicine and history of medicine (1799) at the Medical School of Paris, who evolved radically mechanistic and materialistic theory of biology. The phrase is from "Rapports du physique et du moral de l'homme" (1799, published 1802).

But for everyone who has the capacity to observe [18] thinking—and, with good will, every normally constitut- ed human being has this capacity—the observation of thinking is the most important observation that can be made. For in thinking we observe something of which we ourselves are the producers. We find ourselves facing something that to begin with is not foreign to us, but our own activity. We know how the thing we are observing comes about. We see through the relationships and the connections. A secure point has been won, from which we can reasonably hope to seek an explanation of the other world phenomena.

The feeling of having such a secure point caused the [19] founder of modern philosophy, René Descartes, to base the whole of human knowledge on the sentence, "I think, therefore I am."[3] All other things, all other events, exist without me, but whether as truth or as fantasy and dream, I cannot say. I am absolutely certain of only one thing, for I myself bring it to its secure existence: my thinking. It might have another source for its existence. It might come from God or somewhere else. But that it exists in the sense that I bring it forth myself—of that, I am certain. Descartes initially had no justification to ascribe a different meaning to his sentence. He could only claim that, in thinking, I lay hold of myself in the activity that is, of all the world' s con- tent, the most my own. What the tacked-on *therefore I am*

---

3. René Descartes (1596–1650). French philosopher and mathemati- cian. Author of the famous *Discourse on Method* (1637). See also Rudolf Steiner, *The Riddles of Philosophy*.

might mean has been much disputed. But it can be meaningful only under one condition. The simplest statement that I can make about a thing is that it *is*, that it exists. I cannot immediately say how the existence of anything entering the horizon of my experience might be characterized more precisely. To determine in what sense an object can be described as existent, it would have to be examined in relation to others. An experienced event can be a series of perceptions, but it can also be a dream, a hallucination, and so forth. In brief, I cannot say in what sense an object exists. I cannot derive its existence from the experienced event itself, but I can learn it when I consider the event in relation to other things. But there, too, I cannot know *more* than how it stands in relation to those things. My search finds firm ground only when I find an object the meaning of whose existence I can draw out of itself. As a thinker, I am myself such an object. I endow my existence with the definite, self-reposing content of thinking activity. From there, I can now proceed to ask whether other things exist in the same or in a different sense.

[20]   When we make thinking into an object of observation, we add to the rest of the observed world-content something that normally escapes our attention, but we do not change the way in which we relate to it, which is the same as to other things. We increase the number of the objects of our observation, but not our method of observing. As we observe other things, a process that is overlooked intermingles in world events (in which I now include the act of observation itself). Something is present that differs from all other events, and is not taken into consideration.

But when I observe my thinking, no such unconsidered element is present. For what now hovers in the background is itself only, once again, thinking. The observed object is qualitatively the same as the activity that directs itself toward it. And this is again a special characteristic of thinking. When we make thinking into an object of observation, we are not compelled to do so with the aid of something that is qualitatively different to it; we can remain within the same element.

If I weave into my thinking an object that is given without my participation, I go beyond my observation, and the question will arise: What gives me the right to do so? Why don' t I simply allow the object to work upon me? How is it possible for my thinking to have a relation to the object? These are questions that all who think about their own thought processes must ask themselves. But they fall away when we think about thinking itself. We add nothing foreign to thinking, and thus need not excuse ourselves for such an addition. *[21]*

Schelling says, "To know nature is to create nature."[4] Anyone who takes these words of the bold na- *[22]*

---

4. Friedrich Wilhelm Joseph von Schelling (1775–1855). German idealist philosopher. After being a fellow student with Hegel and Hölderlin at the Tübingen Stift or Seminary, Schelling was Professor at Jena (1798), Würzburg (1803), München (1827) and Berlin (1841–46). Breaking free first from Fichtean (1801), then from Hegelian (c. 1807) idealism, Schelling, much influenced by the theosophy of Jakob Boehme, finally created a unique dynamical philosophy of nature, myth, creativity, and freedom. The phrase is from *Erster Entwurf eines Systems der Naturphilosophie* (1799).

ture philosopher literally must renounce forever all knowledge of nature. For nature is simply there, and to create it a second time, one would have to know the principles according to which it arose. One would first have to look at the conditions for the existence of nature as it is, in order to apply these to the nature one wished to create. But this "looking," which would have to precede any creating, would be to know nature already, even if, after successfully looking, one did not then go on to create. The only kind of nature that one could create without *previously* knowing it would be a nature that *[23]*   did not yet exist.

What is impossible with nature—creation before cognition—we achieve with thinking. If we waited, before thinking, until we already understood it, then we would never get to that point. We must think resolutely ahead, in order later to arrive by observation at a knowledge of what we have done. We ourselves create the object for the observation of thinking. The presence of all other objects *[24]*   has been taken care of without our participation.

Someone could oppose my proposition that we must think before we can observe thinking with the proposition that we also have to digest before we can observe the process of digestion. That objection would be similar to the

5. Blaise Pascal (1625–1662). French mathematical prodigy, physicist, philosopher, and mystic. He wrote an original work on conic sections at sixteen; studied infinitesimal calculus; solved the problem of the general quadrature of the cycloid; developed the differential calculus; originated (with Fermat) the mathematical theory of probability; invented the first calculator, etc.

one Pascal[5] made to Descartes, claiming that one could also say, "I go for a walk, therefore I am." Certainly, I must also go ahead and digest before I have studied the physiological process of digestion. But this could only be compared with the contemplation of thinking if afterward I did not contemplate digestion in thinking, but wanted to eat and digest it. It is, after all, not without reason that digesting cannot become the object of digesting, but thinking can very well become the object of thinking. *[25]*

Without a doubt: in thinking we hold a corner of the world process where we must be present if anything is to occur. And this is exactly the point at issue. This is exactly why things stand over against me so puzzlingly: because I am so uninvolved in their creation. I simply find them present. But in the case of thinking, I know how it is done. This is why, for the contemplation of the whole world-process, there is no more primal starting point than thinking. *[26]*

I will mention a widespread error regarding thinking. It consists in saying that thinking, as it is in itself, is nowhere given to us. The thinking that links the observations of our experience, interweaving them with a conceptual network, is said to be not at all the same as that which we afterward scoop out of the objects and make into the object of our contemplation. What we first weave unconsciously into things is said to be something completely different from what we then extract from them consciously. *[27]*

Those who reason like this do not understand that they

. As a philosophical, mystical thinker he was the author of the famous *Pensées* and *Lettres Provinciales*.

cannot escape thinking in this way. If I want to look at thinking, I cannot leave thinking behind. If we distinguish preconscious thinking from later, conscious thinking, we should at least not forget that this distinction is quite external and has nothing to do with the matter at hand. I in no way make a thing into something else by contemplating it in thinking. I can imagine that a being with altogether different sense organs and with a differently functioning intellect would have a very different mental picture of a horse than I do, but I cannot imagine that my own thinking becomes something else because I observe it. I myself observe what I myself produce. The issue is not how my thinking appears to an intellect different from my own, but how it appears to me. In any case, the picture of *my* thinking in a different intellect cannot be a truer one than in my own. Only if I were myself not the being who thinks, and this thinking confronted me as the activity of a being alien to me, only then could I say that although my image of its thinking arises in a certain way, I cannot know how its

[28]   thinking is in itself.

For the moment, however, there is not the slightest reason for me to regard my own thinking from a different standpoint. I contemplate the rest of the world with the help of thinking. Why should I make an exception for my

[29]   thinking?

I believe I have now justified beginning my consideration of the world with thinking. When Archimedes had invented the lever, he thought that he could use it to lift the whole cosmos on its hinges, if only he could find a secure point to set his instrument. For this, he needed something that was supported by itself, not by something else. In thinking, we have a principle that exists through itself. Starting with thinking, then, let us attempt to understand the world. We can grasp thinking through itself. The only question is whether we can also grasp anything else through it.   *[30]*

Thus far I have spoken of thinking without giving account of its vehicle, human consciousness. Most contemporary philosophers would object that there has to be a consciousness before there can be thinking. According to them, we should therefore proceed from consciousness and not from thinking, since there would be no thinking without consciousness. To this I would have to reply that if I want to understand the relationship between thinking and consciousness, I must think about it. Therefore I presuppose thinking. One can certainly still reply that, if a philosopher wishes to *understand* consciousness, then he or she makes use of thinking, and presupposes it to that extent; yet, in the normal course of life, thinking arises within consciousness and therefore presupposes the latter. If this answer were given to the creator of the world, who wanted to make thinking from scratch, then it would doubtless be justified. Naturally, the creator could not let thinking arise without first having consciousness come about. For philosophers, however, it is not a question of creating the world but of understanding it. Hence they do not need to seek a starting point for creating the world, but rather one for understanding it. I find it very peculiar when people reproach philosophers for concerning themselves in the first place with the correctness of their principles and not immediately with the objects they want to understand. The creator of the world had to know how to find a vehicle for thinking, but the philosopher has to seek a secure foundation from which to understand what already exists. What good does it do to begin with consciousness and subject it to a thinking contemplation, if before we do so we do not know whether *thinking* contemplation can offer insight into things?

[31]

We must first consider thinking completely neutrally, without reference to a thinking subject or a thought object. For in subject and object we already have concepts that are formed through thinking. We cannot deny that, *before anything else can be understood, thinking must be understood.* Those who deny this forget that, as human beings, they are not the first but the last link in the chain of creation. To explain the world through concepts, we cannot proceed from the earliest elements of existence. Rather, we must proceed from the element that is given to us as the nearest, the most intimate. We cannot, in a single bound, set ourselves at the beginning of the world and begin our study there. Instead, we must proceed from the present moment and see whether we can rise from the later to the earlier. As long as geology spoke of imagined catastrophes to explain the present state of the earth, it groped in the dark. Only when it made its starting point the investigation of those processes that are still active on earth today, and reasoned backward from these to the past, did it win for itself a secure foundation. As long as philosophy assumes all kinds of principles—such as atoms, movement, matter, will, and the unconscious—it will hover in the air.

Only when the philosopher regards the absolutely last thing as the first can the goal be reached. But this absolutely last thing achieved by world evolution is *thinking*.

Some say that, even so, we cannot know for certain [32] whether our thinking in itself is correct, and therefore that, to this extent, the point of departure remains a doubtful one. This statement is just as reasonable as to entertain doubts about whether a tree in itself is correct. Thinking is a fact, and to speak about the correctness or falsehood of a fact is meaningless. At most, I can have doubts about whether thinking is used correctly, just as I can doubt whether a certain tree gives the right wood for a certain tool. The task of the present work is precisely to show how the application of thinking to the world is right or wrong. I can understand someone doubting that thinking can know something of the world, but it is incomprehensible to me that anyone could doubt the intrinsic correctness of thinking itself.

Addendum to the new edition (1918) [1]

The preceding discussion points to the significant difference between thinking and all other activities of the soul, a fact that reveals itself to truly unprejudiced observation. Anyone who does not strive for such unprejudiced observation will be tempted to make such objections as: "When I think about a rose, this thinking expresses only a relationship of my "I" to the rose, just as it does when I feel the beauty of the rose. A relationship exists between the "I" and the object in thinking just as it does, for example, in feeling or perceiving." This objection fails to take into account that it is *only* in the act of thinking that the "I" knows itself as *one* being with what is active in all aspects of the activity. With no other activity of the soul is this completely so. For example, when pleasure is felt, subtler observation can easily distinguish to what degree the "I" knows itself as one with what is active, and to what degree something passive is present within it, with the result that the pleasure simply arises for the "I." And the same is true of the other activities of the soul as well. But we must not confuse "having thought-pictures" with working out thoughts by means of thinking. Thought-pictures can emerge dreamily in the soul, like vague suggestions. But this is not *thinking*.

To be sure, someone could now point out that, if thinking is meant in this way, then there is willing hidden in the thinking, so that not just thinking but also the willing of thinking is involved. But this would only justify our saying that real thinking must always be willed. Yet this is irrelevant to our previous characterization of thinking. It may be that the essence of thinking requires that it always be *willed*. But the point is that in this case nothing is willed that, in its execution, does not appear to the "I" as wholly its own, self-supervised activity. We must even acknowledge that it is precisely *because* of the essential nature of thinking put forward here that thinking appears to the observer as completely willed. Anyone who makes the effort really to see into all that is relevant to an assessment of thinking cannot but notice that the special characteristic discussed here does indeed belong to this activity of the soul.

A person whom the author of this book values very highly as a thinker has objected that one cannot speak of thinking as I have done here, because what we believe we observe as active thinking is only an appearance.[6] In reality, one only observes the results of a non-conscious activity that lies at the basis of thinking. And only because this non-conscious activity is unobserved does the illusion arise that the thinking that we do observe exists in itself, as when we imagine ourselves to see movement in a rapid succession of electrical sparks. This objection, too, rests on an inexact view of the facts. It fails to take into account that it is the "I" itself that—*within* thinking—observes *its own* activity. If it could be fooled, as we are by the rapid succession of electrical sparks, the "I" would have to be *outside* thinking. We could say instead that anyone who makes such a comparison deceives himself or herself mightily, a bit like one who claims that a light perceived to be in motion is re-lit by an unknown hand wherever it appears.—No, whoever wishes to see in thinking something other than what is produced within the "I" itself as surveyable activity must first become blind to the simple state of affairs available to observation, in order then to lay a hypothetical activity at the base of thinking. Those who do not blind themselves must recognize that whatever they "think up" in this way and add to thinking leads away from the essence of thinking. Unprejudiced observation shows that noth-

6. Eduard von Hartmann.

ing can be attributed to the essence of thinking that is not found *within* thinking itself. One cannot arrive at anything that *causes* thinking if one leaves the realm of thinking behind.

CHAPTER 4

THE WORLD AS PERCEPT

Concepts and *ideas* arise through thinking. Words cannot [1]
say what a concept is. Words can only make us notice that
we have concepts. When we see a tree, our thinking reacts
to our observation, a conceptual counterpart joins the object, and we consider the object and the conceptual counterpart as belonging together. When the object disappears
from our field of observation, only the conceptual counterpart remains. The latter is the concept of the object.
The wider our experience extends, the greater the sum of
our concepts. But the concepts by no means stand apart
from one another. They combine into a lawful whole. For
example, the concept "organism" combines with others,
such as "lawful development" and "growth." Other concepts, formed from individual things, collapse wholly
into a unity. Thus, all concepts that I form about lions
combine into the general concept "lion." In this way, individual concepts link together into a closed conceptual
system, in which each has its particular place. Ideas are
not qualitatively different from concepts. They are only

concepts with more content, more saturated, and more inclusive. I emphasize here that it is important to note at this point that my point of departure is *thinking*, not *concepts* or *ideas,* which must first be gained by thinking. Concepts and ideas already presuppose thinking. Therefore, what I have said about the nature of thinking—that it rests within itself and is determined by nothing—cannot simply be transferred to concepts. (I note this explicitly here, because this is where I differ from Hegel, who posits the concept as first and original.)

[2]   Concepts cannot be won by observation. This can already be seen from the fact that children form concepts for the objects in their environment only slowly and gradually. Concepts are added onto observation.

[3]   A popular contemporary philosopher, Herbert Spencer, portrays the spiritual process that we perform in response to observation as follows:

[4]   If, wandering through the fields on a September's day, we hear a noise a few steps in front of us, and see the grass in motion by the side of the ditch whence the noise seemed to proceed, then we will probably approach the place to find out what produced the noise and movement. At our approach, there flutters in the ditch a partridge, and with this our curiosity is satisfied: we have what we call an explanation of the phenomena. Carefully examined, this explanation depends on the following: because in life we have countless times experienced that a disturbance in the peaceful state of small bodies accompanies the movement of other

bodies located among them, and because we have therefore generalized the relationships between such disturbances and such movements, we consider this particular disturbance explained as soon as we find that it represents an example of just this relationship.[1]

Examined more closely, however, the situation looks quite different than this description suggests. When I hear a noise, I first seek the concept that fits this observation. Someone who thinks no more of it simply hears the noise and leaves it at that. But by thinking about it, it becomes clear to me that I must regard the noise as an effect. Only when I combine the concept of *effect* with the perception of the noise am I inclined to go beyond the individual observation itself and seek a *cause*. The concept of effect evokes that of cause, and I then seek the causative object, which I find in the form of a partridge. But I can never gain the concepts of cause and effect by mere observation, no matter how many cases I may observe. Observation calls forth thinking, and it is only the latter that shows me how to link one isolated experience with another.

When people demand of a "strictly objective science" *[5]* that it draw its content from observation alone, then they must at the same time demand that it renounce all thinking. For thinking, by its very nature, goes over and above what has been observed.

This is the moment to move from thinking to the being *[6]* who thinks. For it is through the thinker that thinking is

---

1. Spencer, *First Principles*, Part I, Chapter IV.

linked to observation. Human consciousness is the stage where concept and observation meet and are connected to one another. This is, in fact, what characterizes human consciousness. It is the mediator between thinking and observation. To the extent that human beings observe things, things appear as given; to the extent that human beings think, they experience themselves as active. They regard things as *objects*, and themselves as thinking *subjects*. Because they direct their thinking to what they observe, they are conscious of objects; because they direct their thinking to themselves, they are conscious of themselves, they have *self-consciousness*. Human consciousness must necessarily at the same time also be *self*-consciousness, because it is a *thinking* consciousness. For when thinking directs its gaze toward its own activity, it has before it as its object its very own being, that is, its subject.

[7]   But we must not overlook that it is only with the help of thinking that we can define ourselves as subjects, and contrast ourselves to objects. Therefore, thinking must never be regarded as a merely subjective activity. Thinking is *beyond* subject and object. It forms both of these concepts, just as it does all others. Thus, when we as thinking subjects relate a concept to an object, we must not regard this relationship as something merely subjective. It is not the subject that introduces the relationship, but thinking. The subject does not think because it is a subject; rather, it appears to itself as a subject because it can think. The activity that human beings exercise as *thinking* beings is therefore not merely subjective, but it is a kind of activity

that is neither subjective nor objective; it goes beyond both these concepts. I should never say that my individual subject thinks; rather, it lives by the grace of thinking. Thus, thinking is an element that leads me beyond myself and unites me with objects. But it separates me from them at the same time, by setting me over against them as subject.

Just this establishes the dual nature of the human being: [8] we think, and our thinking embraces ourselves along with the rest of the world; but at the same time we must also, by means of thinking, define ourselves as *individuals* standing over against *things.*

Next, we must ask ourselves how the other element, [9] which until now we have characterized merely as the object of observation, enters consciousness where it encounters thinking.

To answer this question, we must purge our field of ob- [10] servation of everything that thinking has already brought into it. For the content of our consciousness at any moment is always already permeated by concepts in the most varied way.

We must imagine that a being with a fully developed [11] human intelligence arises from nothing and confronts the world. What this being would be aware of, before it brought thinking into action, is the pure content of observation. The world would then reveal to this being only the pure, relation-less aggregate of *sensory objects*: colors, sounds, sensations of pressure, warmth, taste, and smell, and then feelings of pleasure and unpleasure. This aggregate is the content of pure, thought-free observation. Over against it stands thinking, which is ready to unfurl its activity when a point of departure is found. Experience soon teaches that it *is* found. Thinking is able to draw threads from one element of observation to another. It joins specific concepts to these elements and thus brings them into a relationship with each other. We have already seen how a noise we encounter is linked with another observation, in that we characterize the former as the effect of the latter.

[12]   If we recall that the activity of thinking should never be considered subjective, we will not be tempted to believe that such relationships, which are established by thinking, have merely a subjective validity.

[13]   It now becomes a question of discovering, through thinking contemplation, how the immediately given content of observation—the pure, relationless aggregate of sensory objects —relates to our conscious subject.

[14]   Because of shifting habits of speech, it seems necessary for me to come to an agreement with my reader on the use of a word that I must employ from now on. The word is *percept*. I will use the word "*percept*" to refer to "the immediate objects of sensation" mentioned above, insofar as the conscious subject knows these objects through observation. Thus, it is not the process of observation but the *object* of observation that I designate with this name.

[15]   I have not chosen to use the term *sensation*, because sensation has a specific meaning in physiology that is narrower than that of my concept of the percept. I can easily characterize a feeling within myself as a percept, but not as a sensation in the physiological sense. By its becoming *percept* for me, I gain knowledge even of my feeling. And

because we gain knowledge of our thinking, too, through observation, we can even call thinking, as it first appears to our consciousness, a percept.

The naive person considers percepts, as they first ap- *[16]* pear, to be things that have an existence quite independent of the human being in question. If we see a tree, we initially believe that the tree, in the form that we see it, with its various colors, etc., is standing there in the spot to which our gaze is directed. From this naive standpoint, if we see the sun appear in the morning as a disc on the horizon and then follow the progress of this disc, we believe that all of this exists and occurs just as we observe it. We cling fast to this belief until we meet other percepts that contradict the first. The child, with no experience of distances, reaches for the moon, and only when a second percept comes to contradict the first can the child correct what at first seemed real to it. Every extension in the sphere of my percepts makes me correct my image of the world. This is evident in daily life, just as it is in the spiritual evolution of humankind. The ancient image of the relation of the earth to the sun and the other heavenly bodies had to be replaced by that of Copernicus, because the ancient image did not agree with new, previously unknown percepts. When Dr. Franz operated on someone born blind, the latter said that before his operation he had arrived through the sense of touch at a very different image of the size of objects. He had to correct his tactile percepts with his visual percepts.[2]

2. Johann Christoph August Franz, (born 1807), eye surgeon.

[17]   Why are we compelled continually to correct our observations?

[18]   A simple reflection provides the answer to this question. If I stand at the end of an avenue, the trees at the other end appear to me smaller and closer together than those where I am standing. My perceptual picture changes as I change the place from which I make my observations. Thus the form in which the perceptual image confronts me depends on conditions determined not by the object but by me, the perceiver. The avenue does not care where I stand. But the image that I have of the avenue is fundamentally dependent on where I stand. In the same way, it makes no difference to the sun and the solar system that human beings regard them just from the earth. But the perceptual image of the heavens that presents itself to human beings is determined by their living on the earth. This dependence of the perceptual image on our place of observation is the easiest kind of dependence to understand. The issue becomes more difficult when we realize the dependence of our perceptual world on our bodily and spiritual organization. The physicist shows that vibrations of the air are present in the space where we hear a sound, and that even the body in which we seek the source of the sound displays a vibrating movement in its parts. But we become aware of this movement as sound only if we have a normally constructed ear. Without this, the whole world would be forever silent for us. Physiology teaches us that there are some people who perceive nothing of the magnificent splendor of color surrounding us. Their perceptual picture shows only nuances of dark

and light. Others fail to perceive only a specific color, such as red. Their image of the world lacks this hue, and is therefore actually different from that of the average human being. I should like to call the dependence of my perceptual image on my place of observation a "mathematical" one, and its dependence on my organization a "qualitative" one. The relative sizes and distances of my percepts are determined through the former; their quality through the latter. That I see a red surface as red—this qualitative determination—depends on the organization of my eye.

Initially, then, our perceptual images are subjective.   *[19]* This recognition of the subjective character of our percepts can easily lead us to doubt whether anything objective underlies them at all. If we know that a percept, for example the color red or a particular sound, is only possible thanks to the structure of our own organism, then we can easily come to believe that the percept does not exist outside our subjectivity, and that apart from the act of perceiving, whose object it is, it has no kind of existence. This view found its classic expression in George Berkeley, who believed that as soon as we become aware of the importance of the subject for percepts, we can no longer believe in a world that exists apart from the conscious spirit:

> Some truths are so near and so obvious to the mind that man need only open his eyes to see them. Such I take this important truth to be, to wit, that all the choir of heaven and furniture of the earth, in a word, all those bodies which compose the mighty frame of the world, have not any subsistence with-

out a mind, that their *being is* to be perceived or known; that, consequently, so long as they are not actually perceived by me, or do not exist in my mind or that of any other *created spirit*, they must either have no existence at all, *or else subsist in the mind of some Eternal Spirit.*[3]

From this point of view, nothing remains of the percept if we exclude the process of its being perceived. There is no color when none is seen, no sound when none is heard. Outside the act of perception, categories such as extension, form, and movement exist just as little as color and sound. Nowhere do we see extension or form alone; rather, we always see these in conjunction with color or other qualities indisputably dependent on our subjectivity. If the latter disappear with our perception, then so must the former, which are bound to them.

[20]   To the objection that, even if figure, color, sound, and so forth do not exist outside the act of perception, there must still be things that exist without consciousness and are similar to the conscious perceptual images, the Berkeleyan response would be to say that a color can only be similar to a color, a figure similar to a figure. Our percepts can be similar only to our percepts, not to any other kind

---

3. George Berkeley (1685–1753), *A Treatise Concerning the Principles of Human Knowledge* (1710). Berkeley was an Irish philosopher and a lecturer in divinity, Greek, and Hebrew at Dublin University, who lived in America (1728–31) before being made Bishop of Cloyne (1734) and retiring in Oxford (1752). He was the philosopher of immaterialism and (subjective) idealism epitomized in the phrase *esse est percipi* that is, to be is to be perceived.

of thing. Even what we call an object is nothing but than a group of percepts connected in a certain way. If I take away from a table its form, extension, color, and so forth—in fact, everything that is only my percept—then nothing more is left. This view, followed through logically, thus leads to the assertion that the objects of my perception are only present through me; they disappear with my perceiving and have no meaning without it. Apart from my percepts, I know of no objects and can know of none.

There is nothing to object to in this claim, as long as it   [21] remains merely a general consideration of how the percept is partly determined by the organization of the subject. The matter would appear fundamentally different, however, if we were in a position to describe the exact function of our perceiving in the origin of a percept. We would then know what happens to the percept during perceiving, and could also determine what aspect of the percept must already exist before it is perceived.

With this, our investigation is directed away from the   [22] object of perception and toward its subject. I do not perceive only other things; I also perceive myself. In contrast to the perceptual images that continually come and go, *I* am what remains. This, initially, is the content of my percept of myself. When I have other percepts, the percept of the *I* can always appear in my consciousness. However, when I am immersed in the perception of a given object, then for the time being I am conscious only of the latter. The percept of my self can be added to this. I am then not merely conscious of the object, but also of my personality, which stands over against the object and observes it. I not only see a tree, I also know that *I am* the one who sees it. Moreover, I realize that something goes on in me *while* I observe the tree. If the tree disappears from my view, a remnant of this process remains in my consciousness: an image of the tree. As I was observing, this image united itself with my self. My self is thereby enriched: its content has received a new element into itself. I call this element my *mental picture* (Vorstellung) of the tree. There would be no need to speak of *mental pictures* if I did not experience them in the percept of my self. In that case, percepts would come and go; I would let them pass by. It is only because I perceive my self, and notice that with every percept the content of my self also changes, that I find myself compelled to connect the observation of the object with my own changed state, and to speak of my mental picture.

[23]   I perceive mental pictures *in my self* in the same way that I perceive colors, sounds, and so forth *in other objects*. From this point of view, I can now make a distinction, calling these other objects that stand over against me the *outer world,* while designating the content of my self-percept as the *inner world.* Failure to recognize the relation between the mental picture and the object has led to the greatest misunderstandings in modern philosophy. The perception of an inner change, the modification that my self undergoes, has been thrust into the foreground, and the object causing this modification has been lost sight of altogether. It has been said that we do not perceive objects, but only our mental pictures. I am not supposed to know anything of the object of my observation, the table in itself, but only of the change that occurs in my

self while I perceive the table. This view must not be confused with the Berkeleyan view mentioned above. Berkeley asserts the subjective nature of my perceptual content, but he does not say that I can know only my mental pictures. He limits my knowledge to my mental pictures because he believes that there are no objects outside mental picturing. In this view, once I cease directing my gaze toward it, what I regard as a table no longer exists. Hence for Berkeley my percepts arise immediately from the power of God. I see a table because God calls forth this percept in me. Berkeley knows of no real beings other than God and human spirits. What we call the world is present only within spirits. What the naive human being calls the outer world, corporeal nature, does not exist for Berkeley.

Berkeley's view stands in contrast to the currently prevailing Kantian view.[4] This also limits our knowledge of the world to our mental pictures. But it does not do so because of the conviction that no things except these mental pictures can exist. Rather, the Kantian view believes us to be so organized that we can learn only of modifications in our own self, not of the things-in-themselves that cause them. From the circumstance that I know only my mental

---

4. Immanuel Kant (1724–1804). Generally considered to be the founder of epistemology, and indeed, philosophy in the modern sense. Steiner began his "prelude" to *Intuitive Thinking—Truth and Science [Knowledge]* (1892)—with the sentence: "Present day philosophy suffers from an unhealthy faith in Kant." To the extent that it is believed that human beings can only know the forms of their own knowing and that there are therefore limits to the human ability to know, this unhealthy dependence of Kant still prevails today.

pictures, the Kantian view draws the conclusion not that there is no existence independent of these mental pictures, but only that the subject cannot directly receive such an existence into itself. This view then concludes that only through "the medium of its subjective thoughts can it imagine, fantasize, think, cognize, or even perhaps fail to cognize" this existence.[5] This (Kantian) view believes it is saying something absolutely certain, something that is immediately evident without any proof.

> The first fundamental proposition that the philosopher must bring to clear consciousness consists in the recognition that our knowledge does not *initially* extend beyond our mental pictures. Our mental pictures are the only things that we know directly, experience directly; and just because we experience them immediately, even the most radical doubt cannot tear from us our knowledge of them. By contrast, the knowledge that goes beyond our mental pictures—I use this expression in its widest sense, so that it includes all psychical events—is not safe from doubt. Hence, *at the start of philosophizing*, all knowledge that goes beyond mental pictures must be explicitly posited as open to doubt.

---

5. Otto Liebmann, *On the Analysis of Reality*, p.28. Liebmann (1840–1912) was a leading Neo-Kantian. Steiner describes his works as "veritable models of philosophical criticism. Here a caustic mind ingeniously discovers contradictions in the worlds of thought, reveals as half truths what appear as safe judgments, and shows what unsatisfactory elements the individual sciences contain when their results appear before the highest tribunals of thought...." (*The Riddles of Philosophy*).

This is how Volkelt's book, *Immanuel Kant's Episte-mology*, begins.[6] But what is presented in it as if it were an immediate and self-evident truth is really the result of the following kind of thought process. "The naive human being believes that objects, just as we perceive them, also exist outside human consciousness. But physics, physiology and psychology seem to teach that our organization is necessary for our perceptions and that consequently we cannot know anything about things other than what our organization transmits to us. Hence our percepts are modifications of our organization and not things in themselves." Eduard von Hartmann characterizes this train of thought as necessarily leading to the conviction that we can have direct knowledge only of our mental pictures. [7] Because we find, outside our organism, vibrations of bodies and of the air that appear to us as sound, this view reasons that what we call sound is nothing more than a subjective reaction of our organization to these vibrations in the outer world. In the same way, color and warmth are only modifications of our organism. According to this view, the percepts of warmth and color are evoked in us by the effects of processes in the outer world that are utterly different from our experience of warmth or color. When these processes stimulate the nerves in my skin, I have the subjective percept of

---

6. Johannes Volkelt (1842–1930) was another Neo-Kantian. Steiner kept up with the work of Liebmann and Volkelt. See his commentaries in *The Riddles of Philosophy*, Part Two, Chapter IV.
7. Cf. *Fundamental Problems of Epistemology*, pp.16-40.

warmth; when they stimulate the optic nerve, I perceive light and color. Light, color, and warmth are therefore what my sense nerves create as responses to outside stimuli. Even the sense of touch presents me not with objects of the external world, but only with my own states. Following modern physics, we might think that the body consists of infinitesimal particles—molecules—and that these molecules do not border one another immediately but are a certain distance apart. Between them, then, is empty space. They affect one another through this space by means of forces of attraction and repulsion. When I bring my hand near a body, the molecules of my hand never touch those of the body immediately. There always remains a certain distance between body and hand. What I feel as the resistance of the body is nothing more than the effect of the repellent force that its molecules exercise on my hand. I am completely outside the body in question and merely perceive its effect on my organism.

[24]   To complete these considerations, we have the teaching of the so-called specific sense energies proposed by J. Müller.[8] According to this theory, our senses have the peculiar quality that each sense responds to all external stimuli in only one specific fashion. If a stimulus is applied to the optic nerve, then the percept of light arises,

---

8. Johannes Peter Müller (1801–1858), Physiologist and comparative anatomist, introduced concept of specific energy of nerves; explained color sensations produced by pressure on retina; studied blood, lymph, chyle, the voice, and embryology. Author of *Handbuch der Physiologie des Menschen* (1833–40).

whether the excitation occurs through what we call light, through mechanical pressure, or through an electrical current impinging on the nerve. On the other hand, the same external stimuli evoke different percepts in the different senses. It appears to follow from this that our senses can transmit only what occurs within them and transmit nothing from the outer world. The senses determine the percepts according to their nature.

Physiology shows that there can also be no direct [25] knowledge of what effect objects have within our sense organs. When physiologists follow the processes in our own body, they find the effects of external motion already transformed within the sense organs in the most various ways. We see this most clearly in the eye and the ear. Both are very complicated organs, which fundamentally alter an external stimulus before bringing it to the corresponding nerve. From the peripheral nerve ending, the already modified stimulus is now led on to the brain. Here, the central organs must in turn be stimulated. From this, the conclusion is drawn that the external process undergoes a series of transformations before coming to consciousness. What goes on in the brain is connected to the external process through so many intermediate processes that we cannot imagine any similarity between them. What the brain then finally transmits to the soul are neither external processes, nor processes in the sense organs, but only processes within the brain. Yet even these the soul does not perceive directly. What we ultimately have in consciousness are not brain processes at all, but *sensations*. My sensation of *red* has no similarity to the process occurring in the brain when I sense redness. Redness emerges again only as an effect in the soul, and is caused by the brain process alone. Therefore, Hartmann says: "What the subject perceives are therefore always only modifications of its own psychic states and nothing else."[9] When I have the sensations, however, these are still far from being grouped into what I perceive as things. After all, only individual sensations can be transmitted to me through the brain. Sensations of hardness and softness are transmitted to me through the sense of touch; color and light through the sense of sight. Yet these are united in one and the same object. Such union, then, can only be effected by the soul itself. That is, the soul assembles separate sensations, transmitted by the brain, into bodies. My brain conveys to me separately, and by altogether different pathways, sensations of sight, taste, and hearing that the soul then combines into the mental picture of a trumpet. This final stage of a process (the mental picture of the trumpet) is given to my consciousness as the very first. In it, nothing may be found of what is outside me and originally made the impression on my senses. On the way to the brain and, through the brain, to the soul, the external object has been completely lost.

[26]   It would be hard to find another edifice of thought in the history of human culture that has been constructed with more ingenuity and that nevertheless, on closer scrutiny, collapses into nothing. Let us look more closely at how this edifice has been built up. It begins with what is

9. *Fundamental Problems of Epistemology.*

given to naive consciousness of the thing perceived. Then it shows that everything found there would be non-existent for us if we had no senses. No eye, no color. So color is not yet present in what affects the eye. It first arises through the interaction of the eye with the object. The object, then, is colorless. But the color is not present in the eye either. In the eye there is a chemical or physical process that is first led through the nerve to the brain, where it sets off another process. This process is still not yet color. It is only through the brain process that the color is evoked in the soul. There, it still does not yet enter my consciousness, but is first transferred outward by the soul onto a body. Finally I believe I am perceiving it there. We have come full circle. We have become conscious of a colored body. That comes first. Now the thought-operation begins. If I had no eyes, the body would be colorless for me. Therefore I cannot attribute color to the body. I go looking for it. I look for it in the eye, in vain; in the nerve, also in vain; in the brain, again in vain. Finally, I look for it in the soul. There I find it, to be sure, but unconnected with the body. I find the colored body only where I began. The circle has been closed. I recognize as the product of my soul what the naive human being imagines as externally present in space.

As long as we keep to this, everything seems to fit *[27]* beautifully. But we must begin again at the beginning. After all, so far I have been dealing with an entity, the external percept, of which, as a naive human being, I had an altogether false view. I believed that it had an objective permanence just as I perceived it. Now I notice that it disappears with my mental picturing; that it is only a modification of my own soul states. Do I still have the right to take it as a starting point for my reflections? Can I say that it has an effect on my soul? From now on, I must treat the table itself—which I used to believe affected me, and produced a mental picture of itself within me—as a mental picture. But then to be consistent my sense organs and the processes in them must also be only subjective. I have no right to speak of a real eye, only of my mental picture of the eye. It is the same with nerve conduction and brain processes, and no less so with the process, in the soul itself, by which *things* are supposedly built up out of the chaos of the various sensations. If I run through the elements of the act of cognition once again, assuming the correctness of that first circuit of thoughts, then the cognitive act reveals itself as a tissue of mental pictures that, as such, can have no effect on one another. I cannot say: my mental picture of the object has an effect on my mental picture of the eye, and from this interaction there proceeds the mental picture of the color. Nor do I need to do so. For as soon as it is clear to me that even my sense organs and their activities, the processes of my nerves and soul, can be given only through perception, then the above train of thought reveals itself in its perfect impossibility. So much is correct then: I can have no percept without the corresponding sense organ. But neither can I have a sense organ without perception. I can pass from my percept of the table to the eye that sees it, or to the nerves in the skin that touch it; but what takes place within these I can learn, once again, only through perception. Then I soon notice that there is no trace of similarity between the process occurring in the eye and what I perceive as color. I cannot deny my color percept by pointing to the process in the eye that takes place during this perception. Nor can I find the color in the nerve- and brain-processes; I only connect new percepts within my organism to the first percept, which the naive person places outside the organism. I only pass from one percept to the next.

Moreover, there is a gap in the whole train of argument. *[28]* I am in a position to follow the processes within my organism, up to the processes in my brain, even though my assumptions become ever more hypothetical the closer I come to its central processes. The path of *external* observation ends with the process in my brain; more precisely, it ends with what I would perceive if I could examine the brain with physical and chemical means and methods. The path of *inner* observation begins with sensation and goes as far as the construction of things from the material of sensation. At the point of transition from brain process to sensation, the path of observation is interrupted.

This way of thinking, which calls itself "critical ideal- *[29]* ism"—in contrast to the standpoint of naive conscious- ness, which it calls "naive realism"—makes the error of characterizing one percept as a mental picture, while ac- cepting another percept in exactly the same way as the na- ive realism it had ostensibly refuted. Critical idealism seeks to prove that percepts have the character of mental pictures, while naively accepting the percepts of one's own organism as objectively valid facts. What is more, it fails to notice that it is throwing together two fields of observation between which it can find no connection.

[30]   Critical idealism can only refute naive realism if, in naive-realist fashion, it accepts one's own organism as something that exists objectively. The moment it becomes aware that the percepts connected to one's own organism and those assumed by naive realism to exist objectively are completely equivalent, it can no longer base itself on the former as if on a sure foundation. It is forced to regard its own subjective organization, too, as a mere complex of mental pictures. But thereby the possibility of thinking that the content of the perceived world is caused by our mental organization is lost. We would have to assume that the mental picture "color" was only a modification of the mental picture "eye." So-called critical idealism cannot be proved without borrowing from naive realism, while naive realism can be refuted only by accepting its own presuppositions, unexamined, in another sphere.

[31]   This much, then, is certain: investigation in the perceptual realm can neither prove critical idealism, nor strip the percept of its objective character.

[32]   Still less can the proposition, "The perceived world is mental picture," be hailed as self-evident and in need of no proof. Schopenhauer begins his main work, *The World as Will and Representation [Mental Picture]*, with the words:

> The world is my mental picture. This truth applies to every living and cognizing being, though human beings alone can bring it into reflected abstract consciousness. And when they actually do

so, then philosophical understanding has dawned upon them. It is then clear and evident that we know no sun and no earth, but always only an eye that sees a sun, a hand that feels the earth; that the world around us is present only as a mental picture, that is, only in relation to something that pictures it, namely ourselves. If any truth may be asserted *a priori* it is this one: for it expresses the one form of all possible and conceivable experience that is more universal than any other, than time, space, and causality, for all of these presuppose it. . . . [10]

This whole proposition collapses in the face of the fact, noted above, that the eye and hand are percepts no less than the sun and the earth. And thus, in Schopenhauer's sense, and using his style of expression, we could answer: My eye, which sees the sun, and my hand, which feels the earth, are mental pictures in exactly the same way as the sun and the earth are. With this insight and without further ado, it is clear that I cancel out Schopenhauer's proposition. For only my real eye and my real hand could have the mental pictures of sun and earth as their modifications, but my mental pictures of eye and hand could not. Yet critical idealism can speak only of these mental pictures.

Critical idealism is completely unable to gain insight *[33]* into the relationship of percepts and mental pictures. It

10. Arthur Schopenhauer (1788-1860), *Die Welt als Wille und Vorstellung* [The World as Will and Representation]. Schopenhauer was the most influential German philosopher between Hegel and Nietzsche. See *The Riddles of Philosophy*, p. 192 ff.

cannot begin to make the distinction, mentioned above (cf. p. 59), between what happens to the percept during the process of perceiving and what must already be present in it before it is perceived. To do this, we must take a different path.

CHAPTER 5

KNOWING THE WORLD

It follows from our considerations so far that we cannot   *[1]*
prove our percepts are mental pictures by investigating
the content of our observations. Such proof is supposedly
established by showing that—if the perceptual process
occurs as it is believed to do on the basis of naive-realistic
assumptions about the psychological and physiological
constitution of the individual—we have to do not with
things in themselves but only with mental pictures of
things. However, if naive realism, consistently pursued,
leads to results that represent the exact opposite of its assumptions, then those assumptions must be seen as un-
suitable for founding a worldview and dropped. In any
case, it is invalid to reject the assumptions and accept the
consequences, as the critical idealists do who base their
claim that the world is my mental picture on the above
line of argument. (Eduard von Hartmann gives a detailed
presentation of this line of argument in *The Fundamental
Problems of Epistemology.*)

[2]   The correctness of critical idealism is one thing; the power of its proofs to convince us is another. How things stand with the former will emerge later in our discussion. But the power of its proofs to convince is zero. When someone builds a house and the ground floor collapses during construction of the second floor, then the second floor falls along with it. Naive realism is to critical idealism as this ground floor is to the second floor.

[3]   For anyone who believes that the whole perceived world is only a mental picture, and in fact is the effect on my soul of things unknown to me, the real epistemological question of course has to do with the things that lie beyond our consciousness, independent of us, and not with the mental pictures that are present only in our souls. Then the question becomes: Since the things, which are independent of us, are inaccessible to our *direct* observation, how much can we know of them *indirectly*? Those who hold this point of view are concerned not with the inner connection of their conscious percepts but only with the non-conscious *causes* of those percepts. For them, these causes exist independently and, according to their belief, the percepts disappear as soon as their senses are turned away from things. From this point of view, consciousness acts as a mirror whose images of specific things also disappear the moment that its mirroring surface is not turned toward them. But whoever does not see the things themselves but only their mirror images must learn to draw conclusions about the nature of the things *indirectly*, from the behavior of the reflections. Modern natural science takes this position. It uses percepts only as a last resort in

gaining information about the material processes standing behind them. For it, only these truly exist. If philosophers as critical idealists acknowledge existence at all, then their search for knowledge, while making use of mental pictures as a means, aims only at this existence. Such philosophers' interest skips over the subjective world of mental pictures and directs itself to what produces them.

A critical idealist might go so far as to say: "I am enclosed within my world of mental pictures, and I cannot leave it. If I think that there is something behind these mental pictures, then this thought, too, is nothing more than a mental picture." An idealist of this kind will therefore either deny the thing-in-itself entirely, or at least explain that it has no significance for human beings; that is, since we can know nothing about it, it is as good as non-existent. [4]

To a critical idealist of this kind, the whole world appears like a dream, in the face of which every attempt at knowledge would be simply meaningless. In this view, there can be only two kinds of people: biased ones who take their own dreamy fabrications for real things, and wise ones who see through the nothingness of this dream world and gradually lose all desire to bother themselves further about it. From this vantage point, even one's own personality can become a mere dream image. Just as one's own dream image appears among other dream images in sleep, so the mental picture of one's own I joins the mental pictures of the external world. Therefore our consciousness does not contain our real I, but only the mental picture of our I. For those who deny that there are things, or [5] that we can know anything of them, must also deny the existence, or at least the knowledge, of their own personality. Critical idealism thus arrives at the statement, "All reality is transformed into a wonderful dream—without there being a life that is dreamed about or a spirit that is doing the dreaming—a dream that coheres in a dream of itself."[1]

[6]   For those who believe they know immediate life is a dream, it does not matter whether they suspect that nothing exists behind it, or whether they refer their mental pictures to real things. For them, life itself loses all scientific interest. Science is an absurdity to those who believe that the accessible universe is exhausted in dreams, while to those who believe themselves equipped to reason from mental pictures to things, it consists in the investigation of "things-in-themselves." We may call the first view absolute *illusionism*; *transcendental realism* is the name given the second view by its most consistent exponent, Eduard von Hartmann.[2]

---

1. Cf. Fichte, *Die Bestimmung des Menschen* (The Vocation of Man), 1800. Johann Gottlieb Fichte (1762–1814) German philosopher between Kant and Hegel. Rudolf Steiner based his doctoral dissertation, published as *Truth and Science [Knowledge]* (1892), on Fichte's theory of knowledge. See also *The Riddles of Philosophy* and *The Riddle of Man*; also lecture of December 16, 1915, "The Spirit of Fichte in our Midst."

2. Knowledge, in this worldview, is called *transcendental* because it includes the conviction that nothing can be said directly about things in themselves, but that one must draw indirect inferences from the subjective, which is known, to the unknown, which lies beyond the subjective (the transcendent).

These two views agree with naive realism in that they [7] seek to gain a footing in the world by an investigation of percepts. But nowhere in this realm can they find a firm base.

One of the main questions for proponents of transcen- [8] dental realism must be: "How does the I bring the world of mental pictures out of itself?" A world given to us as mental pictures, which disappears as soon as we close our senses to the external world, can still be of interest in the serious search for knowledge, insofar as it is a means for indirectly investigating the world of the self-existent I. If the things we experience were mental pictures, then everyday life would be like a dream, and knowledge of the true state of affairs would be like waking up. Our dream images, too, interest us only as long as we dream and so do not see through their dream nature. The moment we awaken, we no longer ask about the inner connection of our dream images, but about the physical, physiological, and psychological processes that underlie them. In the same way, philosophers who hold the world to be their mental picture cannot interest themselves in the inner connection of its details. If they admit an existent I at all, they will not ask how one of their mental pictures connects with another. Rather, they will ask what is going on

---

On this view, the thing-in-itself is beyond the realm of the world *immediately* knowable to us, i.e., it is transcendent. Our world, however, can be related to the transcendent transcendentally. Hartmann's view is called realism because it goes beyond the subjective, the ideal, to the transcendent, the real. (Author's note)

in the soul that exists independently from themselves, while their consciousness contains a specific sequence of mental pictures. If I dream that I am drinking wine that causes burning in my throat, and then wake up with a cough, the plot of the dream ceases to be of any interest to me at the moment of awakening.[3] My attention is now directed only to the physiological and psychological processes through which the sore throat expresses itself symbolically in the dream. Similarly, as soon as philosophers are convinced that the given world has the character of a mental picture, they should immediately pass over it to the real soul lying behind it. Of course, the matter is worse if illusionism completely denies an I-in-itself behind the mental pictures, or at least holds it to be unknowable. We can be led to such a view very easily if we observe that, in contrast to dreaming, there is a state of waking, in which we have an opportunity to see through dreams and relate them to real events, but that there is no state that stands in a similar relationship to waking consciousness. Those who profess this view, however, lack the insight that there is, in fact, something that relates to mere perception as experiences in the waking state relate to dreaming. That something is *thinking*.

[9]   This lack of insight cannot be attributed to the naive observer. Such people give themselves over to life and consider things to be as real as they seem in experience. But the first step to be taken beyond this naive standpoint can only be to ask: "How does thinking relate to perception?"

---

3. Cf. Weygandt, *Entstehung der Traume*, 1893. (Author's note)

Regardless of whether or not the percept, in the form given to me, persists before and after my mental picturing, it is only with the aid of thinking that I can say anything about it. If I say that the world is my mental picture, then I have spoken the result of a process of thinking, and if my thinking is not applicable to the world, then that result is an error. Between the percept and any kind of statement about it, thinking inserts itself.

I have already indicated the reason why thinking is generally overlooked during the contemplation of things (cf. p. 35). It is because we direct our attention only to the object of our thinking, and not simultaneously to our thinking itself. Naive consciousness therefore treats thinking as something that has nothing to do with things and stands altogether apart from them, making its observations about the world. For naive consciousness, the picture of the phenomena of the world sketched by a thinker does not count as something integral to the things of the world, but as something that exists only in the human head; the world is complete even without this picture. The world is complete and finished with all its substances and forces; and human beings make a picture of this finished world. To those who think like this, we need only ask: "By what right do you declare the world to be finished without thinking? Does not the world bring forth thinking in human heads with the same necessity as it brings forth blossoms on the plant? Plant a seed in the earth. It puts forth roots and stem. It unfolds into leaves and blossoms. Set the plant before you. It links itself to a specific concept in your soul. Why does this concept belong to the

[10]

plant any less than leaves and blossoms do? You might reply that leaves and blossoms are present without a perceiving subject, while the concept appears only when a human being confronts the plant. Very well. But blossoms and leaves arise in the plant only when there is earth in which the seed can be laid and light and air in which leaves and blossoms can unfold. Just so, the concept of the plant arises when thinking consciousness approaches the plant."

[11]   It is quite arbitrary to consider as a totality, a whole, the sum of what we experience of a thing through perception alone, and to regard what results from a *thinking* contemplation as something appended, that has nothing to do with the thing itself. If I am given a rosebud today, then the picture that offers itself to my perception is limited to the present moment. But if I put the bud in water, then I will get a completely different picture of my object tomorrow. And if I can keep my eyes turned toward the rosebud, then I shall see today's state change continuously into tomorrow's through countless intermediate stages. The picture offering itself to me in a specific moment is but an accidental cross-section of an object that is caught up in a continual process of becoming. If I do not put the bud in water, then it will fail to develop a whole series of states lying within it as possibilities. And tomorrow I might be prevented from observing the blossom further, and so form an incomplete picture of it.

[12]   It is completely unrealistic to grasp at accidental elements and to declare, of the picture revealed at a particular time: *that* is the thing.

It is just as untenable to declare the sum of perceptual [13] characteristics to be the object in question. Certainly it would be possible for a spirit to be able to receive a concept at the same time as, and unseparated from, a percept. Such a spirit would then never think of regarding the concept as something not belonging to the object, but would ascribe it an existence inseparable from the object.

Let me make my point clearer with an example. When I [14] throw a stone through the air horizontally, I see it in different places in succession. I connect these places into a line. In mathematics, I come to know various kinds of line, among them the parabola. I know the parabola to be a line that results when a point moves in a certain lawful way. If I investigate the conditions according to which the thrown stone moves, I find that the line of its movement is identical with what I know as a parabola. That the stone moves precisely in a parabola is a consequence of the given conditions, and follows necessarily from them. The parabolic form belongs to the whole phenomenon, like all its other aspects. The spirit described above, which has no need of the detour of thinking, would take as given not only the sum of visual sensations in various places but also, united with the phenomenon, the parabolic form of the trajectory that *we* only add to the phenomenon by means of thinking.

It is not due to the objects that they are initially given to [15] us without the corresponding concepts but to our spiritual organization. Our whole being functions in such a way that for everything in reality, the elements flow to us from two sides—from the side of *perceiving* and from the side of *thinking*.

[16]   How *I* am organized to comprehend things has nothing to do with *their* nature. The divide between perceiving and thinking comes into being only at the instant that I, the observer, come over against things. Yet which elements belong to the thing, and which do not, can in no way depend upon how I come to know those elements.

[17]   Humans are limited beings. First, they are beings among other beings. Their existence belongs to space and time. Therefore, only a limited part of the whole universe is accessible to them. This limited part, however, is linked on all sides, temporally and spatially, to other things. If our existence were so united with the things that every world event was at the same time *our* event, then there would be no difference between us and the things. But then, too, there would be no individual things for us. Everything that happens would continually merge with everything else. The cosmos would be a unity, a self-enclosed whole. The stream of events would be interrupted nowhere. Because of our limitedness, what is not really separate appears separate to us. For example, the individual quality of red never exists in isolation. It is surrounded on all sides by other qualities, to which it belongs and without which it could not exist. We, however, must lift out of the world certain cross-sections of it and consider them on their own. From a many-hued whole, our eye can comprehend only a succession of individual colors. From a connected conceptual system, our reason can grasp only individual concepts. This separation is a subjective act: it depends on the fact that we are not identical with the world-process; rather, we are single beings among other beings.

Everything, then, depends upon determining the relationship between other beings and the being that we ourselves are. This determination must be distinguished from
merely becoming aware of our self. The latter relies upon
perceiving, as does awareness of every other thing. Perceiving myself reveals to me a number of qualities that I
combine into the whole of my personality, just as I combine the qualities yellow, metallically gleaming, hard, etc.
into the unity "gold." Self-perception does not lead me
outside the realm of what belongs to me. Such self-perceiving must be distinguished from self-definition through
thinking. Just as, in thinking, I integrate a single percept
from the external world into the context of the world, so,
likewise through thinking, I also integrate the percepts of
myself into the world process. My self-perceiving enclos-
es me within certain limits; but my thinking has nothing to
do with those limits. In this sense, I am a twofold creature.
I am enclosed within the realm that I perceive as that of my
personality, but I am also the bearer of an activity that determines my limited existence from a higher sphere. Our
thinking, unlike our sensing and feeling, is not individual.
It is universal. Only because it is related to the individual's
feeling and sensing does it receive an individual stamp in
each separate human being. Human beings differentiate
themselves from one another through these particular col-
orations of universal thinking. There is only one concept
"triangle." It makes no difference to the content of this
concept whether it is grasped by A or B—by this or that
human carrier of consciousness. But each bearer of consciousness will grasp it in an individual way.

[19]   A common prejudice that is hard to overcome stands opposed to this thought. This prejudice cannot rise to the insight that the concept of the triangle grasped by me is the same as that grasped by my neighbor. Naive human beings consider themselves the builders of their concepts. Therefore they believe that every person has individual concepts. It is a fundamental requirement of philosophical thinking to overcome this prejudice. The single, unitary concept of the triangle does not become many by being thought by many thinkers. For the thinking of many thinkers is itself a unity.

[20]   In thinking, we are given the element that unites our particular individuality with the whole of the cosmos. When we sense, feel (and also perceive) we are separate; when we think, we are the all-one being that penetrates all. This is the deeper basis of our dual nature. Within us, we see an absolute force come into existence, a force that is universal. Yet we do not come to know it as it streams forth from the center of the world, but only at a point on the periphery. If we came to know it as it streamed forth from the center of the world, then we would know the whole riddle of the world at the instant we came to consciousness. Since we stand at a point on the periphery, however, and find our own existence enclosed within certain limits, we must find out about the realm situated outside our own being with the help of thinking that extends into us from universal world existence.

[21]   The urge for knowledge arises in us because thinking in us reaches out beyond our separateness and relates itself to universal world existence. Beings without thinking do

not have this urge. If other things confront them, no questions arise. Other things remain external to such beings. For thinking beings, a concept arises from the encounter with an external thing. The concept is that part of a thing that we do not receive from without, but from within. *Knowledge, cognition* is meant to accomplish the balance or union of the two elements, inner and outer.

A percept, then, is not something finished or closed off. It is one side of the total reality. The other side is the concept. The act of knowing (cognition) is the synthesis of percept and concept. Only percept and concept together make up the whole thing. [22]

The preceding discussion demonstrates that it is meaningless to look for any common element among the world's individual entities other than the conceptual content presented by thinking. Any attempt to find a world unity other than this self-consistent conceptual content—which we gain by thinking contemplation of our percepts—must fail. For us, neither a human, personal God, nor force, nor matter, nor even the idealess will (Schopenhauer) can be considered the universal element of the world. All these entities belong merely to a limited area of our observation. We perceive a humanly limited personality only in ourselves; force and matter only in external things. As for the will, it can be seen only as an expression of our limited personality's activity. Schopenhauer wants to avoid making "abstract" thinking the bearer of the universal world element, and instead seeks something that presents itself to him immediately as real. This philosopher believes that we misjudge the world if we see it as external: [23]

Indeed, the sought-after significance of the world confronting me merely as my mental picture, or the transition from it as a mere mental picture of the cognizing subject to what it may be beyond this, would never be discoverable if the investigator himself were nothing other than the purely cognizing subject (a winged cherub without a body). But he too is rooted in that world, finds himself within it as an *individual*, that is, his cognition, which supports and determines the whole world as mental picture, is mediated throughout by a body whose affections are, as shown above, the intellect's starting point for contemplation of that world. For the purely cognizing subject as such, this body is a mental picture like any other, an object among objects: its movements, its actions are known to him no differently from the changes in all other observable objects, and would be just as strange and incomprehensible to him, if their meaning were not deciphered for him in a completely different way.... For the subject of cognizing, which appears as an individual through its identity with the body, this body is given in two quite distinct ways: first as mental picture for the intellect's contemplation, as object among objects and subject to their laws; but at the same time in a quite different way, namely as that which is known immediately to everyone by the word *will*. Every true act of his will is instantly and unfailingly a movement of his body as well: he cannot really will the act without at the same time perceiving that it appears as movement of the body. The act of will and the action of the body are not two different, objectively known states linked by the tie of causality; their relationship is not one of cause and effect; rather, they are one and the same thing, but given in two altogether different ways: once quite immediately and once for the intellect's contemplation.[4]

With this analysis, Schopenhauer feels justified in locating the "objectivity" of the will in the body. He believes that one can feel a reality—the thing-in-itself *in concreto* —*immediately* in the actions of the body. Against this analysis, we must point out that the actions of our body only come to our awareness through self-percepts, and as such have no advantage over other percepts. If we wish to *know* their essence, then we can only do so through *thinking* observation; that is, by organizing them within the conceptual system of our concepts and ideas.

The view that thinking is abstract, without any concrete *[24]* content—that it offers at most a "conceptual" mirror image of world unity, but not this unity itself—is very deeply rooted in naive human consciousness. Whoever believes this has never become clear about what a percept without a concept really is. Let us consider the world of percepts by itself. It appears as a mere juxtaposition in space, a mere succession in time, an aggregate of unconnected details. None of the things that enter and exit from

4. Schopenhauer, *The World as Will and Representation.*

the perceptual stage appears to have anything to do with any another. In the world of percepts considered by itself, the world is a multiplicity of uniform objects. None plays a greater role than any other in the hurlyburly of the world. If we are to have the insight that this or that fact has greater significance than another, then we must consult our thinking. Without the function of thinking, a rudimentary organ that is without significance for an animal's life appears equal in value with the most important limb of its body. The separate facts emerge in all their significance, both in themselves and for everything else, only when thinking weaves its threads from entity to entity. This activity of thinking is *full of content*. It is only through a very specific, concrete content that I can know why a snail stands at a lower level of development than a lion. The mere sight—the percept—gives me no content that could inform me about any relative perfection in their organization.

[25]   Thinking brings this content to the percept out of the human being's world of concepts and ideas. In contrast to perceptual content, which is given us from without, thought-content appears within. We shall call the form in which thought-content first arises *intuition*. Intuition is to thinking as *observation* is to perception. Intuition and observation are the sources of our knowledge. We remain alienated from an object we have observed in the world as long as we do not have within us the corresponding intuition, which supplies us with the piece of reality missing from the percept. Full reality remains closed off to anyone without the ability to find intuitions corresponding to

things. Just as a colorblind person sees only shades of brilliance without hue, so a person without intuition observes only unconnected perceptual fragments.

To *explain* a thing, to *make it comprehensible*, means [26] nothing other than to place it into the context from which it has been torn by the arrangement of our organization, described above. There is no such thing as an object cut off from the world-as-a-whole. All separation has merely a subjective validity for us, for the way we are organized. For us, the world-whole splits into above and below, before and after, cause and effect, object and mental picture, matter and force, object and subject, and so forth. What meets us in observation as separate details is linked, item by item, through the coherent, unitary world of our intuitions. Through thinking we join together into one everything that we separated through perceiving.

The enigmatic quality of an object lies in its separate [27] existence. But this separate existence is called forth by us and can, within the conceptual world, be dispelled and returned to unity again.

Nothing is given to us directly except through thinking [28] and perceiving. The question now arises: "What is the significance of the percept according to the reasoning here?" We have, to be sure, recognized that critical idealism's proof of the subjective nature of percepts collapses in itself. But insight into the incorrectness of the proof does not yet confirm that the doctrine itself is based on error. Critical idealism's proof does not proceed from the absolute nature of thinking; rather, it is based on the fact that naive realism, if followed consistently, cancels itself out. But how do things stand if the absoluteness of thinking is recognized?

[29]   Let us suppose that a specific percept—for example, red—appears in my consciousness. On continued investigation, this percept proves to be linked with other percepts—for example, to a specific form and to certain percepts of temperature and touch. I call this combination: "an object in the sense world." I can now ask myself what else is located in that section of space where these percepts appear to me aside from what has been listed so far. I find mechanical, chemical, and other processes within that part of space. Going further, I investigate the processes that I find on the path from the object to my sense-organs. I find processes of motion in an elastic medium that by their nature have nothing in common with the original percepts. If I investigate the further mediation occurring between the sense organs and the brain, I obtain the same result. I form new percepts in each of these areas, but what weaves through all of these spatially and temporally disparate percepts as the unifying medium—is thinking.

The vibrations of the air that mediate sound are given to me as percepts in exactly the same way as the sound itself. Thinking alone links all such percepts to one another and shows them in their mutual relationships. Other than what is immediately perceived, we cannot speak of there being anything except what is known through the conceptual connections between the percepts—connections that are accessible to thinking. Therefore any relationship between perceived objects and perceived subjects that goes beyond what is merely perceived is purely ideal, that is, it is expressible only through concepts. Only if I could *perceive* how the percept of an object affects the percept of the subject, or—conversely—only if I could observe the construction of a perceptual form by the subject, would it be possible to speak like modern physiology and the critical idealism built upon it. This view confuses an ideal relation (of the object to the subject) with a process that could only be spoken of if it were perceived. Therefore the phrase, "no color without a color-sensing eye" cannot mean that the eye produces color, but only that a conceptual connection, knowable through thinking, exists between the percept "color" and the percept "eye." Empirical science will have to ascertain how the qualities of the eye and those of color relate to one another and how the organ of sight transmits the perception of colors, etc. I can track how one percept follows another and how it stands in spatial relation to others. I can then bring this to conceptual expression. But I cannot perceive how a percept proceeds out of the unperceivable. All efforts to seek other than conceptual relations between percepts must necessarily fail.

What, then, is a percept? Asked in this general way, the *[30]* question is absurd. A percept always appears as a quite specific, concrete content. This content is immediately given and is limited to what is given. Of what is given, we can ask only what it is apart from perception—that is, what it is for thinking. Therefore the question of *what* a percept is can aim only at the conceptual intuition corresponding to it. From this perspective, the question of the subjectivity of the percept, in the sense meant by critical idealism, cannot be raised at all. Only what is perceived as belonging to the subject can be characterized as subjective. The link between the subjective and the objective is not built by any real process (in the naive sense)—that is, by any perceptible event. It is built by thinking alone. For this reason what seems to lie outside the perceived subject is objective for us. The percept of myself as subject remains perceivable for me when the table now before me has vanished from my observational field. But observation of the table has evoked in me an alteration that also remains. I retain the capacity to create an image of the table again later. This capacity to produce an image remains united with me. Psychology calls this image a memory-picture. Yet it is the only thing that can properly be called the *mental picture* of the table. For it corresponds to the perceptible alteration in my own state through the presence of the table in my field of sight. It does not, in fact, signify a change in some "I-in-itself" standing behind the perceived subject, but rather a change in the perceptible subject itself. The mental picture is thus a subjective percept in contrast to the objective percept of a thing lying within the perceptual horizon. The confusion of subjective percepts with objective percepts leads in idealism to the misunderstanding that the world is my mental picture.

[31]   We must now define the concept of mental picture more narrowly. What we have put forward about it so far is not its concept, but merely points the way toward finding the mental picture within our perceptual field. The exact concept of the mental picture will then make it

possible for us also to achieve a satisfactory understanding of the relationship between the mental picture and its object. This will also lead us over the boundary where the relationship between the human subject and the object belonging to the world is brought down from the purely conceptual field of cognition into concrete, individual *life*. Once we know what to make of the world, it will be easy for us to behave accordingly. We can act with our full strength only when we know the object belonging to the world to which we are devoting our activity.

Addendum to the new edition (1918)

The view characterized here can be regarded as one to which at first we are driven quite naturally when we begin to reflect on our relationship to the world. But we then see ourselves entangled in a thought-structure that dissolves itself as we build it. This thought-structure is such that it requires more than merely theoretical refutation. It must be *lived through*, so as to find a way out through insight into the error to which it leads. It must appear in any discussion of the relationship between human beings and the world, not because we wish to refute others whom we believe have an incorrect view of this relationship, but because we realize what confusion any initial reflection on such a relationship can bring. The insight we must achieve is of how, in such reflections, we can refute *ourselves*. The preceding discussion was meant from just such a point of view. *[1]*

Anyone who wishes to work out a view of the relationship of human beings to the world becomes aware that we *[2]* ourselves produce at least a part of this relationship through making mental pictures of the things and processes in the world. Our attention is thereby withdrawn from what is *outside i*n the world, and turned toward our inner world. We can begin by reflecting that we cannot have a connection to a thing or person if a mental picture does not arise within us. From this, it is but a step to the realization that, after all, we experience only our mental pictures; we know of a world outside ourselves only to the extent that it is a mental picture *within us*. And with this, the naive attitude toward reality, taken up before any reflection on our relation to the world, is abandoned. From a naive standpoint, we believe that we are dealing with real things. Self-reflection drives us from this point of view. It does not allow us to look at a reality such as naive consciousness believes it has before it. Such self-reflection allows us to look only at our mental pictures; *these* insert themselves between our own being and a supposedly real world of the kind that the naive standpoint imagines it can assert. Because of the intervening mental pictures, we can no longer look upon such a reality. We must assume that we are blind for that reality. Thus the thought of a thing-in-itself, that is unattainable to cognition, arises.

Indeed, as long as we continue to focus on the relationship to the world that we enter through the life of mental pictures, we shall never escape this thought-construction. Unless we wish to close off the urge for knowledge artificially, we cannot remain at the viewpoint of naive reality. The very existence of this urge for knowledge of the relation between human beings and the world shows us that this naive standpoint must be abandoned. If the naive standpoint gave us something that could be recognized as truth, then we would not feel this urge.

Yet we do not arrive at something which could be seen as truth merely by abandoning the naive standpoint while at the same time—without noticing it—retaining the style of thought that it requires. We fall into this kind of error when we think that we experience only mental pictures— that though we believe we are dealing with realities, we are in fact conscious only of our mental pictures of realities—and therefore suppose true realities to lie beyond the scope of our consciousness, as "things-in-themselves," of which we know nothing directly, and which somehow approach and influence us, with the result that a world of mental pictures comes to life within us. Those who think in this way only add another world, in thought, to the world lying before them; but with regard to this world they really have to begin at the beginning again. For they do not think about the *unknown* "thing-in-itself" any differently, as far as its relationship to the individual human being is concerned, than about the *known* thing of the naive view of reality.

We avoid the confusion we fall into through critical reflection about this view only when we notice that there is something *within* what we can experience through perception in ourselves and outside in the world—something that cannot fall prey to the problems that arise when a mental picture interposes itself between the process and the observing human being. *This something is thinking.* In relation to thinking, a human being *can* remain with the naive view of reality. If we do not keep to this view, it is only because we notice that we have abandoned this viewpoint for another, but are unaware that the insight we have achieved is inapplicable to thinking. If we do become aware of this, then we allow ourselves entry into the other insight—that *in thinking* and *through thinking* we must recognize that to which we apparently blinded ourselves by interposing our life of mental pictures between the world and ourselves.

Someone highly esteemed by the author of this book has raised the objection that during his explication of thinking the author maintains a naive realist view of thinking, as if the real world and the mentally pictured world were one and the same. Yet the author believes that he has proved by the present discussion that the validity of "naive realism" *for thinking* follows necessarily from an unprejudiced observation of thinking; and that naive realism, which is invalid elsewhere, is overcome through knowledge of thinking's true essence.

CHAPTER 6

HUMAN INDIVIDUALITY

In explaining mental pictures, philosophers have had the greatest difficulty with the fact that we are not ourselves external things, but our mental pictures are supposed to have a form corresponding to them. On closer inspection, however, this difficulty turns out to be non-existent. To be sure, we are not external things, but we belong with them to one and the same world. The segment of the world that I perceive as my subject is run through by the stream of the universal world process. With regard to my perception, I am at first confined within the boundary of my skin. But what is contained within this skin belongs to the cosmos as a whole. Therefore, for a relationship to exist between my organism and an object outside me, it is not at all necessary for something of the object to slip into me or to impress itself on my mind like a signet ring on wax. Thus the question, "How do I learn anything about the tree that stands ten paces from me?" is all wrong. It arises from the view that the boundaries of my body are absolute barriers, through which news about things filters into me. *[1]*

The forces acting within my skin are the same as those existing outside it. Therefore, I really am the things: to be sure, not "I" as a perceived subject, but "I" as a part of the universal world process. The percept of the tree lies with my I in the same whole. The universal world process calls forth equally the percept of the tree *there*, and the percept of my I *here*. Were I a world-creator, not a world-knower, then object and subject (percept and I) would arise in one act. For they determine each other mutually. As world-knower, I can find the common element of the two, as two sides of being that belong together, only through thinking, which relates them to each other through concepts.

[2]   The so-called physiological proofs of the subjectivity of percepts will be the hardest of all to drive from the field. If I exert pressure on my skin, I perceive it as a sensation of pressure. The same pressure may be experienced by me through the eye as light, and through the ear as sound. I perceive an electric shock through the eye as light, through the ear as sound, through the nerves of the skin as impact, and through the nose as an odor of phosphorus. What follows from this? Only that I perceive an electric shock (or pressure) and then a quality of light, or a sound, or a certain smell, and so forth. If there were no eye, there would be no percept of light accompanying the percept of mechanical change in the environment; without an ear, no percept of sound, etc. What right have we to say that, without organs of perception, the whole process would not exist? Those who conclude—from the fact that an electrical process in the eye evokes light—that what we sense as light is, outside our organism, only a

mechanical process of motion, forget that they are merely passing from one percept to another and not at all to something outside perception. Just as we can say that the eye perceives a mechanical process of motion in its environment as light, so we could just as well claim that any systematic change in an object is perceived by us as a process of motion. If I draw twelve pictures of a horse on the circumference of a rotating disc, in exactly the positions that its body assumes in the course of a gallop, then I can by rotating the disc evoke the illusion of movement. I need only look through an opening in such a way that I see the successive positions of the horse at appropriate intervals. Then I see, not twelve pictures of a horse, but the image of a single horse galloping.

Thus, the physiological fact mentioned above can throw no light on the relation of percepts to mental pictures. We must find our way by some other means. *[3]*

The moment a percept emerges on the horizon of my observation, thinking, too, is activated in me. An element of my thought-system—a specific intuition, a concept—unites with the percept. Then, when the percept disappears from my field of vision, what remains? What remains is my intuition, with its relationship to the specific percept that formed in the moment of perceiving. How vividly I can then later re-present this relationship to myself depends upon how my spiritual and bodily organism is functioning. A *mental picture* is nothing but an intuition related to a specific percept. It is a concept, once linked to a percept, for which the relation to that percept has remained. My concept of a lion is not formed *out of* *[4]* my percepts of lions. Yet my mental picture of a lion is certainly formed by means of perception. I can convey the concept of a lion to those who have never seen a lion. But without their own perceiving, I will not succeed in conveying a vivid mental picture.

[5]   A *mental picture*, then, is an individualized concept. We can now understand how mental pictures can represent the things of reality for us. The full reality of a thing is revealed to us in the moment of observation, out of the merging of a concept and a percept. Through a percept, the concept receives an individualized form, a relationship to that specific percept. The concept survives in us in this individual form, with its characteristic relationship to the percept, and forms the mental picture of the corresponding thing. If we encounter a second thing and the same concept combines itself with it, then we recognize it as belonging to the same species as the first, for we find not only a corresponding concept in our conceptual system, but the individualized concept with its characteristic relationship to this same object, and we recognize the object once again.

[6]   Thus, a mental picture stands between a percept and a concept. A mental picture is the specific concept that points to the percept.

[7]   The sum of everything of which I can form mental pictures I can call my "experience." Hence, the greater the number of individualized concepts a person has, the richer their experience will be. A person lacking intuitive capacity, on the other hand, is unsuited to acquire experience. For such a person, once objects are out of sight they are

lost, because the concepts that ought to be brought into relationship with them are lacking. A person whose capacity to think is well developed but who perceives poorly because of coarse sensory equipment will be equally incapable of gathering experience. Such persons might acquire concepts somehow, but their intuitions will lack a vivid relationship to specific things. A thoughtless traveler and a scholar living in abstract conceptual systems are equally unable to have rich experience.

Reality reveals itself to us as percepts and concepts; the subjective representation of that reality reveals itself as mental pictures. [8]

If our personality manifested only cognitively, the sum of everything objective would be given in percepts, concepts, and mental pictures. [9]

Yet we are not satisfied with relating a percept to a concept by means of thinking. We also relate it to our particular subjectivity, to our individual *I*. The expression of this individual relation is feeling, which manifests as pleasure or displeasure. [10]

Thinking and *feeling* correspond to the dual nature of our being, on which we have already reflected. *Thinking* is the element through which we participate in the universal process of the cosmos; *feeling* is the element through which we can withdraw into the confines of our own being. [11]

Our thinking unites us with the world; our feeling leads us back into ourselves and makes us individuals. If we were only thinking and perceiving beings, then our whole life would flow past in monotonous indifference. If we could only *know* ourselves as selves, then we would be [12] completely indifferent to ourselves. It is only because we have self-feeling along with self-cognition, and pleasure and pain along with the perception of things, that we live as individual beings whose existence is not limited to our conceptual relation to the rest of the world, but who also

[13] have a special value for ourselves. Some might be tempted to see in the life of feeling an element more richly imbued with reality than thinking contemplation of the world. The reply to this is that the life of feeling has this richer meaning only for my individuality. For the world as a whole, my feeling life can attain value only if the feeling, as a percept of my self, combines with a concept and so integrates itself indirectly into the cosmos.

[14]   Our life is a continual oscillation between our individual existence and living with the universal world process. The farther we rise into the universal nature of thinking, where what is individual continues to interest us only as an example, an instance of a concept, the more we let go of our character as particular entities—as completely specific, separate personalities. The more we descend into the depths of our own life, allowing our feelings to resonate with the experiences of the outer world, the more we separate ourselves from universal being. A true individual will be the person who reaches highest, with his or her feelings, into the region of ideals. There are people for whom even the most universal ideas entering their heads still retain a special coloring that shows them unmistakably connected with their bearer. There are others whose concepts meet us so completely without trace of ownership as to seem unconnected to anyone of flesh and blood.

Making mental pictures already gives our conceptual [15] life an individual stamp. After all, each of us has a standpoint from which to view the world. Our concepts connect themselves to our percepts. We think universal concepts in our own special way. This characteristic quality is a result of our standpoint in the world, of the sphere of perception connected to our place in life.

In contrast to this particularity is another, dependent on [16] our individual constitution. How we are constituted, after all, makes for a special, well-defined entity. We each connect special feelings with our percepts, and do so in the most varying degrees of intensity. This is the individual aspect of our personality. It remains left over after we have accounted for the specificities of the stage on which we act out our lives.

A feeling-life completely devoid of thought must grad- [17] ually lose all connection with the world. Yet for human beings, oriented as they are toward wholeness, knowledge of things will go hand in hand with education and development of the life of feeling.

Feeling is the means by which concepts first gain con- [18] crete *life*.

CHAPTER 7

ARE THERE LIMITS TO COGNITION?

[1]   We have established that the elements needed to explain
reality are to be drawn from the two spheres of perceiving
and thinking. As we have seen, we are so organized that
the full, total reality (including that of ourselves as subjects) initially appears to us as a duality. Cognition overcomes this duality by composing the thing as a whole out
of the two elements of reality: the percept, and the concept
worked out by thinking. Let us call the way in which the
world meets us, before it has gained its true form through
cognition, "the world of appearance," in contrast to the
unified reality composed of percepts and concepts. We
can then say that the world is given to us as a duality, and
cognition assimilates it into a (monistic) unity. A philosophy that proceeds from this fundamental principal can be
characterized as monistic philosophy or *monism*. In contrast to it stands two-world theory or *dualism*. The latter
does not, for example, assume that there are two sides to a
unitary reality that are separated merely by our organization, but that there are two worlds that are absolutely

distinct from one another. Dualism then seeks the explanatory principles for one world in the other.

Dualism rests on a false conception of what we call [2] cognition. It separates the whole of existence into two regions, each of which has its own laws, and lets those regions confront one another outwardly.

The distinction between the perceived object and the [3] thing-in-itself, which Kant introduced into science and which has not been overcome to this day, originates from this kind of dualism. Following what we have said, the nature of our spiritual organization is such that a separate thing can be given only as percept. Thinking then overcomes this separation by assigning to each percept its lawful place in the world totality. As long as the separated parts of the world totality are designated as percepts, we are simply following a law of our subjectivity when we make this separation. But if we consider the sum of all percepts as one part of the world, and then oppose to these percepts a second part, the "things-in-themselves," we are philosophizing into thin air. We are just playing a game with concepts. We construct an artificial contrast and then can find no content for its second term—since such content can be created for a separate, particular thing only out of perception.

Every kind of existence assumed outside the realm of [4] percepts and concepts must be relegated to the sphere of unjustified hypotheses. The "thing-in-itself" belongs to this category. It is only too understandable if dualistic thinkers can find no link between the world principle assumed hypothetically and what is given by experience.

We can give content to this hypothetical world principle only by borrowing content from the world of experience and then deceiving ourselves about this fact. Otherwise, it remains a concept devoid of content and has only the form of a concept. At this point, dualistic thinkers usually maintain that the content of the concept is inaccessible to our cognition: we can know only *that* such content exists; we cannot know *what* exists. In either case, overcoming dualism is impossible. Even if we import a few abstract elements from the world of experience into the concept of the thing-in-itself, it still remains impossible to trace back the rich, concrete life of experience to a few qualities that themselves are only borrowed from perception.

Du Bois-Reymond thinks that unperceivable atoms of matter create sensation and feeling by their position and movement. [1] He uses this to arrive at the conclusion that we can never have a satisfying explanation of how matter and motion create sensation and feeling. Thus he writes:

> It is completely and forever incomprehensible that a number of atoms of carbon, hydrogen, nitrogen, oxygen, etc., should be other than indifferent as to how they are lying and moving, how they lay and moved, and how they will lie and move. There

1. Emil Du Bois-Reymond (1818–96), German physiologist, known both for his investigations of animal electricity, the physiology of muscles and nerves, and metabolic processes and his famous "ignorabimus"—we cannot know. See *The Riddles of Philosophy* (p. 319 ff.) and, for instance, *The Boundaries of Natural Science,* lecture one, September 27, 1920 (Spring Valley, NY: Anthroposophic Press, 1983).

is no way to understand, from their interaction, how consciousness could arise. [2]

Du Bois-Reymond's argument is characteristic of this whole orientation of thought. Position and motion are separated out from the rich world of percepts. They are then transferred to the notional world of atoms. And astonishment follows that it is impossible to develop concrete life out of this homemade principle, imitated from the perceptual world.

From the definition of the principle of dualism given [5] above, it follows that dualists, working with a completely contentless concept of the "in-itself," cannot arrive at an explanation of the world.

In every instance, the dualist is constrained to set insur- [6] mountable barriers to our capacity for cognition. The follower of a monistic worldview knows that everything necessary to explain a given world phenomenon must lie within this world. What prevents us from achieving such an explanation can be only accidental temporal or spatial limits, or deficiencies in our organization—deficiencies *not* in human organization in general, but only in our own particular organization.

It follows from the concept of cognizing, as we have [7] defined it, that we cannot speak of limits to cognition. Cognizing is not the business of the world in general, but

---

2. From *Über die Grenzen des Naturerkennens* [On the Limits to Knowledge of Nature], a lecture given to the second open session of the forty-fifth meeting of German natural science researchers and doctors, Leipzig, August 14, 1872. Published in that same year.

a transaction that we must each accomplish for ourselves. Things demand no explanation. They exist and work on one another according to laws that thinking can discover. They exist in indivisible unity with these laws. Our I-hood then confronts them, initially comprehending in them only what we have described as the percept. But within this I-hood also lies the power to find the other part of reality. Cognitive satisfaction is attained only when the I has united for *itself* both the elements of reality that are indivisibly connected in the world—for then the I has reached reality once again.

[8]   The preconditions for cognizing exist *through* and *for* the I. The I itself poses the questions of cognition. In fact, it draws them from the element of thinking, which is completely clear and transparent within itself. If we ask ourselves questions that we cannot answer, their content cannot be clear and distinct in every aspect. It is not the world that poses questions to us; we pose them to ourselves.

[9]   I can easily imagine that I would be quite incapable of answering a question that I happened to find written down somewhere if I did not know the sphere from which its content came.

[10]   Our cognition involves questions that emerge for us because a conceptual sphere, pointing to the totality of the world, confronts a perceptual sphere conditioned by place, time, and subjective organization. Our task is to balance these two spheres, both of which we know well. This has nothing to do with a limit to cognition. At a particular time, this or that might remain unexplained because the

place of our vantage point in life prevents us from perceiving the things in question. But what is not found today may be found tomorrow. The limits determined in this way are only temporary, and they can be overcome by progress in perception and thinking.

Dualism mistakenly transfers the contrast between objects and subjects, which has meaning only within the perceptual realm, to purely imagined entities outside this realm. But things separated in the perceptual field are separate only as long as the perceiver refrains from thinking—for thinking suspends all separation and reveals it to be merely subjective. Therefore a dualist is really transferring—to entities behind the percepts—categories that have no absolute but only a relative validity, even for the percepts. A dualist splits percept and concept, the two factors involved in the cognitive process, into four: 1) the object in itself, 2) the subject's percept of the object, 3) the subject, and 4) the concept that relates the percept to the object-in-itself. *[11]*

For the dualist, the relationship between an object and a subject is a *real* one; the subject is really (dynamically) influenced by the object. This real process is said not to emerge into our consciousness. It is supposed to evoke a response in the subject to the stimulus proceeding from the object. The result of this response is supposed to be the percept, which alone emerges into consciousness. The object is supposed to have an objective reality (that is, a reality independent of the subject), while the percept is supposed to have a subjective reality. This subjective reality supposedly relates the subject to the object. That relationship is said to be ideal (conceptual). Thus, dualism splits the cognitive process into two parts. One of them, the creation of the perceptual object out of the thing-in-itself, is assigned a place *outside* consciousness, and the other, the connection of the percept to the concept and the relation of the concept to the object, is assigned a place *within* consciousness.

Given these presuppositions, it is clear why dualists believe it possible to attain only subjective representations of what lies *before* our consciousness. For dualists of this kind, the objective/real process in the subject, through which the percept arises, and, all the more so, the objective relationships of things-in-themselves, are not directly knowable. In their view, human beings can only construct conceptual representations of what is objectively real. The bond of unity that links things, both among themselves and to our individual spirit (as a thing-in-itself), lies beyond consciousness in a being-in-itself of whom, likewise, we can only have a conceptual representative in our consciousness.

[12]   Dualism believes that the whole world would evaporate into an abstract conceptual schema if "real" connections were not affirmed alongside the conceptual connections of objects. In other words, the conceptual principles discoverable through thinking appear too airy to dualists, and so they look for additional, real principles by which to support them.

[13]   Let us look more closely at these real principles. The naive person (that is, a naive realist) regards the objects of external experience as realities. The evidence for their reality is that they can be grasped by the hand and seen by

the eye. "Nothing exists that cannot be perceived" is actually the first axiom of the naive human being, and its
converse is seen as equally valid: "Everything that can be
perceived exists." The best proof of this assertion is the
naive human belief in immortality and in spirits. The naive realist imagines the soul as fine, sense-perceptible
matter, which under certain circumstances, can even become visible to ordinary human beings (i.e., the naive belief in ghosts).

Compared to their "real world," naive realists see ev-   *[14]*
erything else, such as the world of ideas, as unreal, as
"merely conceptual." What we add to objects through
thinking are mere thoughts about things. Thought adds
nothing real to a percept.

But naive persons hold sense perception to be the sole   *[15]*
evidence of reality, not only for the existence of *things*,
but also for events. In this view, one thing can only affect
another if a sense-perceptible force proceeds from the one
and touches the other. In ancient physics, it was believed
that very fine matter streams out from objects and penetrates our souls through our sense organs.[3] Actually seeing such matter was said to be impossible only because of
the crudeness of our senses in comparison to the fineness
of the matter. In principle, this kind of matter was accord-
ed reality on the same grounds by which reality is accord-
ed to the objects of the sense-world— namely, because of
its mode of existence, which was thought of as analogous
to that of sense-perceptible reality.

---

3. For instance, Plato's *Timaeus.*

[16]   For naive consciousness, the self-sufficient existence of what can be experienced through ideas is not considered to be real in the same way as what can be experienced through the senses. Until conviction of its reality is supplied by sense-perception, an object grasped in "idea alone" is a mere chimera. In brief, the naive person demands, in addition to the conceptual evidence of thinking, the real evidence of the senses. The basis for the development of primitive forms of belief in revelation lies in this naive human need. To naive consciousness, the god given through thinking always remains merely a "thought" god. Naive consciousness demands revelation through means accessible to sensory perception. God must appear bodily, and the testimony of thinking counts little. Rather, divinity must be confirmable by the senses through such things as the transformation of water into wine.

[17]   The naive person imagines that cognition is itself a process analogous to sensory processes. Things make an *impression* on the soul, or they emit images that penetrate through the senses, and so forth.

[18]   What naive human beings can perceive with their senses is considered real, and what cannot be perceived in this way (god, the soul, cognition, etc.) is imagined to be analogous to what *is* perceived.

[19]   If naive realism wants to establish a science, it can do so only through the exact *description* of perceptual contents. For naive realism, concepts are only means to this end. They exist to provide conceptual counter-images of the percepts. They have no significance for the things

themselves. For the naive realist, only individual tulips that are seen, or that can be seen, count as real; the idea of a tulip counts only as an abstraction, as an unreal thought-image that the soul assembles from characteristics common to all tulips.

Naive realism, with its fundamental principle of the re-[20] ality of everything perceived, is contradicted by experience, which teaches us that the content of perception is transient. The tulip that I see is real today; a year hence, it will have vanished into nothingness. What lasts is the *species* of tulip. But, for naive realism, this species is "only" an *idea*, not a reality. Thus, the naive realist world-view is in the position of seeing its realities come and go, while what it regards as unreal is more lasting than the real. In addition to percepts, naive realism has to acknowledge something conceptual. It has to include entities that cannot be perceived with the senses. It reconciles itself to this by conceiving their mode of existence as analogous to that of sense objects. The invisible forces through which sense perceptible things affect one another are just such hypothetically assumed realities. So, too, is heredity, which has effects above and beyond the individual, and which is the reason for the development out of one individual of a new individual that is similar to the first, so that the species persists. The life principle permeating the organic body is another such assumed reality; so is the soul (for which naive consciousness always forms a concept analogous to sense realities); and so, finally, is the naive human's Divine Being. This Divine Being is thought to act in a fashion that exactly corresponds to the *perceptible* ways in which human beings act—that is, anthropomorphically.

[21]   Modern physics traces sense impressions back to processes in the smallest parts of the body and in an infinitely fine substance, the ether—or something similar. For example, what we sense as warmth is the movement of the parts within the space occupied by the body that is the source of warmth. Here, too, something imperceptible is thought of by analogy to what is perceptible. The sensory analogue of the concept "body" might be, in this sense, the interior of an enclosed space, in which elastic spheres move in every direction, hitting one another, bouncing off the walls, and so forth.

[22]   Without such assumptions, the world of naive realism disintegrates into an incoherent aggregate of percepts, without mutual relationships and constituting no unity. But it is clear that naive realism can arrive at its assumptions only through inconsistency. If it remains true to its fundamental proposition that only the perceived is real, then it may not assume something real where it perceives nothing. From the standpoint of naive realism, those imperceptible forces operating out of perceptible things are actually unjustified hypotheses. Because such a theory knows of no other realities, it equips its hypothetical forces with perceptual content. It attributes a form of existence (perceptual existence) to a realm where sense perception—the sole means of making an assertion about this form of existence—is lacking.

[23]   This self-contradictory worldview leads to metaphysical realism. Alongside perceptible reality, metaphysical

realism constructs another, imperceptible reality that it conceives as analogous to the first. Therefore, metaphysical realism is necessarily dualistic.

Wherever metaphysical realism notices a relationship [24] between perceptible things (approaching something through movement; something objective entering consciousness, etc.) it posits a reality. Yet the relationship it notices cannot be perceived; it can only be expressed through thinking. This conceptual relationship is arbitrarily made into something akin to the perceptible. For this line of thinking, then, the real world is composed of perceptual objects that emerge and disappear in eternal flux, and of imperceptible forces that produce the perceptual objects and endure.

Metaphysical realism is a contradictory mixture of naive realism and idealism. Its hypothetical forces are imperceptible entities with perceptual qualities. Beyond that region of the world for whose form of existence a means of cognition is present in perception, it is determined to acknowledge still another region, for which this means is inadequate, and which can be ascertained only by thinking. Metaphysical realism, however, cannot, at the same time, decide to recognize that the form of existence transmitted by thinking—the concept or idea—is an equally valid factor with perception. To avoid the contradiction of imperceptible percepts, we must admit that the relationships between percepts, as transmitted through thinking, can have no other form of existence for us than that of concepts. If we reject the invalid components of metaphysical realism, the world presents itself as the sum of percepts and their conceptual (ideal) relations. Thus, metaphysical realism arrives at a worldview that requires, as a matter of principle, that we be able to perceive percepts, while it requires us to be able to think the relations among percepts. Beside the world of percepts and concepts, this metaphysical realism can validate no third region of the world for which both principles, the so-called principle of the real and the principle of the ideal, are simultaneously valid.

[26]   When metaphysical realism claims that, along with the ideal relation between the perceptual object and its subject, there must exist a real relationship between the "thing-in-itself" of the percept and the "thing-in-itself" of the perceptible subject (the so-called individual spirit), then this claim rests on the false assumption of the existence of a process analogous to the processes of the sense world but imperceptible. When metaphysical realism further states that we enter into a conscious-ideal relationship with our perceptual world but can enter into a dynamic relationship (of forces) only with the real world, it commits the same error again. We can speak of a relationship of forces only within the perceptual world (in the area of the sense of touch), but not outside this world.

[27]   The worldview into which metaphysical realism merges when it eliminates its contradictory elements can be called *monism*, because it combines one-sided realism with idealism into a higher unity.

[28]   For naive realism, the real world is a sum of perceptual objects. For metaphysical realism, imperceptible forces as well as percepts attain reality. Monism replaces these

forces with the conceptual connections achieved through thinking. But these connections are the *laws of nature*. A natural law, after all, is nothing other than a conceptual expression for the connection between certain percepts.

Monism never has to seek for explanatory principles of reality outside percepts and concepts. Monism realizes that, in the whole realm of reality, there is never *occasion* to do so. It sees the perceptual world, as it appears immediately to our perceiving, as something half-real. It finds full reality in the union of that world with the conceptual world. The metaphysical realist may object to the monist: "As far as your organism is concerned, it may be that your cognition is perfect in itself, that it lacks nothing; but you do not know how the world would be reflected in an intelligence organized differently from your own." To this monism will respond: "If there are non-human intelligences whose percepts have a form different from our own, what has meaning for me is still only what reaches me through my perceiving and concepts." [29]

Through my perceiving—in fact, through specifically human perceiving—I am located as a subject over against an object. The connection between things is thus interrupted. The subject then restores that connection through thinking. Thereby it reintegrates itself into the world as a whole. Since it is only through our own subject that the whole appears to be torn apart at the place between our percept and our concept, it is also in the union of those two that true cognition is given. For beings with a different perceptual world (for example, beings with double the number of sense organs), the connection would appear interrupted at a different place, and its reunion would accordingly have to take a form specific to those beings. The question of limits to cognition exists only for naive and metaphysical realism, both of which see in the soul's content only a conceptual representation of the world. For them, what exists outside the subject is something absolute, something self-existent, and the content of the subject is a picture of this absolute, standing completely apart from it. The completeness of the cognition depends on the degree of similarity between the picture and the absolute object. A being with fewer senses than human beings have will perceive less of the world; one with more senses will perceive more. The former will therefore have less complete knowledge than the latter.

[30]   For monism, things are otherwise. The organization of the perceiving being determines where the connectedness of the world will seem torn apart into subject and object. The object is not absolute, merely relative to the particular subject. By the same token, the opposition can be bridged only in the specific way appropriate to human subjects. As soon as the I, which is separated from the world in perceiving, reintegrates itself into the connectedness of the world through its thinking contemplation, then all further questioning ceases—since it was only a result of the separation.

[31]   A differently constituted being would have a differently constituted cognition. Our own cognition is sufficient to answer the questions posed by our own nature.

[32]   Metaphysical realism must ask: How is what is given to us as perception given? How is the subject affected?

For monism, the percept is determined by the subject. *[33]*
But, at the same time, the subject has the means in thinking to cancel out what it has itself determined.

Metaphysical realists face a further difficulty when *[34]*
they seek to explain the similarity of the world pictures of
different human individuals. They have to ask themselves: "How is it that the world picture that I construct
out of my subjectively determined percepts and concepts
is equivalent to those that other human individuals construct from the same two factors that are subjective to
them? From my own subjective world picture, how can I
draw any conclusions about that of another human being?" Because people manage to get along with one another in practice, the metaphysical realist believes it
possible to infer the similarity of their subjective world
pictures. From the similarity of these world pictures, a
further inference is then drawn regarding the similarity of
the individual spirits —the "I-in-itself"—underlying the
separate human perceptual subjects.

This kind of conclusion infers, from a sum of effects, the *[35]*
character of their underlying causes. After a sufficient
number of cases, we believe that we understand the situation enough to know how the inferred causes will operate
in other cases. We call such an inference an inductive inference. If further observation yields something unexpect-
ed, we will find ourselves forced to modify its results,
because the character of the result is, after all, determined
only by the individual form of our observations. Yet, according to the metaphysical realist, this conditional knowledge of causes is perfectly sufficient for practical life.

[36]   Inductive inference is the methodological foundation of modern metaphysical realism. Once people believed that, from concepts, they could evolve something that was no longer a concept. They believed that, through concepts, they could know the metaphysically real entities that metaphysical realism necessarily requires. Today, this kind of philosophy belongs to a vanquished past. Instead, we believe that from a sufficient number of perceptual facts we can infer the character of the thing-in-itself underlying those facts. Just as earlier people sought to develop the metaphysical from concepts, they seek today to develop it from percepts. Since concepts were present to people in transparent clarity, they believed that they could deduce the metaphysical from them, too, with absolute certainty. But percepts are not so transparent to us. Each successive percept appears somewhat different from those of the same kind that preceded it. What is inferred from the earlier ones is consequently somewhat modified by each successive percept. Therefore, the form that we thus give to the metaphysical can be called only relatively correct. It is subject to correction by future cases. Eduard von Hartmann's metaphysics is characterized by this methodological principle. Hence, on the title page of his first major work, he placed the motto: "Speculative results following the inductive method of natural science."

[37]   The form that metaphysical realists give to things-in-themselves today is arrived at through inductive inferences. By reflecting on the process of cognition they have convinced themselves of the existence of an

objectively real world continuity alongside what is "subjectively" cognizable through percept and concept. They believe they can determine how this objective reality is constituted by inductive inference from their percepts.

Addendum to the new edition (1918)

Certain ideas based on natural-scientific study will always pose distractions for the kind of unprejudiced observation of experience in percepts and concepts that I have tried to present in the preceding discussion. According to modern science, for instance, the eye perceives colors in the light spectrum from red to violet. Beyond violet, there are forces of radiation corresponding to no color-percept in the eye, but rather only to a chemical effect. In the same way, beyond the red limit, there are radiations that manifest only as warmth. Consideration of these and similar phenomena leads to the view that the range of the human perceptual world is determined by the range of the human senses, and humans would face an altogether different world if they had additional, or completely different, senses. Anyone who indulges in extravagant fantasies, for which the brilliant discoveries of current natural science offer quite seductive opportunities, can easily conclude that, after all, nothing enters the human field of observation but what can affect the senses formed by our bodily organization. We have no right, then, to regard what we perceive because of our bodily organization as any standard of reality. Each new sense would place before us a different picture of reality. [1]

Within appropriate limits, this view is thoroughly justified. But those who allow themselves to be misled by this opinion and prevented from an unprejudiced observation of the relationship between percepts and concepts expressed here are sealing off the path to a knowledge of the world and of human beings that is rooted in reality. To experience the essence of thinking—that is, actively to elaborate the conceptual world—is something completely different from the experience of something perceptible through the senses. Whatever senses human beings might have, not one could give us reality if our thinking did not permeate what is perceived through them with concepts. However constituted, any sense permeated by concepts in this way offers human beings the possibility of living in reality. The fantasy of the completely different perceptual picture possible with other senses has nothing to do with the question of how human beings stand in the real world. We must realize that *every* perceptual picture takes its form from the organization of the perceiving entity, but that the perceptual picture permeated by an actually experienced thinking contemplation leads us into reality. It is not the fantasy depiction of how differently a world would look for other than human senses that can enable us to seek knowledge of our relationship to the world; rather, it is the insight that *every* percept gives only a part of the reality hidden within it, and that it thus directs us away from its *own* reality. This insight is then joined by another—that thinking leads us into the part of the percept's reality that was hidden by the percept itself.

In the field of experimental physics, it is sometimes necessary to speak not of elements that are immediately perceptible, but of unobservable quantities such as lines of electric or magnetic force. This can also distract us from the unprejudiced observation of the relationship described here between the percept and the concept worked out in thinking. It can *appear* as if the elements of reality that physics describes have nothing to do either with what is perceptible or with the concept worked out in active thinking. Yet such a view would be based on self-deception. We must realize, in the first place, that *everything* worked out in physics—except unjustified hypotheses that ought to be excluded—is achieved with percepts and concepts. A physicist's accurate cognitive instinct transposes what is apparently an unobservable content to the field where percepts exist, where it is then thought out in familiar concepts from that field. The strengths of electric or magnetic fields, for example, are not obtained through an *essentially* different cognitive process than that which operates between percepts and concepts.

An increase or alteration in the human senses would result in a different perceptual picture, an enrichment or alteration of human experience. But real knowledge must be achieved, even in regard to *this* experience, by the interaction of concept and percept. The *deepening* of cognition depends on the forces of intuition that live in thinking (cf. p. 88). In the *experience* of thinking, such intuition can immerse itself either more or less deeply in reality. The extension of the perceptual picture can stimulate this immersion and so, indirectly, promote it. Yet

this immersion in the depths — this attainment of reality—should *never* be confused with encountering a
broader or narrower perceptual picture, in which there is
always only a half reality, as determined by the cognizing organism. Anyone not lost in *abstractions* will realize how relevant it is for our knowledge of human nature
that physics has to *infer* elements in the perceptual field
to which no sense is attuned as directly as for color or
sound. *Concretely*, the essence of the human is determined not only by the kind of immediate perception with
which we confront ourselves through our organization,
but also by our excluding other things from this immediate perception. Just as both the conscious waking state
and the unconscious state of sleep are necessary for life,
so both the sphere of sense percepts and a (much greater)
sphere of elements that are not sense-perceptible, in the
field from which sense percepts originate, are necessary
for human self-experience. All of this was already expressed indirectly in the original presentation of this text.
I add this extension of its content here because I have
found that many readers have not read it with sufficient
precision.

It should also be kept in mind that the idea of the *percept*, as developed in this text, must not be confused with
that of external sense perception, which is only a special
case of it. Readers will see from what has been said, but
still more so from what will be said later, that everything
both sensory *and spiritual* that meets a human being is
here taken to be a "percept" until it is grasped by the actively elaborated concept. "Senses" of the kind normally

meant by the word are not necessary to have percepts of soul or spirit. One could object that such an extension of normal linguistic usage is illegitimate. But it is *absolutely necessary* unless we want our cognitive growth in certain areas to be held in chains by linguistic custom. Anyone who speaks of perception *only* as sense perception will not arrive at a concept appropriate for knowledge—even knowledge of this same sense perception. Sometimes we *must* extend a concept so that it can have an appropriate meaning in a narrower field. Sometimes, too, we must add something to what a concept initially calls to mind so that what is thought of initially can be justified or adjusted. Thus, on page 100 of this book we read that "A mental picture, then, is an individualized concept." I have heard the objection that this is an unusual use of words. But if we are to understand what a mental picture really is, this usage is necessary. What would become of the progress of knowledge, if everyone who has to adjust concepts meets with the objection, "That is an unusual use of words"?

THE FACTORS OF LIFE

Let us recapitulate what we have gained through the previous chapters. The world comes to meet me as a multiplicity, a sum of separate details. As a human being, I am myself one of these details, an entity among other entities. We call this form of the world simply *the given* and—insofar as we do not develop it through conscious activity but find it ready-made—we call it *percept*. Within the world of percepts, we perceive ourselves. But if something did not emerge out of this self-percept that proved capable of linking both percepts in general and also the sum of all other percepts with the percept of our self, our self-percept would remain simply one among many. This emerging something, however, is no longer a mere percept; nor is it, like percepts, simply present. It is produced through activity and initially appears linked to what we perceive as our self, but its inner meaning reaches beyond the self. It adds conceptual determinates to individual percepts, but these conceptual determinates relate to one another and are grounded in a whole. It determines conceptually what is

[1]

achieved through self-perception conceptually, just as it determines all other percepts. It places this as the subject or "I" over against objects. This "something" is thinking, and the conceptual determinates are concepts and ideas.

Thus, thinking first expresses itself in the percept of the self, but it is not merely subjective, for the self characterizes itself as subject only with the help of thinking. Such self-reference in thought is one way that we determine our personality in life. Through it, we lead a purely conceptual existence. Through it, we feel ourselves as thinking beings. Were it unaccompanied by other ways of determining our self, this determination of our personality would remain purely conceptual (logical). Then we would be beings whose lives were limited to establishing purely conceptual relationships among percepts, and between percepts and ourselves. Now, if we call the establishment of such a relationship in thought *cognition*, and the state of the self achieved through it *knowledge*, then—if the assumption just mentioned applied—we would have to regard ourselves as *merely* cognizing or knowing beings.

[2]   But this assumption does not hold. As we have seen, we do not relate percepts to ourselves only through concepts, but also through feeling. Therefore we are not beings with merely conceptual content to our lives. The naive realist, in fact, sees in the feeling-life a *more real* expression of the personality than in the purely conceptual element of knowledge. And if the matter is judged from that standpoint, this view is quite correct. At first, feeling is exactly similar on the subjective side to the percept on the objective side. Therefore, according to the

fundamental proposition of naive realism (everything that can be perceived is real), feeling guarantees the reality of one's own personality. Yet monism, as understood here, must acknowledge that a feeling, if it is to appear to us in its full reality, requires the same kind of completion as any other percept. For monism, feeling is an incomplete reality that, in the form in which it is given to us at first, does not yet contain its second factor, the concept or idea. This is why feeling, like perceiving, always appears *before* cognizing. First, we merely feel ourselves as existing; and, in the course of our gradual development, we reach the point at which, out of our own dimly felt existence, the self concept dawns upon us. But what emerges *for us* only later is originally inseparably united with feeling. This is what makes naive persons believe that existence reveals itself directly in feeling, but only indirectly in knowledge. Exercising the life of feeling will therefore seem more important to them than anything else. They believe themselves to have grasped the pattern of the universe only when they have received it into their feeling. They try to make feeling, not knowing, the means of cognition. Since feeling is something altogether individual, something equivalent to perception, philosophers of feeling make something that has significance only within their own personality into the principle of the universe. They try to permeate the entire universe with their own selves. What monism, as described in this book, attempts to grasp *conceptually*, the philosophers of feeling seek to achieve with feeling. They see that kind of connection with things as more immediate.

[3]   This tendency—the philosophy of feeling—is often called *mysticism*. A mystical view based solely on feeling errs in wanting to *experience* what it ought to *know*; it wants to make something that is individual, feeling, into something universal.

[4]   Feeling is a purely individual act. It is a relationship of the outer world to our subject, insofar as that relationship finds expression in a purely subjective experience.

[5]   There is yet another expression of the human personality. Through its thinking, the I participates in general, universal life. Through thinking, it relates percepts to itself, and itself to percepts, in a purely conceptual way; in feeling, it experiences a relationship of the object to its subject. But in *willing*, the reverse is the case. In willing, too, we have a percept before us: namely, that of the individual relation of our self to what is objective. And whatever is not a purely conceptual factor in our will is just as much a mere object of perception as anything in the outer world.

[6]   Yet here, too, naive realism believes that it has before it a far realer kind of existence than can be attained through thinking. In contrast to thinking, which formulates the event only afterward in concepts, naive realism sees an element in the will in which we are *immediately* aware of an event or cause. From this point of view, what the I achieves through its will is a process that is experienced immediately. Adherents of this philosophy believe that, in the will, they have hold of a corner of the world process. They believe that in willing we experience a real event quite immediately, while we can only follow other events from the outside. They make the form of existence

in which the will appears within the self into an actual principle of reality. Their own willing appears to them as a special case of the universal world process; and the universal world process appears as a universal will. Here the will becomes a world principle, just as feeling becomes a cognitive principle in mysticism. This point of view is called the *philosophy of the will* (or *thelism*). It makes something that can be experienced only individually into a constitutive factor of the world.

The philosophy of will can no more be called "science" *[7]* than can the mysticism of feeling, for both maintain that to permeate the world with concepts is inadequate. In addition to a conceptual principle of existence, both demand a real principle as well. There is some justification in this. But since we can grasp these so-called real principles only through our perception, the claims of both mysticism of feeling and philosophy of the will are identical with the view that we have two sources of knowledge—thinking and perceiving, the latter expressing itself as individual experience in feeling and in will. According to this view, since what flows from one source (our experiences) cannot be received directly into what flows from the other (thinking), both kinds of cognition, thinking and perceiving, remain side by side without any higher mediation between them. Beside the conceptual principle attainable through knowledge, there is supposed to exist a real principle of the world that can be experienced, but not grasped by thinking. In other words, because they subscribe to the proposition that what is directly perceived is real, mysticism of feeling and the philosophy of will are both types of naive realism. Yet, compared to the original naive realism, they commit the further inconsistency of making a specific form of perceiving (feeling or willing) into the sole means of cognizing existence—but they can do so only by subscribing to the general proposition that what has been perceived is real. On that basis, however, they would also have to ascribe an equivalent cognitive value to external perceiving.

[8]   The philosophy of will becomes metaphysical realism when it transfers the will into those realms of existence where immediate experience of it is not possible in the same way as it is in one's own subject. It assumes the existence, outside the subject, of a hypothetical principle, the sole criterion for whose reality is *subjective* experience. As metaphysical realism, the philosophy of the will succumbs to the criticism given in the previous chapter, which the contradictory aspect of every metaphysical realism must recognize and overcome, that the will is only a universal world process to the extent that it relates to the rest of the world conceptually.

Addendum to the new edition (1918)

[1]   The difficulty of grasping thinking in its essence by observing it consists in this: when the soul wants to bring it into the focus of attention, this essence has all too easily already slipped away from the observing soul. All that is left for the soul then is the dead abstraction, the corpse of living thinking. If we look only at this abstraction, we can easily feel drawn to the mysticism of feeling or the

metaphysics of will, which seem so "full of life." We find it strange if anyone seeks to grasp the essence of reality in "mere thoughts." But whoever truly manages to experience *life within thinking* sees that dwelling in mere feelings or contemplating the element of will cannot even be compared with (let alone ranked above) the inner richness and the *experience*, the inner calmness and mobility, in the life of thinking. It is precisely the richness, the inner fullness of experience, that makes its reflection in normal consciousness seem dead and abstract. No other activity of the human soul is as easily misunderstood as thinking. Feeling and willing warm the human soul even when we look back and recollect their original state, while thinking all too easily leaves us cold. It seems to dry out the life of the soul. Yet this is only the sharply contoured shadow of the reality of thinking—a reality interwoven with light, dipping down warmly into the phenomena of the world. This dipping down occurs with a power that flows forth in the activity of thinking itself—the power of love in spiritual form. One should not object that to speak of love in active thinking is to displace a feeling, love, into thinking. This objection is actually a confirmation of what is being said here. For whoever turns toward *essential* thinking finds within it both feeling and will, and both of these in the depths of their reality. Whoever turns aside from thinking toward "pure" feeling and willing loses the true reality of feeling and willing. If we *experience* thinking *intuitively*, we also do justice to the experience of feeling and will. But the mysticism of feeling and the metaphysics of will cannot do justice to the penetration of existence by intuitive thinking. Those views all too easily conclude that it is *they* who stand within reality, while intuitive thinkers, devoid of feeling and estranged from reality, form only a shadowy, cold picture of the world in "abstract thoughts."

CHAPTER 9

THE IDEA OF FREEDOM

For cognition, the concept of a tree is determined by the percept of a tree. Faced with a specific percept, I can select only a very specific concept out of the general conceptual system. The connection between a concept and a percept is indirectly and objectively determined by thinking about the percept. The percept's connection with its concept is recognized *after* the act of perception; but their belonging together is determined by the situation itself. [1]

The process presents itself differently when we examine cognition itself or the relationship between human beings and the world through cognition. In the preceding discussion, an attempt was made to show that it is possible to clarify this relationship through unprejudiced observation. A proper understanding of such observation leads to the insight that thinking can be beheld directly as a self-enclosed entity. Those who find it necessary to explain thinking as such by appealing to something else—such as physical processes in the brain or unconscious mental processes lying behind observed, conscious thinking— [2]

misunderstand what the unprejudiced observation of thinking provides. To observe thinking is to live, during the observation, immediately within the weaving of a self-supporting spiritual entity. We could even say that whoever wants to grasp the essence of the spirit in the form in which it *first* presents itself to human beings can do so in the self-sustaining activity of thinking.

[3]   In examining thinking itself, two things coincide that otherwise *must* always appear as separated: concepts and percepts. If we do not understand this, the concepts developed in response to percepts will seem to us to be shadowy copies of these percepts, while the percepts themselves will seem to present us with true reality. We will also build a metaphysical world for ourselves on the pattern of the perceived world. Following the style of our mental imagery, we will call this metaphysical world the atomic world, the world of the will, or of the unconscious spirit, and so forth. And we will fail to see how, in all of this, we have built up only a hypothetical metaphysical world on the pattern of *our* perceptual world. But, if we see what is really present in thinking, we will recognize that only one part of reality is present in the percept and that we *experience* the other part—which belongs to it and is necessary for it to appear as full reality—in the permeation of the percept by thinking. We shall then see, in what appears in consciousness as thinking, not a shadowy copy of reality, but a spiritual essence that sustains itself. Of this spiritual essence we can say that it becomes present to our consciousness through *intuition*. *Intuition* is the conscious experience, within what is purely spiritual, of a

purely spiritual content. The essence of thinking can be grasped only through intuition.

Only when, by means of unprejudiced observation, we [4] have wrestled through to a recognition of this truth about the intuitive essence of thinking can we obtain a clear path to insight into the human organization of body and soul. We then recognize that this organization can have no effect on the *essence* of thinking, even though the facts initially *seem* to contradict this. In normal experience, human thinking appears only in and through the organization of body and soul. This organization makes itself felt so strongly in thinking that its true significance can only be seen by someone who has recognized that *nothing* of that organization plays a part in the essential nature of thinking. But such a person will also see what a peculiar kind of relationship exists between this human organization and thinking. For our organization has no effect on the essence of thinking but rather retreats when the activity of thinking appears. Our organization suspends its own activity—it makes room—and, in the space that has been made free, thinking appears. The effective essence in thinking has a double function. First, it represses the human organization's own activity and, second, it replaces that activity with itself. Even the first of these, the repression of the bodily organization, is a result of thinking activity—of the part of that activity that prepares the *appearance* of thinking. We can see from this in what sense thinking is reflected in the bodily organization. Once we see this, we will no longer be able to mistake the significance of that reflection and take it for thinking itself. If we walk over softened ground, our footsteps dig into the earth. We are not tempted to say that the footprints are driven upward from below by forces in the ground. We will not attribute to *those* forces any share in the origin of the footprints. Similarly, if we observe the essence of thinking without prejudice, we will not attribute any part of this essence to traces in the bodily organism that arise because thinking prepares its appearance by means of the body.[1]

[5]   Here a significant question emerges. If the human organization plays no part in the *essence* of thinking, what significance does this organization play in the totality of the human being? The answer is that what happens in human organization as a result of thinking has nothing to do with the essence of thinking, but it does have something to do with the origin of I-consciousness out of thinking. The real "I" certainly lies in thinking's own essence, but I-consciousness does not. Anyone who observes thinking without prejudice sees this is the case. The "I" is to be found in thinking; but "I-consciousness" appears because the traces of thinking activity are engraved in general consciousness, as characterized above. (I-consciousness therefore arises through the bodily organization. But let us not confuse this with the claim that I-consciousness, once arisen, remains dependent on the bodily organization. Once arisen, it is

---

1. In writings subsequent to this one, the writer has shown how the above view has been confirmed in psychology, physiology, etc. Here, only what comes from the unprejudiced observation of thinking itself was to be addressed. (Author's note)

taken up into thinking, and thereafter shares in thinking's spiritual being.)

"I-consciousness" is based on the human organization, [6] from which our acts of will flow. Following the preceding discussion, insight into the connection between thinking, the conscious I, and acts of will can be achieved only if we first observe how an act of will proceeds from the human organization.[2]

For an individual act of will, we must consider both the [7] motive and the motive power. The motive is a conceptual or mentally pictured factor; the motive power is the factor of willing that is conditioned directly within the human organization. The conceptual factor, or motive, is the momentary determining principle of willing; the motive power is the abiding determining principle of the individual. A motive can be a pure concept or a concept with a specific relation to perceiving, that is, a mental picture. By affecting a human individual and by determining that individual to act in a certain direction, general and individualized concepts (mental pictures) become motives of willing. Yet one and the same concept, or one and the same mental picture, has different effects on different individuals. The same concept (or mental picture) can cause different people to perform different acts. Willing, then, is not merely the result of the concept or mental picture, but also of the individual human make-up. We shall call this individual make-up, following Eduard von Hartmann, the

2. From p.132 through the above, passages were added, or reworked, for the new edition of 1918. (Author's note)

characterological disposition. The way in which concepts and mental pictures work upon someone's characterological disposition gives that person's life a specific moral or ethical stamp.

[8]   Our characterological disposition is shaped by the more-or-less lasting content of our subjective life—in other words by the content of our mental pictures and feelings. Whether or not a mental picture currently arising within me stimulates my willing depends on how it relates itself to the rest of my mental pictures, as well as to my idiosyncracies of feeling. My store of mental pictures is determined, in turn, by the sum of concepts that have come into contact with percepts in the course of my individual life, that is, by the concepts that have become mental pictures. These, again, depend on my greater or lesser capacity for intuition and on the range of my observations—that is, on the subjective and objective factors of my experiences, on my inner character, and on my life-setting. My feeling life is especially important in determining my characterological disposition. Whether or not I make a particular mental picture or concept a motive for action depends upon whether it gives me joy or pain.

These are the elements to be considered in an act of will. The immediate mental picture or concept becomes a motive and determines the goal or purpose of my willing; my characterological disposition determines whether or not I will direct my activity toward that goal. The mental picture of taking a walk during the next half hour determines the goal of my activity. This mental picture, however, is elevated into a motive of willing only if it encounters a suitable characterological disposition; that is, if in my life to date I have developed mental pictures of, for example, the usefulness of taking walks and the value of health and, further, if the mental picture of taking walks is linked in me with feelings of pleasure.

Thus, we must distinguish between (1) the possible   *[9]*
subjective dispositions that are suited to making specific mental pictures and concepts into motives and (2) the possible mental pictures and concepts that are capable of influencing my characterological disposition so that an act of will results. The former represent the *motive powers*, the latter the *goals* of morality.

By identifying the elements that compose an individual   *[10]*
life, we can discover the motive powers of morality. The   *[11]*
first level of individual life is *perceiving*, particularly the perceiving of the senses. In this region of individual life, perceiving is immediately—without any intervening feeling or concept—transformed into willing. The motive power under consideration here is simply called *drive*. Satisfaction of our lower, purely animal needs (hunger, sexual intercourse, etc.) occurs in this way. The special characteristic of the life of the drives is the immediacy with which the individual percept activates our willing. This immediacy, originally belonging only to the lower sense life, can also be extended to the percepts of the higher senses. We react to the percept of some event in the external world without further reflection and without linking a special feeling to it—as occurs in conventional social behavior. We call the motive power here *tact* or *moral taste*. The more such an immediate reaction to a

percept occurs, the more suited the person in question will be to act purely under the influence of tact: that is, *tact* becomes the characterological disposition.

[12]   The second sphere of human life is *feeling*. Particular feelings accompany percepts of the external world. These feelings can become motive powers for action. If I see a hungry person, my compassion can form the motive power to act. Such feelings include shame, pride, sense of honor, humility, remorse, compassion, vengeance, gratitude, piety, loyalty, love, and duty.[3]

[13]   Finally, the third level of life is *thinking and mental picturing*. Through mere reflection, a mental picture or concept can become a motive for action. Mental pictures become motives because, in the course of life, we constantly link certain goals of our will to percepts that recur repeatedly in more or less modified form. Therefore people who are not without experience are always aware, along with certain percepts, of mental pictures of actions they themselves have performed or seen others perform in similar cases. These mental pictures float before them as defining patterns for all later decisions; they become part of their characterological disposition. We can call this motive power of the will *practical experience*. Practical experience merges gradually into purely tactful action. This happens when certain typical pictures of actions

---

3. A complete catalogue of the principles of morality (from the standpoint of metaphysical realism) can be found in Eduard von Hartmann's *Die Phänomenologie des sittlichen Bewusstseins*. (Author's note)

have become so firmly connected in our consciousness with mental pictures of certain situations in life that we may, in any given instance, skip over all deliberation based on experience and go immediately from the percept into willing.

The highest stage of individual life is conceptual think- *[14]* ing without reference to a specific perceptual content. We determine the content of a concept out of the conceptual sphere through pure intuition. Such a concept initially contains no reference to specific percepts. If we enter into willing under the influence of a concept referring to a percept—that is to say, a mental picture—then it is this percept that determines our willing through the detour of conceptual thinking. If we act under the influence of intuitions, then the motive power of our action is *pure thinking*. Since it is customary in philosophy to designate the capacity for pure thinking as "reason," we are fully justified in calling the moral driving force characteristic of this stage *practical reason*. The clearest account of this motive force of the will has been given by Kreyenbuehl.[4] I count his essay on the topic among the most significant creations of contemporary philosophy, particularly of ethics. Kreyenbuehl calls the motive power in question

---

4. *Philosophische Monatshefte*, Band XVIII, Heft 3, 1882. Available as Kreyenbuehl, *Ethical-Spiritual Activity in Kant* (translated by Harold Jurgens), Spring Valley: Mercury Press, 1986. Kreyenbuehl (1846–1929) was a Swiss scholar, teacher, journalist, seeker after truth, and lecturer on Platonic philosophy. He wrote, among others, on Schiller, Plato, Pestalozzi, the Gospel of Saint John, and the history of philosophy.

practical a priori, that is, an impulse to act flowing directly from my intuition.

[15]   Clearly, such an impulse no longer belongs, strictly speaking, to the realm of characterological dispositions. For what is active here as the motive power is no longer something merely individual in me, but the conceptual, and therefore universal, content of my intuition. As soon as I recognize the justification for making this content the basis and starting-point for an action, I enter into willing, regardless of whether the concept was already present in me beforehand or only entered my consciousness immediately before the action—that is, regardless of whether or not it was already present in me as disposition.

[16]   An act of will is real only if a momentary impulse of action influences the characterological disposition in the form of a concept or mental picture. Such an impulse then becomes a motive of willing.

[17]   The motives of morality are mental pictures and concepts. There are ethicists who also see a motive of morality in feelings. They claim, for example, that the aim of moral action is to promote the greatest possible amount of pleasure in the acting individual. But only the *mental picture of pleasure,* not pleasure itself, can become a motive. The *mental picture* of a future feeling, but not the feeling itself, can affect my characterological disposition. For the feeling itself is not present in the moment of action; rather, it must first be produced through the action.

[18]   The *mental picture* of one's own or another's well-being is quite properly recognized as a motive of willing. The principle of producing through one's actions the

greatest amount of pleasure for oneself—that is, of attaining individual happiness—is called *egoism*. This individual happiness is sought either through thinking ruthlessly only of one's own welfare and striving for it even at the expense of the happiness of other individuals (pure egoism), or through promoting the good of others because one hopes for indirect advantages from their happiness, or through fear of endangering one's own interests by harming others (morality of prudence). The particular content of egoistic moral principles will depend on what mental picture we form of our own or others' happiness. We will determine the content of our egoistic striving according to what we regard as good in life (luxurious living, hope of happiness, deliverance from various evils, and so forth).

The purely conceptual content of an action should be   *[19]* seen as a different kind of motive. Unlike the mental picture of one's own pleasure, this content relates not just to a single action, but to the derivation of an action from a system of moral principles. These moral principles can regulate ethical conduct in the form of abstract concepts, without an individual's worrying about the origin of the concepts. We then feel that our subjection to the moral concept, which hovers over our actions as a commandment, is simply a moral necessity. We leave the establishment of this necessity to whoever demands our moral subjection; that is, to whatever moral authority we recognize (the head of our family, the state, social custom, ecclesiastical authority, divine revelation). A special kind of moral principle is involved when the commandment does not announce itself to us through outer authority, but from within ourselves. We may call this moral autonomy. We then hear within ourselves the voice to which we must submit. The expression of this voice is *conscience*.

[20]   Moral progress occurs when a person does not simply accept the commandment of an outer or inner authority as a motive for action, but rather strives to see why any given principle should work as a motive. This is to progress from an authoritarian morality to action based on ethical insight. At this level of morality, we consider the needs of a moral life and allow our actions to be determined by knowledge of them. Such needs are (1) the greatest possible welfare of all humanity, purely for the sake of that welfare; (2) the progress of civilization or the moral *evolution* of humanity to ever greater perfection; and (3) the realization of individual moral goals that have been grasped purely intuitively.

[21]   The *greatest possible welfare of all humanity* will naturally be formulated differently by different people. This phrase does not refer to a particular mental picture of such welfare but to the idea that those individuals who recognize this principle strive to do whatever they think will most promote the welfare of all humanity.

[22]   For those who associate a feeling of pleasure with the benefits of civilization, *the progress of civilization* turns out to be a special case of the moral principle of greatest possible welfare. But they will have to accept into the bargain the demise and destruction of many things that also contribute to the welfare of humanity. However, it is also possible that someone could see ethical necessity in the progress of civilization, quite apart from the feeling

of pleasure associated with it. For such a person, then, it is a distinct moral principle in addition to the previous one.

The principle of the welfare of all, like that of the progress of civilization, depends on a mental picture; that is to say, on the relationship that we make between the content of ethical ideas and particular experiences (percepts). But the highest ethical principle of which we can think is that which contains no such relationship *in advance*, but rather springs from the source of pure intuition and only afterward seeks a relationship to a percept (to life). Here, the determination of *what* is to be willed proceeds from a different source than in the previous examples. Those who honor the ethical principle of the good of all will, in all their actions, ask first what their ideals contribute to that good. Those who adhere to the ethical principle of the progress of civilization will do the same. Yet there is a higher way that does not proceed from one definite, single ethical goal in each case, but assumes a certain value to all ethical maxims and in each case asks whether one or the other moral principle is more important. In certain circumstances, I might regard promotion of cultural progress as right and make it into the motive of my action; in others, promotion of the good of the whole; and in a third case, promotion of my own welfare. But, if all other reasons determining action move to second place, then conceptual intuition itself has primary consideration. The other motives now step down from the leading position, and the ideal content of the action alone operates as its motive.

[23]

[24]   We described the stage of characterological disposition that works as *pure thinking*, or *practical reason*, as the highest. We have now described *conceptual intuition* as the highest motive. More exact reflection soon reveals that motive power and motive coincide at this level of morality. That is, neither a previously determined characterological disposition nor an outer ethical principle taken as a standard influences our action. The action is therefore not executed robotically according to certain rules, nor is it action performed automatically in response to outer pressure, but rather it is action determined solely by its own conceptual content.

[25]   Such an action presupposes the capacity for moral intuitions. Whoever lacks the capacity to experience the particular ethical principle of each individual case will also never achieve truly individual willing.

[26]   The exact opposite of this ethical principle is the Kantian: Act in such a way that the bases of your action are applicable to all human beings. This sentence is the death of all individual impulses of action. My standard cannot be how *all* humans would act but rather what I am to do in the individual case.

[27]   A superficial judgment might perhaps object to these arguments by asking: How can an action be formed individually, for the particular case and the particular situation, and yet simultaneously be determined purely conceptually, out of intuition? This objection rests on confusing the ethical motive with the perceptible content of an action. The latter *can* be a motive, and even is so, for example, in the case of the progress of civilization, in

egoistic actions, etc. In actions based on purely ethical intuition, it is *not* the motive. Naturally, my I directs its gaze toward the perceptual content but it does not allow itself to be *determined* by it. The content is used only to form a *cognitive concept* for oneself; the corresponding *moral concept* is not derived by the I from the object. The cognitive concept of a particular situation that I encounter is also a moral concept only when I come from the standpoint of a particular moral principle. If I wanted to base all of my actions on the moral evolution of civilization, then I would have fixed marching orders. From every event that I perceive and that can possibly concern me, an ethical duty immediately arises; namely, to do my part so that the event in question serves the evolution of civilization. In addition to the concept, which reveals to me the context of an event or thing in natural law, the event or thing also has an ethical label with instructions addressed to me, the moral being, about how I should behave. Such a moral label is legitimate in its sphere, but on a higher level it coincides with the idea that reveals itself to me when I face a concrete situation.

People vary in their capacity for intuition. For one person, ideas just bubble up, while another achieves them by much labor. The situations in which people live, and which serve as the scene of their activity, are no less varied. How I act will therefore depend on how my capacity for intuition works in relation to a particular situation. The sum of ideas active within us, the real content of our intuitions, constitutes what is individual in each of us, *[28]* notwithstanding the universality of the world of ideas. To the extent that the intuitive content turns into action, it is the ethical content of the individual. Allowing this intuitive content to live itself out fully is the highest driving force of morality. At the same time, it is the highest motive of those who realize that, in the end, all other moral principles unite within it. We can call this standpoint *ethical individualism*.

[29]   What is decisive in an intuitively determined action in a concrete instance is the discovery of the corresponding, completely individual intuition. At this level of morality, we can speak of general moral concepts (norms or laws) only to the extent that they result from the generalization of individual impulses. General norms always presuppose concrete facts from which they can be derived. But facts are first *created* by human action.

[30]   When we seek for laws (or concepts) in the actions of individuals, peoples, and eras, we discover an ethics that is not a science of ethical norms but a natural history of morality. Only the laws obtained in this way relate to human conduct as natural laws relate to a particular phenomenon. But they are by no means identical with the impulses on which we base our actions. If we want to understand how a human action springs from *ethical* willing, we must look first to the relationship of that willing to the action in question. First, we must focus on actions for which this relationship is decisive. If I or another later reflect upon such an action, then we can discover which ethical principles are relevant. While I am acting, an ethical principle moves me to the extent that it can live within me

intuitively; it is united with *love* for the goal that I wish to realize through my action. I do not consult any person or code with the question, "Should I perform this action?" — I perform the action as soon as I have grasped the idea. Only in this way is it *my* action.

The actions of those who act only because they recognize particular ethical norms result from the principles present in their moral code. They are mere executors, a higher form of robot. Toss an opportunity to act into their awareness and, right away, the clockwork of their moral principles sets itself in motion and runs its course in a lawful fashion to produce a Christian, humane, or apparently selfless action or one for the sake of the progress of civilization. Only when I follow my love for an object is it I myself who act. At this level of morality, I do not act because I acknowledge a lord over me or an external authority or a so-called inner voice. I acknowledge no outer principle for my action, because I have found within myself the basis of my acting—love for the action. I do not check rationally whether the action is good or evil; I do it because I *love* it. My action becomes "good" if my intuition, steeped in love, stands in the right way in the intuitively experienceable world continuum; it becomes "bad" if that is not the case. I do not ask myself, "How would another person act in my situation?" Rather, I act as I, this particular individuality, want (or will). What directs me is not common usage, not general custom, not a universal human principle, and not an ethical norm, but my love for the deed. I feel no compulsion, neither the compulsion of nature, which guides me in my drives, nor the compulsion of ethical commandments. I simply want to carry out what lies within me.

[31]   Defenders of universal ethical norms might object to these arguments as follows: If all people strive merely to express themselves, and to do as they please, then there is no difference between a good action and a crime; every bit of knavery within me has equal claim to expression with the intention to serve the universal good. As an ethical human being, what should be decisive for me is not the mere fact that I have focused on the idea of an action, but rather my determination of whether the action is good or evil. Only if I have determined that it is good should I carry it out.

[32]   My response to this objection, which seems plausible, but arises only from a misunderstanding of what is meant here, is this: Anyone who wants to know the essence of human willing must distinguish between the path that brings willing up to a certain stage of development and the special form that it assumes when it nears its goal. On the path to this goal, norms play their justifiable role. The goal consists in the realization of ethical aims that are grasped purely intuitively. Humans achieve such aims to the degree that they possess any capacity to lift themselves to the intuitive-conceptual content of the world. In any individual act of willing, other things are generally mixed in with such aims, as motive or motive power. But intuition can still determine, or co-determine, human willing. What we *should* do, we do; we offer the stage upon which "should" becomes "do." An action is our own if we allow it to emerge as such from within ourselves. Here, the impulse

can only be completely individual. In truth, only an act of will emerging from intuition can be individual. Only if blind drives are reckoned to belong to the human individuality can we see a criminal deed, or evil, as an expression of individuality equivalent to the incarnation of pure intuition. But the blind drive that drives someone to commit a crime does not come from intuition. It does not belong to what is individual within a person. It belongs to what is commonest, to what is equally present in all individuals and out of which we must work our way with our individuality. What is individual in me is not my organism, with its drives and feelings, but my own world of ideas that lights up within this organism. My drives, instincts, and passions establish no more in me than that I belong to the general species *human being*. The fact that something conceptual expresses itself in a special way in those drives, passions, and feelings establishes my individuality. Through my instincts, my drives, I am the kind of person of whom there are twelve to the dozen; I am an individual by means of the particular form of the idea by which, within the dozen, I designate myself as *I*. Only a being other than myself could distinguish me from others by differences in my animal nature. I distinguish myself from others by my thinking, that is, by actively grasping what expresses itself in my organism as conceptuality. Thus, we cannot say that the action of a criminal proceeds from an idea. In fact, what is characteristic of criminal acts is precisely that they derive from non-conceptual elements within a human being.

Insofar as an action proceeds from the conceptual part *[33]* of my individual being it is felt to be free. Every other portion of an action, whether it is performed under the compulsion of nature or according to the requirement of an ethical norm, is felt to be *unfree*.

[34]   Humans are free to the extent that they are able to obey themselves at each instant of their lives. An ethical deed is only *my* deed if it can be called a free deed in this sense. We have examined under which conditions a willed act is felt to be free. What follows will show how this purely ethically understood idea of freedom realizes itself in human nature.

[35]   To act out of freedom does not exclude moral laws, but rather includes them. Still, it stands on a higher level than action dictated by moral laws alone. Why should my action serve the welfare of the whole any less if I have acted out of love than if I acted *only* because I feel a duty to serve the welfare of the whole? The simple concept of duty excludes *freedom*, because duty does not recognize individuality but demands instead subjection of individuality to a general norm. Freedom of action is thinkable only from the standpoint of ethical individualism.

[36]   But how is it possible for humans to live together socially if everyone is striving merely to express his or her own individuality? This objection is characteristic of misguided moralism, which imagines that a society of human beings is only possible if they are all united by a commonly determined ethical order. Such moralism fails to understand the unity of the world of ideas. It cannot conceive that the world of ideas that is active in me is none other than the one that is at work in my neighbor. To be sure, this unity is merely a result of experience in the world.

But it *must* be so. For, if it were to be recognized in any way other than observation, then general laws rather than individual experience would give the stamp of validity in that realm. Individuality is possible only if each individual being knows another being by individual observation alone. The difference between me and my neighbor consists not in our living in two completely distinct spiritual worlds, but in my neighbor's receiving intuitions other than my own out of the world of ideas common to us both. My neighbors want to live out *their* intuitions, I *mine*. If we all really draw from the Idea, and follow no external (physical or spiritual) impulses, then we cannot but meet in the same striving, the same intentions. An ethical misunderstanding, a clash, is impossible among ethically *free* human beings. Only someone who is ethically unfree, who obeys natural drives or the conventional demands of duty, will thrust aside someone else who does not follow the same instincts and the same demands. *To live* in love of action, and *to let live* in understanding of the other's will, is the fundamental maxim of *free human beings*. They know no other *"should"* than the one with which their willing is intuitively in harmony. Their capacity for ideas tells them how they are to *will* in any given case.

If the basic source of compatibility did not lie within [37] human nature, we could not implant it by any outward laws! Only because individuals *are* of one spirit can they live out their lives side by side. A free person lives in trust that the other free person belongs to the same spiritual world and that they will concur with each other in their intentions. Those who are free demand no agreement from their fellows, but they expect it, because it is inherent in human nature. This is not meant to indicate the necessity of this or that outer arrangement. Rather, it is meant to indicate the *attitude*, the *state of the soul*, with which a human being, experiencing himself or herself amidst esteemed fellow human beings, can best do justice to human dignity.

[38]   There are many who will object: The concept of the *free* human being that you sketch is a chimera; it has been realized nowhere. We have to deal with real people, and the only morality to hope for in them comes when human beings obey an ethical commandment, when they formulate their ethical task as duty and do not freely follow their inclinations and their love. I do not doubt this at all. Only a blind man could. But if this is supposed to be the *final* insight, then away with all hypocrisy about "ethics." You should then simply say that, as long as human nature is not *free*, it must be *forced* into action. From a certain standpoint, it is irrelevant whether unfreedom is enforced through physical means or through moral laws, whether humans are unfree because they obey their limitless sexual drive or because they are enchained by conventional morality. But let us not claim that people can correctly call their actions *their own,* if they are driven to them by a power other than themselves. Still, right in the midst of compulsion, certain human beings lift themselves up, *free spirits*, who, in the welter of custom, legal stricture, religious practice, and so forth, find *themselves*. They are *free* to the extent that they obey only themselves; they are *unfree* to the extent that they subject themselves to something

else. Who of us can say that they are really free in all their actions? But in each of us there dwells a deeper being in whom the free human comes to expression.

Our life is made up of free and unfree actions. Yet we cannot think the concept of the human through to the end without arriving at the *free spirit* as the purest expression of human nature. Indeed, we are only truly human to the extent that we are free.   *[39]*

That is an ideal, many will say. No doubt. But it is an ideal that works as a real element in our being and manifests its effects on the surface. It is no thought-up or dreamed-up ideal, but one that has life and makes itself clearly known in even its most imperfect form of existence. Were human beings merely natural creatures, it would be absurd to look for ideals—that is, ideas that are not currently effective and requiring realization. With things of the external world, the idea is determined by the percept, and we have done our part once we have recognized the connection between idea and percept. But this is not so with humans. The totality of human existence is not determined apart from the human beings themselves; their true concepts as *ethical* human beings (free spirits) are not united in advance, objectively, with the perceptual picture of "human beings," needing merely to be confirmed afterward by cognition. As human beings, we must each unite our own concept with the percept of "human" through our own activity. Concept and percept coincide here only if we ourselves make them coincide. But we can only do so if we have discovered the concept of the free spirit, which is our own concept. In the objective   *[40]* world, the percept is divided from the concept by the way we are organized; in cognition we overcome this division. The division is no less present in our subjective nature; we overcome it in the course of our development by bringing our own concept to full outward manifestation. Thus, the intellectual as well as the moral life of human beings leads us to the dual nature of humans: perceiving (immediate experience) and thinking. Intellectual life overcomes the duality through cognition; moral life overcomes it through the actual realization of the free spirit. Every being has its inborn concept (the law of its being and activity); but in external things the concept is inseparably bound up with the percept, and only separated from it in our spiritual organism. In human beings, the concept and the percept are *actually* separate at first, to be just as *actually* united by human beings themselves. It could be objected that a particular concept corresponds to our percept of a human being at every instant of a person's life, just as it does to every other thing; that I can create the concept of a stereotypical human for myself, and can also have such a human given me as percept. Were I then to add to that the concept of the free spirit, I would have two concepts for one and the same object.

[41]   This is one-sided thinking. As a perceptual object, I am subject to continual transformation. As a child I was one thing, as a youth another, as an adult still another. In fact, at every moment the perceptual picture of myself is different from what it was a moment before. These changes can take place in such a way that the same person (the stereotypical human) is always expressed in them or in such

a way that they represent the expression of the free spirit. My actions, too, as objects of perception, are subject to such changes.

There is a possibility for the human perceptual object to [42] transform itself, just as within the plant seed there lies the possibility of becoming a whole plant. The plant will transform itself because of the objective lawfulness lying within it. Humans remain in an incomplete state if they do not take in hand the transformative substance within themselves, and transform themselves through their own power. Nature makes human beings merely natural creatures; society makes them law-abiding actors; but they can only make *themselves* into *free* beings. At a certain stage of their development, nature releases human beings from her chains; society carries this development up to a further point; but human beings must give themselves the final polish.

The standpoint of free morality does not claim that the [43] free spirit is the only form in which a human being can exist. Free morality sees in free spirituality only the final stage of human evolution. This is not to deny that acting in accordance with norms has its justification as one stage in evolution. But it cannot be acknowledged as the absolute standpoint of morality. The free spirit overcomes such norms in that free spirits do not merely feel commandments as motives, but order their actions according to their impulses (intuitions).

Kant says, "Duty! You exalted, mighty name, you who [44] contain nothing lovable, nothing ingratiatingly agreeable, but who demand submission, (you who) establish a law... before which all inclinations fall dumb, though in secret they might work against it!"[5] To this, a human being, out of the consciousness of the free spirit, replies: "Freedom! You friendly, human name, you who contain everything morally beloved, everything that most dignifies my humanity, and who make me into no one's servant, you who do not merely establish a law, but wait for what my moral love itself will recognize as law, because it feels unfree in the face of every merely imposed law!"

[45]   This is the contrast between morality that is merely lawful and morality that is free.

[46]   Philistines, who see morality embodied in something externally fixed, might even see a free spirit as a dangerous person. They will do so, however, only because their view is limited to a particular epoch. If they could look beyond it, they would immediately find that free spirits need to move beyond the laws of the state as little as the philistines themselves, and that they never have to place themselves in real opposition to these laws. For the laws of the state, like all other objectively ethical laws, all sprang from the intuitions of free spirits. There is no law enforced by family authority that was not once intuitively conceived and formulated as such by an ancestor. Even the conventional laws of morality are first established by specific persons. And the laws of the state always arise in the heads of state officials. These minds have set up laws over other people, and no one becomes unfree except by forgetting that origin and making the

5. *Critique of Practical Reason*, 1.3.

laws either into extra-human commandments, into objective ethical concepts of duty independent of human participation, or into the commanding voice of one's own falsely conceived, mystically compelling inner self. But those who do not overlook the origin, but seek the human being within it, will see it as belonging to the same world of ideas from which they too draw their moral intuitions. If they believe that they have better intuitions, then they try to substitute their own for the existing ones; if they find that the existing ones are justified, then they act in accordance with them as if they were their own.

We must not establish the formula that human beings [47] exist to realize an ethical world order cut off from themselves. Anyone who claimed as much would still be standing, in relation to the science of humankind, at the same point at which natural science stood when it believed that a bull has horns in order to butt. Fortunately, natural scientists have done away with such concepts of purpose. It is harder for ethics similarly to free itself. But just as horns do not exist *because* of butting, but butting exists *through* the horns, so human beings do not exist because of morality, but morality exists *through* human beings. Free human beings act morally because they have moral ideas, but they do not act in order for morality to arise. Human individuals, with the moral ideas belonging to their being, are the precondition for the moral world order.

The human individual is the source of all morality and [48] the center of earthly life. States and societies exist because they turn out to be the necessary consequence of individual life. That states and societies then react upon individual life is just as understandable as the fact that butting, which exists because of the bull's horns, reacts upon the further development of the horns which would otherwise become stunted with prolonged disuse. In the same way, individuals would become stunted if they led isolated existences outside human community. It is precisely for this that the social order is formed, so that it can then react favorably on the individual.

CHAPTER 10

FREEDOM-PHILOSOPHY
AND MONISM

Simple people, who acknowledge as real only what they [1] can see with their eyes and touch with their hands, also require reasons that are perceptible to the senses for their moral lives. Such people need someone to communicate the grounds for action to them in a way that is understandable to their senses. And they will allow these grounds for action to be dictated to them, as commandments, by a person whom they consider wiser and mightier than themselves, or whom they acknowledge for some other reason as a power over them. In this way, as principles of morality, arise the principles of family, state, church, or divine authority that were mentioned in the last chapter. Those who are the most limited in their horizons put all their faith in some one other person; those who are somewhat more advanced allow their ethical conduct to be dictated to them by a majority (state or society). They always rely on powers they can perceive. Those for whom the conviction finally dawns that these powers are basically human beings as weak as themselves will seek guidance from a

higher power, from a divine being, whom they nevertheless endow with sense-perceptible qualities. They let the
conceptual content of their moral life be communicated to
them by this being, once again, in perceptible ways—
whether the god appears in a burning bush, or dwells in a
bodily/human form among humans and audibly declares
for their ears what they should and should not do.

[2]   At the highest ethical stage of development of naive realism, the moral commandment (moral idea) is separated
from any entity foreign to oneself and is thought of hypothetically as an absolute power within oneself. What people first understood as the outer voice of God, they now
understand as an independent power in their inner selves,
speaking of this inner voice in a way that equates it with
conscience.

[3]   But, with this, the level of naive consciousness has already been left behind, and we have entered the region
where moral laws become independent norms. They then
no longer have a bearer, but become metaphysical entities
that exist through themselves. They are analogous to the
invisible-visible forces of metaphysical realism, which
does not seek reality by way of human participation in it
through thinking but imagines a hypothetical reality added
onto experience. Extra-human ethical norms always appear as accompaniments to this metaphysical realism.
Such metaphysical realism has to seek the origin of morality in the area of extra-human reality. There are various
possibilities here. If we assume an entity, conceived of as
having no thought of its own and operating under purely
mechanical laws, as must be the case for materialism, then

this entity will also produce out of itself—by purely mechanical necessity—human beings and everything associated with them. The consciousness of freedom can then be only an illusion. For, although I consider myself the creator of my action, what operates within me is the matter of which I am composed and its inner processes. I believe myself to be free, but actually all my actions are merely results of material processes underlying my bodily and spiritual organism. This view holds that we have the feeling of freedom only because we do not know the motives that compel us. "We must. . . emphasize that the feeling of freedom depends upon the absence of externally compelling motives. Our action, like our thinking, is necessitated." [1]

Another possibility is to see a spiritual being as the extra- *[4]* human absolute behind phenomena. We would then also seek the impulse for action in such a spiritual power. We would regard the moral principles in our reason as an expression of this being-in-itself, which has its own particular goals for humanity. To the dualist of this persuasion, moral laws appear to be dictated by the absolute. Human beings through their intelligence need only discover and carry out the decrees of this absolute being. To the dualist, the moral world order appears as the perceptible reflection of a higher order standing behind it. Earthly morality is the manifestation of the extra-human world

---

1. Ziehen, *Leitfaden der physiologischen Psychologie*, First Edition, p. 207f. For the way in which "materialism" is discussed here, and the justification for discussing it in this way, see the "Addition" at the end of this chapter. (Author's note)

order. In this moral order, it is not human beings who are important but the being-in-itself, the extra-human entity. Human beings *have to do* what this being *wills*.

Eduard von Hartmann imagines the being-in-itself as a divinity whose own existence is suffering. He believes that this divine being created the world so that, through the world, it might be released from its infinite suffering. Von Hartmann therefore regards human moral evolution as a process whose purpose it is to redeem the Divinity:

> The world process can be brought toward its goal only through the construction of an ethical world order by reasoning, self-aware individuals. Real existence is the incarnation of divinity; the world process is at the same time both the Passion of the God who has become flesh and the path of redemption of Him who was crucified in the flesh; *morality, however, is cooperation in the shortening of this path of suffering and redemption.* [2]

In this view, human beings do not act because they will it, but *have to* act because it is God's will to be redeemed. Just as materialist dualists make human beings into automata whose actions are merely results of purely mechanical laws, so spiritualist dualists make human beings into slaves to the will of the absolute (because they see the absolute, the being-in-itself, as something spiritual in which human beings do not participate with their conscious experience). Freedom has no place either in materialism or in one-sided spiritualism, nor has it a place

2. Hartmann, *Die Phänomenologie des sittlichen Bewusstseins.*

in metaphysical realism, which infers something extra-human as true reality, but does not experience it.

For one and the same reason, naive and metaphysical [5] realism must both logically deny freedom. Both see in human beings merely executors of principles that have been necessarily imposed upon them. Naive realism kills freedom through subjection to the authority of a perceptible being, to a being thought of as analogous to a percept or, finally, to the abstract inner voice that it *interprets* as conscience. Metaphysical realists, who merely infer something extra-human, cannot acknowledge freedom because they see human beings as determined, mechanically or morally, by a "being-in-itself."

Because it acknowledges the validity of the world of [6] percepts, monism must acknowledge the partial validity of naive realism. Anyone incapable of producing moral ideas through intuition must receive them from others. To the extent that humans receive their ethical principles from without, they are in fact unfree. But monism ascribes equal significance to ideas and to percepts. Ideas, however, can become manifest in human individuals. To the extent that human beings obey impulses from that side, they feel themselves to be free. But monism denies any validity to a merely inferential metaphysics, and therefore also to impulses to action deriving from so-called "beings-in-themselves." According to the monistic view, human beings can act unfreely if they obey perceptible, external compulsion; they can act freely if they only obey themselves. But monism cannot acknowledge an unconscious compulsion lying behind both percepts and concepts. If one person maintains that another's action was *unfree*, then the first must show the thing or person or situation in the perceptible world that occasioned the action. If the assertion is based on causes for action lying outside the world that is real to the senses and the spirit, then monism cannot accept such an assertion.

[7]   In the monistic view, human action is part unfree, part free. We find ourselves *unfree* in the world of percepts and realize within ourselves the *free* spirit.

[8]   For the monist, ethical commandments, which the merely inferential metaphysician must regard as expressions of a higher power, are *human thoughts*. For the monist, the ethical world order is the imprint neither of a purely mechanical natural order nor an extra-human world order. It is entirely the free work of human beings. Humans have to carry out their own will, not that of a being outside them in the world. They realize their own resolves and intentions, not those of some other being. Monism does not see, behind an active human being, the goals of an external world executive who determines human actions according to its will; rather, to the extent that they realize intuitive ideas, human beings pursue only their own, *human* goals. In fact, each individual pursues his or her special goals. For the world of ideas is expressed not in a human community, but only in human individuals. What emerges as the common goal of a human collective is only a result of separate deeds of will by its individual members, usually a few select individuals whom the others obey as authorities. Each of us is meant to be a *free spirit*, just as each rose seed is meant to be a rose.

Therefore, in the realm of truly ethical action, monism [9] is a *freedom philosophy*. As a philosophy of reality, monism rejects metaphysical, unreal restrictions on the free spirit—just as it recognizes the physical and historical (naive realistic) restrictions on the naive person. Because monism does not regard human beings as finished products who reveal their full being at every moment of life, it views as inconsequential the argument over whether a human being as such *is or is not free*. Monism sees an evolving essence in humans and asks whether, on this path of evolution, the stage of the free spirit can be attained.

Monism knows that nature does not release human be- [10] ings from her arms as ready-made free spirits, but leads them to a certain stage. From this, as still unfree beings, they must develop themselves further, to the point where they discover themselves.

Monism understands that a being acting under physical [11] or moral compulsion cannot be truly ethical. It considers the passage through automatic actions (following natural drives and instincts) and the passage through obedient action (following ethical norms) as necessary preliminary stages in morality, but it also understands the possibility of overcoming both transitional stages through the free spirit. Monism liberates a truly moral world view both from the inward fetters of naive ethical maxims and from the outward ethical maxims of speculative metaphysicians. Monism cannot eliminate these naive ethical maxims, just as it cannot eliminate the percept. But it rejects the outward maxims of speculative metaphysicians because it seeks within the world, not outside it, all explanatory principles for the illumination of world phenomena. Just as monism declines even to think of cognitive principles other than human ones (cf. p. 87), it also decisively rejects the thought of ethical maxims other than those applying to human beings. Human morality, like human cognition, is conditioned by human nature. And just as other beings will have a different understanding of cognition, so they will also have a different morality. For the follower of monism, morality is a specifically human quality and *freedom* is the human way of being moral.

Addenda to the new edition (1918)

[1]   1. One difficulty in evaluating what has been presented in the last two chapters is that readers may think they have encountered a contradiction. On the one hand, the discussion mentions the experience of thinking, which is felt to be of universal significance, equally valid for every human consciousness. On the other hand, it is noted that the ideas realized in moral life, which are of the same kind as the ideas worked out in thinking, are expressed in an individual way in each human consciousness. But if we feel compelled to remain at the level of this "contradiction"— if we do not recognize that a piece of the essence of human beings is revealed precisely *in the living contemplation of this actually present contrast*—then we shall be able to see neither the idea of cognition nor that of freedom in their true light. For those who think of its concepts as merely borrowed (abstracted) from the sense world,

and who do not give intuition its full weight, what is claimed here as a reality remains "mere contradiction." For those who understand how ideas are intuitively *experienced* as a kind of self-sufficient essence, it is clear that, *when we cognize* in the world of ideas, we live our way into something that is the same for all human beings; but that, when we borrow intuitions from that world of ideas for our acts of will, we individualize an element of that world *through the same activity* that we develop in the spiritual-conceptual process of cognition as something universally human. What appears as a logical contradiction—the universal formation of cognitive ideas and the individual formation of ethical ideas—becomes, when it is beheld in its reality, a living concept. Here lies something characteristic of the human entity: what can be grasped intuitively in the human being moves back and forth, as in a living pendulum, between universally valid cognition and individual experience of the universal. For those who cannot see one half of the pendulum's movement in its reality, thinking remains a merely subjective human activity; for those who cannot grasp the other, all individual life seems lost in the human activity of thinking. For a thinker of the first kind, cognition is an unintelligible fact; for the other, moral life. Both will contribute inadequate notions of all kinds to the explanation of one or the other, either because they do not actually grasp that thinking can be experienced, or because they misunderstand it as a merely abstracting activity.

2. Materialism is mentioned on pages 164 –65. I am *[2]* well aware that there are thinkers—such as Ziehen,

mentioned above—who do not call themselves materialists at all but who, from the point of view put forward in
this book, must be labeled as such. What matters is not
whether people claim not to be materialists because, for
them, the world is not limited to merely material existence.
Rather, what matters is whether they develop concepts that
are applicable *only* to material existence. Those who say,
"Our action, like our thinking, is determined," express a
concept that applies neither to action nor to existence, but
only to material processes. If they thought through their
concept to the end, they would have to think materialisti-
cally. That they do not do so is merely a result of the inconsistency that so often comes from thinking that is not
carried through to the end. Today, we often hear that science has abandoned nineteenth-century materialism. But
actually this is not true. It is simply that, at present, we often fail to notice that our ideas apply only to material
things. Nowadays, materialism is veiled; in the second half
of the nineteenth century, it showed itself openly. The
veiled materialism of the present is no less intolerant toward a view that grasps the world spiritually than was last
century's admitted materialism. But materialism today deceives many into thinking that they can reject a worldview
involving spirituality because, after all, natural science
"has long since abandoned materialism."

CHAPTER 11

WORLD PURPOSE AND LIFE PURPOSE
(Human Destiny)

Among the many currents in humanity's spiritual life, we [1] may follow up one that may be described as the overcoming of the concept of purpose in areas where it does not belong. *Purposefulness* represents a particular kind of sequence of phenomena. It is only truly real when, in contrast to the relationship of cause and effect in which an earlier event determines a later one, just the opposite happens and a later event has a determining effect upon an earlier one. This only happens with human actions. Human beings perform actions of which they have *previously* made mental pictures, and they allow themselves to be determined in their actions by those mental pictures. With the help of a mental picture, what comes later (the action) has an effect upon what came earlier (the actor). Yet the detour through the mental picture is absolutely necessary for a purposeful chain of events.

In processes that break down into causes and effects, we [2] must distinguish percepts from concepts. The percept of the cause precedes the percept of the effect; if we could not connect them through their corresponding concepts, cause and effect would remain simply side by side in our consciousness. The percept of an effect must always *follow* the percept of a cause. An effect could have a real influence on the cause only through a conceptual factor. For the perceptual factor of an effect simply does not exist before the perceptual factor of the cause. Anyone claiming that a blossom is the purpose of a root—that the former influences the latter—can do so only with regard to the factor in the blossom that can be established by thinking. At the time of the root's origin, the perceptual factor of the blossom does not exist yet. A purposeful connection, however, requires not merely the conceptual, lawful connection of the later with the earlier, but the concept (the law) of the effect must actually influence the cause by a perceptible process. But we can observe a concept's perceptible influence on something else only in the case of human actions. Only there, then, is the concept of purpose applicable. As we have repeatedly noted, naive consciousness, which gives validity only to what is perceptible, seeks to transpose the perceptible even to where only the conceptual can be known. It seeks perceptible connections in perceptible events or, if it does not find them, it *dreams them up*. The concept of purpose appropriate to subjective action is well suited for such dreamed up connections. Naive persons know how they bring about an event, and conclude from this that nature will do the same. They see not only invisible forces but imperceptible, real purposes in the purely conceptual connections of nature. Human beings make their tools for a purpose; naive realists have the creator construct organisms according to the same formula. This false concept of purpose is disappearing from the sciences only very gradually. To this day, it still works quite a bit of mischief in philosophy, where the question is raised as to the extra-worldly purpose of the world, of the extra-human destiny (and consequently also the purpose) of human beings, and so forth.

Monism rejects the concept of purpose in all spheres—   [3]
with the single exception of human action. It looks for laws of nature, but not purposes of nature. *Purposes of nature,* like imperceptible forces (pp.114 ff.), are arbitrary assumptions. From the standpoint of monism, purposes of life, if not set by humans for themselves, are likewise unjustified assumptions. Only what a human being has made purposeful is purposeful, for it is only through the realization of an idea that purposefulness arises. But the idea becomes effective in a realistic sense only in human beings. Therefore human life has only the purpose and direction that human beings give it. To the question: What kind of task do human beings have in life? Monism can answer only: the one that they set for themselves. My mission in the world is not predetermined but, at each moment, it is the one I choose for myself. I do not enter my life's path with fixed marching orders.

Ideas are realized purposefully only through human be-   [4]
ings. It is therefore invalid to speak of the embodiment of ideas through history. From a monistic point of view, such phrases as, "History is the evolution of human beings toward freedom," or "the realization of the moral world order" and so forth, are untenable.

[5]   Advocates of the concept of purpose believe that if they relinquish this concept they must also abandon all order and unity in the world. Here is Robert Hamerling:

As long as there are drives in nature, it is foolish
[6]   to deny *purposes* there. Just as the formation of a limb in the human body is not determined and conditioned by an *idea* of this limb hovering in the air, but by its connection with the greater whole—the body to which the limb belongs—so too the formation of every natural creature, whether plant, animal or human, is not determined and conditioned by an *idea* of it hovering in the air, but by the formative principle of the greater whole of nature, which lives itself out and organizes itself purposefully.[1]

And again, in the same volume:

The theory of purpose claims only that, *despite* the thousand discomforts and distresses of this creaturely life, a high purposefulness and planfulness is unmistakably present in the forms and evolutions of nature—but a planfulness and purposefulness that realizes itself only within natural laws and cannot aim at a sluggard's world in which life would face no death, and growth no decay, with all of the more or less unpleasant, but finally unavoidable interme-
[7]   diate stages. If opponents of the concept of purpose oppose, to the miraculous world of purposefulness that nature reveals to us in all areas, a laboriously

---

1. *Atomistik des Willens*, Vol. 2.

assembled heap of partial or complete, imagined or real *un*-purposefulnesses, I find this just as silly.[2]

What is meant here by "purposefulness"? The coher- [8] ence of percepts into a whole. But since laws (ideas) that we find through our thinking lie at the base of all percepts, the planful coherence of the members of a perceptual whole is precisely the *conceptual* coherence of the members of a *conceptual* whole contained within this perceptual whole. Saying that animals or human beings are not determined by *ideas hovering in the air* is a skewed expression, and the view condemned in this way loses its absurd character as soon as we correct the expression. Of course, animals are not determined by ideas hovering in the air, but animals *are* determined by an inborn idea that makes up their lawful being. Precisely because this idea is not outside the object, but works within it as its essence, there can be no talk of purposefulness. Precisely those who deny that natural creatures are determined from without (whether through an idea hovering in the air or an idea existing *outside* the creature in the mind of a world-creator is, in this context, completely irrelevant) must admit that such natural creatures are not determined purposefully and planfully from without, but causally and lawfully from within. I construct a machine purposefully when I bring its parts into a relationship that they do not have by nature. The purposefulness of the arrangement consists in my having set the operation of the machine, as its idea, at its base. In this way, the machine becomes a

---

2. Ibid.

perceptual object with a corresponding idea. Natural objects are just such entities. Whoever calls a thing purposeful because it is formed according to law might just as well apply the same label to natural objects. But this kind of lawfulness must not be confused with that of subjective human actions. For a *purpose*, it is absolutely necessary that the effective cause be a concept—in fact, the concept of the effect. But nowhere in nature can we establish that concepts are causes. The concept always proves to be merely the conceptual link between a cause and an effect. In nature, causes exist only in the form of percepts.

[9]   Dualism may talk of world purposes and the purposes of nature. Where a lawful linkage of cause and effect communicates itself to our perception, the dualist may assume that we are seeing only a faint copy of a connection in which the absolute world-being has realized its purposes. For monism, any reason to assume the existence of world purposes and purposes of nature falls away, along with the assumption of an absolute world-being that cannot be experienced but only inferred hypothetically.

Addendum to the new edition (1918)

[1]   No one who has thought through this discussion in an unprejudiced way can conclude that, in rejecting the concept of purpose for extra-human facts, I have placed myself among the thinkers who, by discarding that concept, enable themselves to interpret everything outside human action—and finally that too—as *only* a natural process. This should be clear from my portrayal of the

process of thinking as purely spiritual. If the concept of purpose is rejected here even in relation to the *spiritual* world lying outside human action, it is because in that world something is revealed that is *higher* than the kind of purpose that could be realized in humanity. And if I say that the thought of a purposeful destiny for the human race, conceived on the pattern of human purposefulness, is false, I mean that individual humans set themselves purposes, and the outcome of the total activity of humanity is composed from these. This outcome is then something *higher* than the purposes of individual humans that are its parts.

CHAPTER 12

MORAL IMAGINATION
(Darwinism and Ethics)

[1]   *Free spirits* act out of their impulses—that is, from intuitions chosen by thinking from the totality of their world of ideas. The reason that *unfree* spirits separate particular intuitions from their world of ideas, to make them the basis of an action, lies in what the *perceptual* world has given them—that is, in their previous experiences. Before coming to a decision, unfree spirits remember what someone did, or recommended, or what God commanded in such a case, and so forth. Then they act accordingly. Free spirits have other sources of action than these preconditions. They make absolutely *original* decisions. They worry neither about what others have done in their situation, nor about what they have been commanded to do. Purely conceptual reasons move them to select a particular concept from the sum of their concepts and translate it into action. Their action, however, belongs to perceptible reality. What they perform there will thus be identical to a quite specific perceptual content. The concept will have to realize itself in a concrete, individual

event. But, as a concept, it cannot contain that event. It can relate to it only as any concept relates to a percept—for example, as the concept of "lion" relates to an individual lion.

The link mediating between a concept and a percept is the *mental picture* (cf. p. 100). For an unfree spirit, this link is given in advance—motives are present in advance as mental pictures in consciousness. When unfree spirits want to do something, they do it as they have seen it done, or as they have been told to do in this particular case. Authority, therefore, works best through *examples*, that is, through the transmission of quite specific, individual acts to the consciousness of unfree spirits. A Christian acts less in accordance with the teachings than with the *model* of the Redeemer. With regard to positive action, rules have less value than they do for the restraint of particular actions. Only when they forbid actions, and not when they command them to be done, do laws take on universal conceptual form. Laws concerning what unfree spirits should do must be given to them in quite concrete form: Clean the street in front of your doorway! Pay your taxes at just this rate at tax-office X! and so forth. The laws forbidding actions take the conceptual form: Thou shalt *not* steal! Thou shalt *not* commit adultery! But these laws, too, affect unfree spirits only by their appeal to concrete mental pictures, such as that of the corresponding secular punishment, torments of conscience, eternal damnation, and so forth.

As soon as an impulse to action is present in the form *[2]* of a general concept—for example, thou shalt do good to thy neighbor, or thou shalt live so as best to further thy well-being—then a concrete mental picture of the action (the relation of the concept to a perceptual content) must first be found in each individual case. This translation of concept into mental picture is always necessary for a *free spirit*, who is driven neither by a model nor by fear of punishment.

[3]   Imagination is the chief means by which human beings produce concrete mental pictures from the sum of their ideas. Free spirits need *moral imagination* to realize their ideas and make them effective. Moral imagination is the source of a free spirit's actions. Therefore, only people who have moral imagination are really morally productive. Simple moral preachers—that is, people who spin out codes of ethics without being able to condense them into concrete mental pictures—are morally unproductive. They are like critics who can rationally discuss what works of art should be like, but cannot themselves produce anything at all.

[4]   To turn a mental picture into a reality, moral imagination must set to work in a specific field of percepts. Human action does not create percepts, it recasts already-existing percepts and gives them a new form. To be able to transform a specific perceptual object or group of objects in accordance with a moral mental picture, one must have understood the laws of the perceptual picture to which one wants to give new form or new direction—that is, one must have understood how it has worked until now. Further, one must find the method by which those laws can be transformed. This part of moral efficacy depends on knowledge of the phenomenal world with which

one is dealing. This knowledge must therefore be sought in a branch of general scientific knowledge. Hence, along with the faculty[1] for moral ideas and imagination, moral action presupposes the capacity to transform the world of percepts without interrupting its coherence in natural law.

The capacity to transform the world of percepts is *moral technique*. It is learnable in the sense that any knowledge is learnable. Generally, people are better equipped to find concepts for the world that is already finished than to determine productively, out of their imagination, future, not-yet-existent actions. Therefore, those without moral imagination may well receive the moral mental pictures of other people and skillfully work them into reality. The reverse can also occur: people with moral imagination can lack technical skill and may have to make use of others to realize their mental pictures.

Insofar as knowledge of the objects within our field of action is necessary for moral action, our actions are based upon this kind of knowledge. What is relevant here are *natural laws*. We are dealing with natural science, not with ethics. *[5]*

Moral imagination and the moral capacity for ideas can become objects of knowledge only *after* an individual has produced them. By then, they no longer regulate life; they *[6]*

---

1. Only a superficial view could see, in the use of the word "faculty" here and in other passages, a return to an older psychology's teaching of soul faculties. Connecting it with what was said on pp. 88–89 ff. yields the exact meaning of the word. (Author's note)

have already regulated it. They can be regarded as effective causes like any others—they are purposes only for the subject. Hence, we deal with them as with a *natural history of moral ideas.*

[7]   Apart from this, there can be no science of ethical norms.

[8]   Some people have tried to retain the normative character of moral laws—at least, to the extent that they have understood ethics as if it were analogous to dietetics. Dietetics derives general rules from the organism's requirements for life, so as then to affect the body on the basis of these rules.[2] But the comparison between ethics and dietetics is false because our moral life cannot be compared with the life of the organism. The organism's activity exists without any contribution on our part. We find its laws already present in the world. Hence we can seek the laws and apply those that we have found. But moral laws are first created by us. Before they are created, we cannot apply them. The error arises because moral laws are not created at each moment with a new content, but are inherited. Thus moral laws, inherited from one's ancestors, appear to be given, like the natural laws of the organism. But they are in no way applied by a later generation with the same legitimacy as the rules of diet. For moral laws deal with the individual and not, like natural law,

---

2. Cf. Paulsen, *System der Ethik* [*System of Ethics*](1889). Friedrich Paulsen (1846–1908) was a German philosopher, educator, and professor, who elaborated a theory of "panpsychism" and wrote on Kant and the history of German education.

with an example of a species. I, as an organism, am just such an example of a species; I will live according to nature if I apply the natural laws of the species to my particular case. But, as a moral being, I am an individual and have laws of my very own.[3]

The view presented here seems to contradict the fundamental teaching of modern natural science known as the *theory of evolution*. But it only *seems* to be so. People understand *evolution* to mean the *real* development, according to natural laws, of what is later from what was earlier. People understand evolution in the organic world to mean that later (more perfect) organic forms are real descendants of earlier (more imperfect) forms and developed from them according to natural laws. Adherents of the theory of organic evolution must actually imagine that there was once a time on earth when a being—if it were present as an observer endowed with a sufficiently long life-span—could have followed with its own eyes the gradual development of reptiles from proto-amniotes. In the same way, evolutionists imagine that a being—if it could have remained in an appropriate spot in the world-ether during that infinitely long time—could have observed the development of the solar system out of the

[9]

---

3. When Paulsen says (*System der Ethik*, p. 15), "Different natural predispositions and life conditions require both a different corporeal diet and a different spiritual-moral diet," he is quite close to the right understanding, yet he misses the decisive point. To the extent that I am an individual, I do not need a diet. Dietetics is the art of bringing the particular example into harmony with general laws. But as an individual I am not an example of a species. (Author's note)

Kant-Laplace primordial nebula. In order to picture things in this way, however, the nature of the proto-amniotes, like the Kant-Laplace primordial nebula, would have to be thought of *differently* than materialists think of them. But that is irrelevant here.

Evolutionists could never claim that, without having ever seen a reptile, they could derive the concept of reptiles, with all of their features, from the concept of proto-amniotes. Nor can the solar system be derived from the concept of the Kant-Laplace primordial nebula, if that concept is understood to be directly determined only by the percept of the primordial nebula. In other words, if they think consistently, evolutionists must assert that later phases of evolution really follow from earlier ones, and that if we have the *concept* of the imperfect *and* that of the perfect given to us, we will be able to see the connection. But on no account can evolutionists affirm that the concept attained from the earlier is sufficient to develop the concept of the later from it. It follows that, while ethicists can certainly see the connection between earlier and later moral concepts, not even a single new moral idea can be drawn forth from earlier ones. As moral beings, individuals produce their own content. For an ethicist, this content is just as much a given as reptiles are a given for the natural scientist. Reptiles developed from proto-amniotes, but natural scientists cannot get the concept of reptiles from out of the concept of proto-amniotes. Later moral ideas develop from earlier ones, but ethicists cannot draw forth the ethical concepts of later cultural epochs from those of earlier epochs.

The confusion arises because as natural scientists we already have the facts before us and afterward investigate them cognitively, while for ethical action we must ourselves first create the facts that we cognize afterward. In the evolutionary process of the ethical world order, we accomplish something that, on a lower level, is accomplished by nature: we alter something perceptible. Thus, initially, the ethical norm cannot be *cognized* like a natural law; rather, it must be created. Only once it is present can it become the object of cognition.

But can we not measure the new against the old? Are not all of us forced to measure what we produce by our moral imagination against received ethical teachings? If we are to be ethically productive, this is as absurd as if we were to measure a new natural form against an old one and say: reptiles are an unjustifiable (pathological) form because they do not match proto-amniotes. *[10]*

Thus, ethical individualism does not contradict a theory of evolution when it is properly understood, but follows directly from it. Haeckel's genealogical tree, running from protozoa to human beings as organic beings, ought to be traceable—without interrupting natural law or breaking the uniformity of evolution—right up to the individual as an ethical being in a specific sense. [4] *[11]*

---

4. Ernst Heinrich Philipp August Haeckel (1834–1919), German biologist and philosopher. The first German advocate of Darwin's theory of evolution, Haeckel formulated the famous dictum, "ontogeny recapitulates phylogeny." Haeckel was the first to draw up a genealogical tree, relating all the various orders of animals, and proposed that all life was a unity, originating in crystals and evolving to humanity.

But nowhere could we derive the *nature* of a subsequent species from the *nature* of an ancestral species. It is true that an individual's ethical ideas evolve from those of his or her predecessors, but it is equally true that individuals are ethically sterile if they lack moral ideas of their own.

[12]   The same ethical individualism that I have developed on the basis of the preceding views could also be derived from the theory of evolution. The final conviction would be the same. Only the path by which it was attained would be different.

[13]   To the theory of evolution, the emergence of completely new ethical ideas from moral imagination is no more amazing than the development of a new animal species from an old one. But, as a monistic worldview, evolutionary theory must reject—in ethics, as in science—every merely inferred, otherworldly (metaphysical) influence that cannot be experienced conceptually. In so doing, it is following the same principle as when it seeks causes of new organic forms without appeal to the interference of an otherworldly being who—by supernatural influence— summons each new species according to a new creative thought. Just as monism cannot employ supernatural creative thoughts to explain living creatures, so likewise it cannot derive the ethical order of the world from causes lying outside the experienceable world. For monism, the moral essence of someone's will is never fully explained

---

. Out of this he formulated a philosophy of *monism*. In the early twentieth century, this monism took a quasi-religious form in Germany and meetings of monists were held throughout the country.

by tracing it back to some continuous supernatural influence on ethical life (divine world rule from without), to a specific temporal revelation (transmission of the ten commandments), or to the appearance of God on earth (Christ). What happens in a human being and to a human being by means of these becomes ethical only if is appropriated in human experience by individuals who make it their own. For monism, ethical processes are products of the world like everything else that exists, and their causes must be sought in the world—that is to say, in human beings, because humans are the bearers of morality.

Thus, ethical individualism becomes the pinnacle of the edifice that Darwin and Haeckel sought to build for natural science. It is spiritualized evolutionary theory, transferred to moral life. *[14]*

Those who narrow-mindedly confine the concept of what is *natural* to an arbitrarily limited region easily reach the point of not being able to find any room there for free individual action. Consistent, systematic evolutionists cannot fall into any such narrow-mindedness. They cannot close the natural path of evolution with the apes, and then give humanity a "supernatural" origin. Evolutionists must seek the spirit, too, in nature, even in the search for natural human ancestors. They cannot stop at human organic processes, finding those alone to be natural. They must also regard the morally free life as a spiritual continuation of organic life. *[15]*

According to their fundamental principles, theorists of evolution can claim only that present ethical behavior follows from other kinds of occurrences in the world. To *[16]*

characterize an action—for instance, to define it as *free*—
must be left to *immediate observation* of the action itself.
After all, evolutionists also claim only that humans
evolved from non-human ancestors. What humans are actually like must be ascertained through observation of human beings themselves. The results of such observation
cannot come into conflict with a properly understood history of evolution. Only the claim that these results were
such as to preclude a natural world order could not be
aligned with the current trend of natural science.[5]

[17]   Ethical individualism has nothing to fear from a natural
science that understands itself: observation shows that
freedom is characteristic of the perfected form of human
action. This freedom must be ascribed to the human will
insofar as the will realizes pure conceptual intuitions. For
these intuitions do not result from necessity working upon
them from without; they are self-sustaining. We feel the
action to be *free w*hen we find that it is the *image* of such
an ideal intuition. The freedom of an action lies in this
characteristic.

[18]   From this standpoint, what can be said about the dis-
tinction made in Chapter One between the two sentences
"To be free means to be able to *do* what one wills" and
"The real meaning of the dogma of free will is to be able

---

5. It is quite proper that we speak of thoughts (ethical ideas) as
objects of observation. For even if the products of thinking do not
enter into consciousness during thought-activity, they can still
become the object of observation afterward. It is in this way that we
have been able to characterize human action. (Author's note)

to desire or not desire as one pleases"? Hamerling based his view of free will precisely on this distinction, describing the first of these as correct and the second as an absurd tautology. He says, "I can *do* what I will. But to say that I can will what I will is an empty tautology." Whether I do—transform into reality—what I will—that is, what I have intended as the idea of my action—depends on outer circumstances and on my technical skill (cf. p.182). To be free means: to be able—on my own, through moral imagination—to determine the mental pictures (motives) underlying an action. Freedom is impossible if something outside myself (whether a mechanical process or a merely inferred, otherworldly God) determines my moral mental pictures. Therefore, I am free only when *I* produce these mental pictures myself, not merely when I *can* carry out motives that another has placed within me. Free beings are those who can *will* what they themselves hold to be right. Those who do something other than what they want must be driven to it through motives that do not lie within them. They are acting unfreely. To choose to will or want what I consider right or not right therefore means to choose to be free or unfree. But this, naturally, is just as absurd as to see freedom in the capacity to do what one *has to* will. Yet this is exactly what Hamerling claims when he says that it is perfectly clear that the will is always determined by motives, but it is absurd to say that it is therefore unfree; for we can neither wish for, nor think of, a greater freedom of the will than for it to realize itself according to its own strength and determination.

But we *can* wish for a greater freedom, and only then is it true freedom: namely, to determine for ourselves the motive of our will.

[19]   Under certain circumstances, we can be induced to refrain from what we want to do. To allow ourselves to be told what we *ought to* do, that is, to want what others, and not we ourselves, consider to be right—to this we submit only to the extent that we do not feel *free*.

[20]   Outer forces can prevent me from doing what I will. In that case, they simply condemn me to inaction or to unfreedom. Only if they subjugate my spirit, drive my motives from my head, and replace them with their own— only then do they really intend to make me unfree. This is why the Church is not merely against *actions*, but particularly against *impure thoughts*, the motives for my actions. The Church makes me unfree when it sees as impure all motives it has not itself decreed. A church or any other community creates unfreedom when its priests or teachers turn themselves into keepers of conscience, so that the faithful (in the confessional) *must* take the motives for their actions from them.

Addendum to the new edition (1918)

[1]   This discussion of human will shows what human beings can experience in their actions so that, through this experience, they arrive at the awareness: "My will is free." It is especially significant that the justification for calling a will "free" comes from the experience that a conceptual intuition realizes itself in the will. This *can* result only

from observation; and it *does* so only when human willing observes itself in a stream of development whose aim is precisely to make possible willing carried by purely conceptual intuition. This is achievable because in conceptual intuition nothing but its own self-based essence is at work. Whenever such an intuition is present in human consciousness, it has not developed from the processes of the organism (cf. pp. 135 ff.). Rather, organic activity has withdrawn to make room for conceptual activity. If I observe willing that is the image of an intuition, then all organically necessary activity has withdrawn from that willing. The will is free. Such freedom of will cannot be observed by someone unable to see that free willing consists in the fact that the necessary activity of the human organism is *first* numbed and suppressed by the intuitive element, and then replaced by the spiritual activity of the idea-filled will. Only someone who cannot make *this* observation of the twofold nature of a free act of will believes that *all* willing is unfree. Anyone who can make the observation struggles through to the insight that human beings are unfree to the extent that they cannot complete the process of restraining the organic activity; but that such unfreedom strives toward freedom, which is in no way an abstract ideal, but a guiding power inherent in human nature. Human beings are free to the extent that they can realize, in their willing, the same mood of soul that lives in them when they are conscious of forming purely conceptual (spiritual) intuitions.

CHAPTER 13

THE VALUE OF LIFE
(Pessimism and Optimism)

[1]   A counterpart to the question of life's purpose or vocation
(cf. pp. 173 ff.) is that of life's value. In relation to this
question, we encounter two opposed views, together with
every conceivable attempt at compromise between them.

One view says that this world is the best that could con-
ceivably exist, and that life and action in it are gifts of in-
estimable value. Everything exhibits harmonious and
purposeful cooperation, and everything is worthy of admiration. Even what is apparently bad and evil may be
recognized as good from a higher standpoint: it represents
a beneficial counterpart to what is good. We value the
good all the more for its contrast with evil. Nor is evil
something truly real; we merely sense as evil what is a
lesser degree of good. Evil is the absence of good, not
something significant in itself.

[2]   The other view claims that life is full of trial and tribu-
lation; everywhere unpleasure outweighs pleasure, pain
outweighs joy. Existence is a burden, and in all circumstances non-existence would be preferable to existence.

The main proponents of the first view—optimism—are   [3]
Shaftesbury and Leibniz[1]; of the second view—pessimism—the main proponents are Schopenhauer and Eduard von Hartmann.[2]

Leibniz believes this is the best of all possible worlds.   [4]
A better one is impossible, for God is good and wise. A
good God *wants* to create the best of all worlds; a wise
God *knows* what is best. Such a God can distinguish the
best from all other (worse) possibilities. Only an evil or
unwise God could create a world worse than the best
possible.

Anyone who starts from this viewpoint finds it easy to   [5]
prescribe the direction that human activity must take to
contribute its share to the greatest good of the world. A
human being must only discover the counsels of God
and act accordingly. If we know *what* God intends for
the world and the human race, then we shall also *do* what
is right. And we will gladly add our own good to the
good of the world. From the optimistic standpoint, then,
life is worth living. It must stimulate us to cooperative
participation.

---

1. Anthony Ashely Cooper, third Earl of Shaftesbury (1671–1713),
English philosopher, tutored by Locke and much influenced by the
Cambridge Platonists, wrote *Characteristics of Men, Manners, Opinions Times* (1711) which became a chief source of English deism and
influenced Pope, Coleridge, Kant etc.; Gottfried Wilhelm Leibniz
(1646–1716) German philosopher and mathematician—perhaps the
last "universal" philosopher.
2. See notes p. 11 and p. 71.

[6]   Schopenhauer pictures the matter differently. He thinks of the ground of the universe not as an all-wise and all-good being, but as blind drive or will. The fundamental trait of all willing is eternal striving, ceaseless yearning for satisfaction that can, however, never be attained. For as soon as we attain the goal of our striving, a new need arises, and so on. Satisfaction lasts less than an instant. The whole remaining content of our life is unsatisfied craving—that is, dissatisfaction, suffering. If our blind urge is finally dulled, then we become contentless, and infinite boredom fills our existence. Therefore, the best course is to stifle wishes and needs, to extirpate our wanting. Schopenhauer's pessimism leads to inactivity; his ethical goal is *universal sloth*.

[7]   By a fundamentally different method, von Hartmann tries to found pessimism and then use it for ethics. Following a favored tendency of our time, von Hartmann attempts to found his worldview on *experience*. From *observation* of life, he seeks to discover whether pleasure or pain predominates in the world. Reviewing everything that appears good or fortunate to us in the light of reason, he shows that all supposed contentment proves on closer inspection to be *illusion*. It is illusory to believe that we have sources of happiness and satisfaction in health, youth, freedom, adequate income, love (sexual pleasure), compassion, friendship and family life, self-esteem, honor, fame, power, religious education, pursuit of science and art, hope of life hereafter, or participation in cultural evolution. Soberly considered, every pleasure brings much more evil and suffering into

the world than pleasure. *The displeasure of a hangover is always greater than the pleasure of intoxication.* Pain predominates in the world. No human being, not even the relatively happiest, would, if asked, choose to endure this miserable life a second time. And yet, since von Hartmann does not deny the presence of conceptuality (wisdom) in the world, but rather accords it a validity equal to blind urge (or will), he can attribute the world's creation to his Primordial Being only if he can make the pain of the world serve a wise world-purpose. The pain of the world's creatures, however, is none other than God's pain, for the life of the world as a whole is identical with the life of God. An all-wise being, however, can only have as its goal liberation from suffering and, since all existence is suffering, that means liberation from existence. Thus, the aim of world-creation is to carry being over into the far better state of non-being. The world process is a continual struggle against God's pain and ends finally in the annihilation of all existence. Hence human morality is participation in the annihilation of existence. God created the world to free Himself through the world from His infinite pain. According to von Hartmann, that pain must "be considered in a certain way as an itching rash on the Absolute." Through this itching eruption, the unconscious healing power of the Absolute frees itself from an inner illness; or else we must think of it "as a painful poultice that the all-one Being applies to itself, in order first to draw an inner pain outward and then remove it altogether." Human beings are integral members of the world. God suffers in them. He created them to disperse His infinite pain. The pain that each one of us suffers is only a drop in the infinite ocean of God's pain.[3]

[8]　　Human beings must steep themselves in the awareness that the quest for individual satisfaction (egoism) is foolish. All they need to do is dedicate themselves through selfless devotion to the world process—the redemption of God. Thus, in contrast to Schopenhauer's pessimism, Hartmann's pessimism leads to devoted activity in a lofty task.

[9]　　But what about the claim that this view is based on experience?

[10]　　To strive for satisfaction is to reach, in one's life activity, beyond life's given content. A creature is hungry: that is, when the furtherance of its organic functions requires new life-content in the form of nourishment, it strives to be filled. To strive for honor means to regard one's personal actions and omissions as valuable only when they are recognized from without. The striving for knowledge arises when, before we have understood it, something seems missing from the world we see, hear, and so on. Fulfillment of striving creates pleasure in the striving individual; lack of fulfillment creates pain. It is important to note here that pleasure or pain depend only on the fulfillment or nonfulfillment of striving. Striving itself can in no way count as pain. If it turns out that, in the moment one striving is fulfilled, a new striving immediately appears, I cannot say that, for me, pleasure has given birth

---

3. Cf. Hartmann, *Die Phänomenologie des sittlichen Bewusstseins*, pp. 866 ff. (Author's note)

to pain, because enjoyment always creates a desire for its repetition or for new pleasure. I can speak of pain only when this desire hits up against the impossibility of its fulfillment. Even when an enjoyment that I have experienced creates a longing for a greater or more refined experience of pleasure, I can speak of it as pain created by the earlier pleasure only if I lack the means to experience that greater or more refined pleasure. Only when pain appears as a natural consequence of enjoyment (as when a woman's sexual pleasure is followed by the suffering of childbirth and the cares of child rearing) can I consider enjoyment the creator of pain. If striving by itself evoked pain, then every reduction of striving should be accompanied by pleasure. But the opposite is the case. A lack of striving in our lives produces boredom, which is connected with displeasure. Since striving can, in the nature of things, last a long time before receiving any fulfillment and since, for the moment, it remains content with that hope, it must be acknowledged that pain has nothing to do with striving as such, but depends merely on its non-fulfillment. Schopenhauer, then, is certainly wrong when he holds desire or striving in itself (the will) to be the source of pain.

In reality, it is just the reverse. Striving (desiring), as *[11]* such, brings joy. Who does not know the enjoyment offered by hope of a goal that is distant, but intensely desired? This joy is the companion of work whose fruits will come our way only in the future. Such pleasure is quite independent of attaining our goal. If this goal is finally attained, the pleasure of fulfillment is then added, as something new, to the pleasure of striving. But if anyone claims that the pain of disappointed hope adds to the pain of an unattained goal, and makes the pain of unfulfillment greater in the end than the pleasure there might have been in the fulfillment, we would have to reply that the opposite can also occur. The recollection of pleasure will just as often have a mitigating effect on the pain of unfulfillment. Anyone who cries out, in the face of shattered hopes, "I have done all that I could!" is proof of this. The blissful sense of having tried to do one's best is overlooked by those who, with every unfulfilled desire, assert that not only is the joy of fulfillment absent, but even the enjoyment of desiring itself is destroyed.

[12]   Fulfillment of desire evokes pleasure, and nonfulfillment evokes pain. But we must not conclude from this that pleasure is satisfaction of desire and pain is its nonsatisfaction. Both pleasure and pain can be present in someone without being a consequence of desire. Illness is pain that is not preceded by desire. Anyone claiming that illness is an unsatisfied desire for health errs in seeing the obvious wish not to become sick, a wish that is never brought into awareness, as a positive desire. If we inherit a legacy from a rich relative of whose existence we had no notion, it fills us with a pleasure that had no preceding desire.

[13]   Those who wish to investigate whether there is an excess on the side of pleasure or pain must take into account the pleasure of desiring—the pleasure of the fulfillment of desire—and the pleasure that comes to us without effort. On the other side of the ledger, they must

put the displeasure of boredom, that of unfulfilled striving, and finally, what encounters us apart from our desires. To this column belongs the pain caused by work imposed upon us that we have not chosen for ourselves.

The question now arises: what is the right method for [14] reckoning the *balance* of these credits and debits? Eduard von Hartmann believes that it is reason that weighs them. To be sure, he also says, "Pain and pleasure *exist only* to the extent that they are *felt*." It follows from this that there is no other yardstick for pleasure than the subjective one of feeling. I must *feel* whether the sum of my pleasurable and unpleasurable emotions results in a balance of joy or pain within me. Regardless of this, von Hartmann claims

Though the value of every creature's life can be found only by looking at its own subjective yardstick, this is not to say that every creature calculates the total emotional contents of life *correctly* or, in other words, that *its total estimate* of its own life is correct with regard to its subjective experiences. [4]

Thereby, *rational judgment* about feeling is made once more into the proper evaluator.[5]

Those who adhere more or less exactly to the views of [15] such thinkers as Eduard von Hartmann might believe that,

---

4. *Philosophie des Unbewussten*, 7th Edition Vol. II, p. 290.

5. Anyone who wants to calculate whether the sum total of pleasure or of pain predominates forgets that a calculation is being set up about something that is never experienced. Feeling does not calculate, and for the real evaluation of life what matters is real experience, not the result of an imaginary calculation. (Author's note)

to evaluate life properly, they have to clear away the factors that falsify our *judgment* about the balance of pleasure and pain. There are two ways that they can try to do this.

First, they can show that our desire (drive, will) interferes negatively with a sober evaluation of our feelings. For example, while we ought to realize that sexual enjoyment is a source of troubles, the power of the sexual drive seduces us, promising greater pleasure than it delivers. We want the enjoyment, and so do not admit to ourselves that it makes us suffer.

Second, adherents of this view can submit feelings to a critique and try to demonstrate, in the light of reason, that the objects to which our feelings attach are illusory, and *that they are destroyed as soon as our ever growing intelligence sees through the illusions.*

[16]   In other words, they can consider the question in the following way. If an ambitious man, for instance, wants to know whether pleasure or pain has played the greater part in his life thus far, he must free himself from two sources of error in judgment. Since he is ambitious, this fundamental character trait will make him magnify the joys over the recognition of his achievements and diminish the humiliations caused by his setbacks. But when he actually experienced the setbacks, he felt the humiliations deeply, precisely because he is ambitious. In memory, however, these setbacks appear in a milder light; while the joys of recognition, to which he is so susceptible, engrave themselves all the deeper. Certainly, for the ambitious man, it is a real benefit that this should be so.

Illusion diminishes his displeasure in the moment of self-observation. Yet his judgment is false. The sufferings over which a veil is drawn for him had to be really experienced in all their strength, and so he actually enters them incorrectly on his life's balance sheet. To arrive at a proper judgment, the ambitious man would have to rid himself of his ambition at the moment of contemplation. He would have to review his life with no colored glass before his spiritual eyes. Otherwise, he is like a merchant who enters his own business zeal in the credit column.

Holders of this view can go still further, however. They [17] can say that the ambitious man must also realize that the recognition for which he strives is worthless. Either on his own or with the help of others, he will realize that recognition by others can have no importance for a rational person— after all, we can always be sure that "the majority is wrong and the minority is right in all such matters that are not fundamental questions of evolution or have not already been completely solved by science," so that "whoever makes ambition his guiding star places his happiness in life at the mercy of such a judgment."[6] If the ambitious man can say all this to himself, then he must characterize as illusion what his ambition pictured as reality. And therefore he must also characterize as illusion the feelings that attach to these illusions. On this basis, it may be said that the feelings of pleasure resulting from illusion must also be stricken from the balance. What is left, then, represents the illusion-free sum of pleasure, and this is so

---

6. *Philosophie des Unbewussten*, Vol. II, p. 332.

small in comparison with the sum of pain that life is joy-
less, and nonbeing is preferable to being.

[18]   But, while it is immediately obvious that the interference of ambition deceives us into false calculations concerning pleasure, what has been said about recognizing
the illusory character of pleasure's objects must still be
challenged. It would be an error to remove from the calculation of life's pleasure all feelings of pleasure attached
to real or supposed illusions. For the ambitious man has
really enjoyed the admiration of the masses, regardless of
whether he himself, or someone else, later recognizes this
admiration as illusory. This process does not in the least
diminish the feeling of pleasure that was enjoyed. Elimination of all such "illusory" feelings from life's balance
does not set right our judgment about feelings, but rather
erases from life feelings that were really present.

[19]   And why should those feelings be eliminated? Whoever has these feelings experiences pleasure through
them; whoever has conquered them experiences through
that conquest (not through feeling, in a self-satisfied
way, "What a wonderful person I am!" but through the
objective sources of pleasure that lie within the conquest
itself) a pleasure that is spiritualized, to be sure, but no
less significant. If feelings are struck from the pleasure
column because they attach to objects that turn out to be
illusory, then the value of life is made dependent on not
the quantity but the quality of pleasure, and that, in turn,
is made dependent on the value of the things that cause
the pleasure. However, if I want to determine the value
of life only from the quantity of pleasure or pain, then I

must not presuppose something else by which I first determine the value or valuelessness of the pleasure. If I say, "I want to compare the quantity of pleasure with the quantity of pain to see which is greater," then I must also bring into the calculation all pleasure and pain in their actual amounts, quite apart from whether they are based on illusion or not. Anyone who ascribes less life-value to a pleasure based on illusion than to one that is justifiable by reason is making the value of life dependent on factors other than pleasure.

The person who estimates pleasure at a lower rate because it attaches to a worthless object is like a merchant who enters in his ledger the considerable profits of a toy factory at a quarter of their worth, on the grounds that the factory produces mere playthings for children. [20]

If it is merely a question of weighing the relative quantities of pleasure and pain, then the illusory character of the objects of certain feelings of pleasure should be left completely out of the picture. [21]

With its reasoned consideration of the quantities of pleasure and pain created by life, the path recommended by von Hartmann therefore brings us to this point: we know *how* we are to set up our accounts; we know *what* we have to place on each side of our ledger. But how should the calculation now be made? Is reason, in fact, equipped to reckon the balance? [22]

If the *calculated* profit does not equal a business's demonstrable past profits or future gains, then the merchant has made an error. The philosopher, too, will certainly have made an error of assessment if it is impossible to [23] demonstrate that a cleverly calculated surplus of pleasure or pain is actually felt.

[24]   For the moment, I shall not review the calculations of the pessimists who support their opinions with a rationalist worldview; still, anyone deciding whether or not to carry on with the business of life will first demand to be shown where the calculated surplus of pain is to be found.

[25]   Here we touch the point where reason by itself is *not* in a position to determine the surplus of pleasure or pain, but must rather demonstrate that surplus as a percept in life. For human beings cannot attain reality solely through concepts, but only through the interpenetration, mediated by thinking (cf. pp. 88 ff.), of concepts and percepts (and feelings are percepts). A merchant, likewise, will close his business only if the loss calculated by his accountant is confirmed by the facts. If that does not happen, he will have the accountant calculate again. We conduct the business of life in just the same way. If a philosopher wants to prove that pain is much more common than pleasure, and yet we do not feel this to be so, then we say: you have made a mistake in your brooding; think it through again! But, if, at a given moment, a business really suffers such losses that its credit can no longer satisfy the creditors, then bankruptcy results even if the merchant's bookkeeping obscures the state of his affairs. In the same way, if, at a certain moment, the quantity of a person's pain is so great that no hope (credit) of future pleasure can offer solace, then this must lead to bankruptcy in the business of life.

Yet the number of suicides is still relatively small in [26] proportion to the multitude of those who live bravely on. Only very few people give up the business of life because of the presence of pain. What follows from this? Either it is incorrect to say that the quantity of pain is greater than the quantity of pleasure, or else we simply do not make continuation of life dependent on the quantity of pleasure or pain that we feel.

Eduard von Hartmann's pessimism is unique in ex- [27] plaining life as worthless (because pain predominates), and yet maintaining that we must go through it nonetheless. We must do so because the world purpose mentioned above (p. 197) can be achieved only through ceaseless, devoted human labor. But, as long as human beings still pursue their egotistical desires, they are unsuited to such selfless labor. They can devote themselves to their true task only if they have convinced themselves, through experience and reason, that the pleasures in life striven for by egotism cannot be attained. In this way, the conviction of pessimism is supposed to be a source of selflessness. An education based on pessimism is supposed to eradicate egotism by presenting it with its own hopelessness.

In von Hartmann's view, the striving for pleasure is [28] originally based in human nature. Only insight into the impossibility of fulfillment makes this striving yield to higher tasks for humanity.

But one cannot say that egotism is truly overcome by an [29] ethical worldview that seeks to achieve devotion to non-egotistical life aims by the acceptance of pessimism. Ethical ideals are said to be strong enough to master the will only if a person has seen that a selfish striving for pleasure cannot bring satisfaction. We human beings, whose selfishness has yearned for the grapes of pleasure, find them sour because we cannot reach them. Therefore, we leave them and devote ourselves to a selfless way of life. In the pessimist's view, moral ideals are not strong enough to overcome egotism. Instead, pessimists base their dominion on the ground previously cleared for them by the recognition of the hopelessness of self-seeking.

[30]   If human beings strove for pleasure by nature and were unable to attain it, then annihilation of existence and salvation through non-existence would be the only rational goal. But if we hold that God is the actual bearer of the world's suffering, then human beings have to make it their task to bring about God's salvation. Attainment of that goal is hindered, not furthered, by suicide of the individual. Rationally, God can have created human beings only in order for them to bring about His salvation by their actions. Otherwise, creation would be pointless. And this kind of worldview does think in terms of extra-human goals. Each of us must contribute our specific labor to the universal work of salvation. If we withdraw from this labor through suicide, what we ourselves were meant to do must be undertaken by others who have to bear the torment of existence in our stead. And since God resides in each being as the actual bearer of pain, the suicide does nothing to diminish God's suffering; rather, it imposes on God the new difficulty of creating a substitute.

[31]   All of this presupposes that pleasure is the measure of life's worth. Life is expressed through a number of drives

(needs). If the value of life depended on whether it brought more pleasure or pain, any drive bringing its bearer a surplus of pain would be considered worthless. Let us now look at drives and pleasures to see whether the former can be measured by the latter. To avoid the suspicion that we consider that life begins with "the aristocracy of intellect," we shall begin with a "purely animal" need: hunger.

Hunger arises when our organs can no longer function properly without a new supply of nourishment. What hungry persons strive for first is to satisfy their hunger. As soon as sufficient nourishment has been supplied and hunger ceases, everything striven for by the drive for food has been attained. In this case, the enjoyment that attaches to satisfaction consists initially in the removal of the pain caused by hunger. But an additional need joins itself to the mere drive to satisfy hunger. The person does not want only to bring the disturbed organic functions back into good order through the intake of nourishment, nor simply to overcome the pain of hunger; the person also wants this to be accompanied by pleasant sensations of taste. When we are hungry and half an hour remains before a tasty meal, we might even keep away from less interesting fare that could satisfy our hunger in order to avoid spoiling our pleasure in what is to come. We need hunger to have the full enjoyment of our meal. In this way, hunger becomes the occasion of pleasure for us. If all the hunger in the world could be quieted, it would result in the full measure of enjoyment attributable to the presence of the need for food. But to this we would still

[32]

have to add the special enjoyment at which gourmets aim through an extraordinary cultivation of the palate.

[33]   This kind of enjoyment would have the greatest imaginable value if the need for it never went unsatisfied, and if, along with the enjoyment, we did not have to accept a certain quantity of pain into the bargain.

[34]   Modern science holds that nature produces more life than it can maintain; that is, nature creates more hunger than it is in a position to satisfy. In the struggle for existence, the excess life that is produced must perish painfully. Granted, in each moment, the needs of life are greater than the available means of satisfying them, and therefore the pleasure of life is compromised. Yet this in no way diminishes the pleasure in life that is actually present. Wherever desire finds satisfaction, there is a corresponding quantity of enjoyment—even if there exists, in this creature or others, a huge number of unsatisfied drives. What *is* diminished is the *value* of the enjoyment of life. If only a portion of the needs of a living creature find satisfaction, the creature has a corresponding degree of enjoyment. The smaller the enjoyment is in proportion to the total demands of life in the sphere of the desires in question, the less value that enjoyment will have. We can imagine the value represented by a fraction whose numerator is the enjoyment actually present and whose denominator is the total sum of the needs. When the numerator and the denominator are equal, that is, when all needs are satisfied, then the fraction has a value of one. It becomes greater than one when more pleasure is present in a living creature than its desires demand; it is

smaller if the quantity of enjoyment lags behind the sum of desires. But as long as the numerator (the enjoyment) has even the slightest value, the fraction can never equal *zero*. If, before dying, I were to make a final account, and mentally distribute over my whole life both the quantity of enjoyment related to a particular drive (for example, hunger) and the demands of that drive, then the pleasure experienced might have a very slight value, but it can never be quite valueless. Given a constant quantity of enjoyment, a creature's increased needs diminish the value of the pleasure in life. The same applies to the totality of life in nature. The greater the total number of creatures in relation to the number whose drives are fully satisfied, the lower is the average value of the pleasure in life. Our shares in life's pleasure in the form of instincts fall in value when we cannot hope to cash them in for the full amount. If I have enough to eat for three days and then must go hungry for the next three, the pleasure of those three days of eating is not diminished. But I must then think of it as distributed over the six days, so that its *value* in terms of my food drive is reduced to one half. It is the same with the amount of pleasure in relation to the *degree* of my need. If I have enough hunger for two pieces of buttered bread but I only get one, then the pleasure derived from it has only half of the value that it would have if I had been satisfied by that one piece alone. This is how the *value* of pleasure in life is determined. It is measured against life's needs. Our desires are the yardstick; pleasure is what we measure. The enjoyment of being satisfied has value only because of the existence of hunger. It has value of a specific magnitude depending on its relation to the magnitude of the existing hunger.

[35]   Unfulfilled demands in life cast a shadow even over desires that are satisfied and thus diminish the *value* of pleasurable hours. But we can also speak of the *present value* of a feeling of pleasure. The smaller a pleasure in relation to the duration and the intensity of our desire, the less the present value of a feeling of pleasure will be.

[36]   A quantity of pleasure has full value for us when its duration and degree exactly coincide with our desire. When it is smaller than our desire, the value of a given quantity of pleasure is diminished; when the pleasure is greater, we have an undesired surplus, which is felt as pleasure only for as long as we can heighten our desire during the enjoyment itself. If we are in no position to keep the growth of our desire in step with the increase of pleasure, then pleasure turns into displeasure. The object that would otherwise content us assails us without our wanting it, and we suffer from it. This is one proof that pleasure has value for us only as long as we can measure it against our desire. An excess of pleasant feeling changes into pain. We can observe this especially in persons whose desire for any kind of pleasure is very slight. In persons whose drive for food is stunted, eating quickly leads to nausea. Again, we can see from this that desire is the yardstick for the value of pleasure.

[37]   Pessimists might say that an unsatisfied drive for food brings into the world not merely displeasure because of lost enjoyment, but also positive pain, suffering, and misery. They can appeal here to the nameless misery of

those who are starving, and to the totality of pain arising indirectly, for such people, from lack of food. And, if pessimists want to extend their claim to nonhuman nature as well, they can point to the sufferings of animals who starve at certain times of the year because of lack of nourishment. Pessimists claim that such ills far outweigh the quantity of enjoyment brought into the world by the drive for food.

Doubtless, we can compare *pleasure* and *pain* and determine the surplus of one or the other, just as we can with *profit* and *loss*. But, if pessimists believe that an excess exists in the column of displeasure, and infer the worthlessness of life from that, then they err in making a calculation that is never made in real life. [38]

In a given instance, our desire is oriented toward a specific object. As we have seen, the greater our pleasure is in relation to our desire, the greater is the value of pleasure in satisfying the desire.[7] [39]

But the quantity of pain that we are willing to accept in order to attain the pleasure also depends on the magnitude of our desire. We compare the magnitude of the pain not with the pleasure, but with the magnitude of our desire. Someone who takes great pleasure in eating will, because of enjoyment in better times, be able to sustain a period of hunger better than someone who lacks this joy in eating. A woman who wants children does not compare the pleasure of having one to the quantity of pain in pregnancy,

---

7. We disregard here the case where, due to excessive increase in pleasure, it turns into pain. (Author's note)

childbirth, child rearing, and so forth, but to her desire to have a child.

[40]   We never strive for an abstract pleasure of a certain magnitude but for concrete satisfaction in a very specific way. If we strive for a pleasure that must be satisfied by a specific object or sensation, then we cannot be satisfied by another object or sensation that would offer a pleasure of the same magnitude. For someone who is striving to satisfy hunger, the pleasure in so doing cannot be replaced with an equally pleasurable walk. Only if our desire were for a specific quantity of pleasure *in the abstract* would it disappear as soon as the price of achieving it turned out to be a greater quantity of pain. But, since satisfaction is sought in a specific way, the pleasure of fulfillment arises even if a pain that outweighs the pleasure must also be taken with it. Because the instincts of living creatures move in a specific direction, and aim at a concrete goal, it is impossible to reckon as an equivalent factor the quantities of pain that may obstruct the path to this goal. Provided that the desire is strong enough to be present to some degree after overcoming the pain—however great this may be in absolute terms—the pleasure of satisfaction can still be tasted to its full extent. Thus, desire does not compare pain directly with the attained pleasure; it indirectly compares its own (relative) magnitude with that of the pain. It is not a question of whether the pleasure or the pain involved will be greater, but rather whether the desire for the goal or the hindrance of pain will be greater. If the hindrance is greater than the desire, then the latter bows to the inevitable, weakens, and strives no further.

Since satisfaction is always demanded in a specific way, the pleasure associated with it acquires such a significance that, after satisfaction has occurred, we must take the unavoidable quantity of pain into account only to the extent that it has diminished the quantity of our desire. If I am a passionate devotee of beautiful views, I never calculate how much pleasure I will get from the view from a mountain peak and compare it with the pain of the laborious ascent and descent. I consider only whether, after overcoming these difficulties, my desire for the view will still be sufficiently lively. Only indirectly, through the intensity of the desire, do pleasure and pain together yield a result. The question is never whether pleasure or pain is present in surplus but whether the will for the pleasure is great enough to overcome the pain.

A proof for the correctness of this assertion is the fact *[41]* that we put a higher value on pleasure when it must be purchased at the cost of great pain than when it falls into our lap like a gift from heaven. If pain and torment have diminished our desire, and the goal is nevertheless attained, then the pleasure is that much *greater in proportion* to the remaining quantity of desire. Now, as I have shown (cf. p. 210), it is this proportional relationship that represents the *value* of the pleasure. Further proof is provided by the fact that living creatures (including human beings) express their drives as long as they are in a position to bear the pains and torments that they encounter. The struggle for existence is but a consequence of this fact. Living creatures strive to fulfill themselves; only those whose desires are smothered by the force of the opposing difficulties give up the struggle. Every living creature seeks nourishment until lack of nourishment destroys its life. Human beings, too, only take their own lives if they believe (rightly or wrongly) that the goals of life worth striving for are unattainable. As long as we believe in the possibility of achieving what seems to us to be worth striving for, we will struggle against all torment and pain. Philosophy would have to convince us that wanting makes sense only if the pleasure is greater than the pain; by nature, we want to achieve the objects of our desire if only we can bear the necessary pain, however great it might be. But such philosophy would be in error, because it makes human will dependent on a circumstance (surplus of pleasure over pain) that is originally foreign to us. The original measure of our will is desire, and desire asserts itself as long as it can.

The calculation of the pleasure and pain of satisfying a desire that is set up by *life*—not by rational philosophy—can be looked at in the following way. Suppose that, when buying a certain quantity of apples, I am obliged to take twice as many bad apples as good ones, because the seller wants to unload his merchandise. If the value I place on the smaller quantity of good apples is so high that, in addition to the purchase price, I am willing to assume the cost of disposing of the bad apples, then I will not hesitate for a moment to take the bad apples. This example illustrates the relationship between the quantities of pleasure and pain coming from any of our drives. I determine the value of the good apples not by subtracting their number from that of the bad ones, but by seeing whether, despite the presence of the bad ones, the good ones still retain *some* value.

Just as I disregard the bad apples when I enjoy the good ones, so I give myself up to the satisfaction of a desire after having shaken off the unavoidable suffering. [42]

Even if pessimism were correct in its claim that there is more pain than pleasure in the world, this would have no influence on our willing, for living creatures would still strive after whatever pleasure remains. Empirical proof that pain outweighs joy (if it could be given) would indeed demonstrate the fruitlessness of the philosophical position that sees the value of life in a surplus of pleasure (*eudemonism*), but it could not demonstrate that our will is itself unreasonable; for our will aims not at a surplus of pleasure, but at the quantity of pleasure that remains after the pain has been endured. This always appears as a goal worth striving for. [43]

Attempts have been made to refute pessimism by asserting that it is impossible to calculate the surplus of pleasure or pain in the world. Calculation is possible only if we can compare the magnitudes of the elements of the calculation. Every pain or pleasure has a specific magnitude (intensity and duration). We can even compare the approximate magnitudes of different kinds of pleasurable sensation. We know whether a good cigar or a good joke gives us more pleasure. There can be no objection to comparing different kinds of pleasure and pain with regard to their magnitudes. Researchers who make it their business to determine the surplus of pleasure or pain in the world proceed from thoroughly justifiable premises. We may assert [44] the incorrectness of pessimistic conclusions, but we may question neither the possibility of a scientific estimation of the quantities of pleasure and pain, nor therefore the determination of the balance of pleasure. Yet it is wrong to claim that the results of such calculation have some bearing on human volition. We really evaluate our actions according to whether pleasure or pain predominates only when we are indifferent to the objects of our activity. If it is a matter merely of deciding between enjoying a game or a light conversation after a day's work, and I am indifferent as to which of the two I choose, then I shall ask myself which brings me the greater surplus of pleasure. I shall certainly abandon an activity if the scale dips toward the side of pain. When we buy a toy for a child, our choice depends on what we think will give the most pleasure. In all other circumstances, however, we do not base our decisions exclusively on the balance of pleasure.

[45]   If pessimistic ethicists believe that, by proving that pain exceeds pleasure, they are paving the way for selfless devotion to the work of culture, they are not taking into account that human will, by its very nature, is not influenced by this knowledge. Human striving is governed by the quantity of possible satisfaction after all difficulties have been overcome. Hope of such satisfaction is the basis of all human activity. The work of each individual and the whole work of culture springs from this hope. Pessimistic ethics believes it must present the human pursuit of happiness as impossible, so that people will devote themselves to the proper ethical tasks. But these ethical tasks are nothing other than our actual natural and

spiritual drives, and their satisfaction will be striven for despite the accompanying pain. The pursuit of happiness that pessimism wishes to eliminate is quite nonexistent. We perform the tasks we must because, once we have really recognized their nature, it is in our very nature to *want* to perform them.

Pessimistic ethics asserts that we can devote ourselves to what we recognize as our life's task only once we have abandoned the pursuit of happiness. But no ethics can invent any life tasks other than realizing what human desires demand and fulfilling our ethical ideals. No ethics can take away our pleasure in the fulfillment of our desires. If the pessimist says, "Do not strive for pleasure, you can never attain it, but strive for what you recognize to be your task," the response must be: "But this is how human beings already are." The claim that humans strive merely for happiness is the invention of a philosophy gone astray. We strive for satisfaction of what our essential nature desires, and we have in view the concrete objects of this striving and not some abstract "happiness." Fulfillment of such striving is a pleasure. When pessimistic ethics demands that you strive, not for pleasure, but for what you have recognized as your life's task, it is pointing to what humans by their nature *want*. Human beings do not need to be turned upside down by philosophy; they do not need to throw away their nature in order to be ethical. Morality lies in striving for a goal recognized as just; and it is human nature to pursue the goal as long as the pain involved does not cripple the desire for it. This is the nature of all real willing. Ethics is not based on the extirpation of all striving for pleasure so that bloodless, abstract ideas can assert their dominance unchallenged by a strong yearning for enjoyment in life. Ethics is based on *strong will*, borne by conceptual intuitions, that attains its goal even if the path is thorny.

[46]   Ethical ideas spring from human moral imagination. Their realization depends upon their being desired strongly enough to overcome pain and suffering. Ethical ideals are *human* intuitions, the driving forces that our own spirit harnesses. We *want* them because their realization is our highest pleasure. We do not need ethics to forbid us to strive for pleasure and then tell us what we *should* strive for. We shall strive for ethical ideals if our moral imagination is active enough to endow us with intuitions that give our willing the strength to make its way against the obstacles—including the unavoidable pain—lying within our organization.

[47]   Those who strive toward ideals of sublime greatness do so because such ideals are the content of their being, and to realize them brings an enjoyment compared with which the pleasure that pettiness derives from satisfying everyday drives is trivial. Idealists *revel* spiritually in the transformation of their ideals into reality.

[48]   Whoever would extirpate the pleasure in fulfilling human longing must first make humans into slaves who act *not* because they *want* to, but only because they *ought* to. For the achievement of what we want gives pleasure. What is called "the Good," is not what we *ought* to do, but what we *want* to do when we express our full, true human nature. Those who do not recognize this must first drive

out of us what we want and then must impose *from without* the content we are to give to what we want.

We value the fulfillment of a desire because it springs [49] from our own being. What we have attained has value because it is wanted. If we deny any value to the goal of human willing as such, then we must find valued goals that have value in something that human beings do not want.

The ethics built upon pessimism springs from a neglect [50] of moral imagination. Only those who consider the individual human spirit incapable of providing itself with the content of its striving can see the totality of what we want in the yearning for pleasure. The person without imagination creates no ethical ideas. Such a person must receive these ideas from without. Our physical nature ensures that we strive after satisfaction of our lower desires. But development of th*e whole* human being also includes desire originating in the spirit. Only if we believe that human beings have no such desires can we claim that they must be received from without. We would then be justified in saying that we are duty bound to do something that we do not want. Every ethics that requires us to repress what we want in order to fulfill tasks that we do not want, fails to reckon with the *whole* human being and reckons instead with a human being devoid of the capacity for spiritual desire. For harmoniously developed human beings, so-called ideas of the Good lie not *without* but *within* the circle of their being. Ethical conduct lies not in the elimination of a one-sided self-will but in *full* development of human nature. Anyone who considers ethical ideals attainable only if we kill off our self-will is unaware that such ideals are wanted by human beings just as we want satisfaction of the so-called animal drives.

[51]   There is no denying that the views sketched here may easily be misunderstood. Immature people, with no moral imagination, like to see the instincts of their own half-developed natures as the full content of humanity and dismiss all ethical ideals not of their own making, so that they can "express themselves" undisturbed. It is obvious that what is right for the complete human being does not apply to half-developed human nature. What we would expect of mature human beings cannot also be expected of those who still need to be educated for their ethical nature to pierce the husk of their lower passions. But I have not tried to show here what must be impressed on an unevolved human being, but rather what lies within the nature of a mature human being. The goal was to demonstrate the possibility of freedom, and freedom does not appear in acts based on sensory or psychic constraint, but in acts borne by spiritual intuitions.

[52]   Mature human beings assign themselves their own value. They do not strive for pleasure, handed to them as a gift of grace by nature or by the creator; nor do they fulfill an abstract duty that they recognize as such after having renounced the striving for pleasure. They act as they want to—that is, according to the standard of their ethical intuitions—and they feel their true joy in life to be the achievement of what they want. They determine the value of life by comparing what has been achieved with what was attempted. The ethics that replaces *want* with *should*—that replaces inclination with duty—logically

determines the value of a human being by comparing what duty requires with how he or she fulfilled it. It measures people by a yardstick that lies outside their own being.

The view developed here returns us to ourselves. It recognizes as the true value of life only what we individually regard as such according to the measure of what we want. It knows of no value in life that is not recognized by the individual, just as it knows of no life goal that does not spring from the individual. It sees our own master and our own assessor in the essential individuality of each of us, seen into from all sides.

Addendum to the new edition (1918)

If one clings to the apparent objection that human willing, as such, is irrational and that we must show people this—so that they will see that the goal of ethical striving lies ultimately in liberation from human willing—then what has been presented in this chapter can be misunderstood. Just such an apparent objection was raised to me by a competent critic, who said that it is the business of a philosopher to consider what the thoughtlessness of beasts and most people neglects—namely, to draw up the real balance sheet of life. But whoever raises this objection fails to see the main point. If freedom is to be realized, then the willing within human nature must be sustained by intuitive thinking. At the same time, certainly, willing can be determined by other things than intuitions; yet morality and moral value come about only in the free realization of intuition flowing from the human [1] essence. Ethical indi-vidualism is suited to portray ethics at its full worth, for it does not take the position that there is anything truly ethical in what brings about an outward agreement between our willing and a given norm, but rather in what arises from out of human beings when they develop ethical willing as an element of their full natures. To do something immoral appears to them then as a maiming, a crippling of their essence.

CHAPTER 14

INDIVIDUALITY AND GENUS

The view that human beings are capable of self-enclosed, *[1]* free individuality seems to be contradicted by the fact that, as human beings, we both appear as parts within a natural whole (race, tribe, people, family, male or female gender) and act within that whole (state, church, and so forth). We bear the general characteristics of the community to which we belong and we give to our actions a content that is determined by the place that we occupy within a larger group.

Given all this, is individuality possible at all? If human *[2]* beings grow out of one totality and integrate themselves within another, can we consider separate human beings as wholes unto themselves?

The qualities and the functions of a part are determined *[3]* by the whole. An ethnic group is a whole, and all who belong to it bear the characteristics determined by the nature of the group. How the individual is constituted and how the individual behaves are determined by the character of the group. Thus, the physiognomy and the activity of the individual have a generic quality. If we ask why this or that about a person is this or that way, we must refer back from the individual to the genus. This explains to us why something about the individual appears in the form we observe.

[4]   But human beings free themselves from what is generic. If we experience it properly, what is humanly generic does not limit our freedom, nor should it be made to do so artificially. As human beings, we develop qualities and functions of our own, whose source can only be sought within ourselves. What is generic about us serves only as a medium through which we can express our own distinct being. We use the characteristics nature gives us as a basis, and we give these the form that corresponds to our own being. We look in vain to the laws of the genus for an explanation of that being's actions. We are dealing with an individual, and individuals can be explained only individually. If a human being has achieved such emancipation from the generic, and we still want to explain everything about that person in generic terms, then we have no sense for what is individual.

[5]   It is impossible to understand a human being fully if one bases one's judgment on a generic concept. We are most obstinate in judging according to type when it is a question of a person's sex. Man almost always sees in woman, and woman in man, too much of the general character of the other sex and too little of what is individual. In practical life, this does less harm to men than it does to women. The social position of women is unworthy, for the most part, because it is at many points determined not, as it should be, by the individual characteristics of an individual woman, but by the general mental picture that others

form of the natural duties and needs of the female. The activity of a man in life is determined by his individual capacities and inclinations; that of a woman is supposed to be determined exclusively by the fact that she is, precisely, a woman. Woman is supposed to be a slave of the generic, of what is universally womanish. As long as men debate whether women are suited to this or that profession "according to their natural disposition," the so-called woman question cannot evolve beyond its most elementary stage. What women are capable of according to their nature should be left to women to decide. If it is true that women are suited only to the profession that is currently allotted to them, then they will hardly be able to attain any other on their own. But they must be allowed to decide for themselves what is appropriate to their nature. Anyone who fears a cataclysm in our social conditions if women are accepted not as generic entities but as individuals should be told that social conditions in which one half of humanity leads an existence unworthy of human beings are conditions that stand in great need of improvement.[1]

---

1. As soon as this book appeared (1894), the objection was raised against these comments that, within what is appropriate to their sex, women can already live as individually as they like and much more freely than men, who become de-individualized through school, war and profession. I know that this objection will be raised today (1918) perhaps even more strongly then ever. Still, I must let these sentences stand, and hope that there are readers who understand how completely such an objection runs counter to the concept of freedom developed in this book, and who judge the above sentences of mine by standards other than the de-individualization of men through school and profession. (Author's note)

[6]   Those who judge human beings according to generic characteristics stop before the boundary beyond which people begin to be beings whose activity is based on free self-determination. What lies short of that boundary can, of course, be an object of scientific investigation. Racial, tribal, national, and sexual characteristics form the content of specific sciences. Only persons who want to live merely as examples of a genus can fit themselves into a generic picture derived from such scientific investigation. But all these sciences together cannot penetrate to the specific content of single individuals. Where the region of freedom (in thinking and action) begins, determination of individuals by the laws of the genus comes to an end. The conceptual content that, in order to have full reality, human beings must connect with a percept through thinking (cf. pp.81 –82) cannot be fixed once and for all, and bequeathed in finished form to humanity. Individuals must gain their concepts through their own individual intuitions. How an individual should think cannot be derived from some generic concept. Each individual must set the standard all alone. Nor is it possible to tell, from general human traits, which concrete goals an individual chooses to seek. Anyone who wishes to understand a particular individual must penetrate to that individual's particular being, not remain at the level of typical characteristics. In this sense, every single human being is a separate problem. All science concerned with abstract thoughts and generic concepts is only a preparation for the kind of cognition imparted to us when a human individuality communicates to us its way of viewing the world. And all

such science is only preparatory for the kind of cognition we attain from the content of a human individuality's willing. When we have the sense that we are dealing with the aspect of a person that is free from typical styles of thought and generic desires, then we must make use of no concept from our own mind if we want to understand that person's essence. Cognition consists in linking a concept with a percept through thinking. For all other objects, the observer must penetrate to the concept by means of his or her own intuition. Understanding a free individuality is exclusively a question of bringing over into our own spirit in a pure form (unmixed with our own conceptual content) those concepts by which the individuality determines itself. People who immediately mix their own concepts into any judgment of others can never attain understanding of an individuality. Just as a free individuality frees itself from the characteristics of the genus, cognition must free itself from the approach appropriate to understanding what is generic.

People can be considered free spirits within the human *[7]* community only to the degree that they free themselves from the generic in this way. No human is all genus; none is all individuality. But all human beings gradually free a greater or lesser sphere of their being both from what is generic to animal life and from the controlling decrees of human authorities.

Our remaining part, where we have yet to win such *[8]* freedom, still constitutes an element within the total organism of nature and mind. In this regard, we live as we see others live or as they command. Only the part of our action that springs from our intuitions has moral value in the true sense. And what we have in the way of moral instincts through inheritance of social instincts becomes something ethical through our taking it up into our intuitions. All the moral activity of humanity arises from individual ethical intuitions and their acceptance in human communities. We could also say that the ethical life of humanity is the sum total of what free human individuals have produced through their moral imagination. This is the conclusion reached by monism.

THE CONSEQUENCES OF MONISM

The unitary explanation of the world—the monism por- *[1]*
trayed here—takes the principles needed to explain the
world from human experience. It also looks for the sources
of action in the observable world: that is, in the human nature accessible to our self-cognition, particularly in moral
imagination. Monism refuses to seek the ultimate causes
of the world that appear to our perceiving and thinking by
making abstract inferences about something *outside* that
world. For monism, the unity brought to the manifold multiplicity of percepts through the experience of thinking observation is both what our human urge for cognition
demands, and the means by which this urge for cognition
seeks entry into the physical and spiritual regions of the
universe. Those who seek another unity behind the one
sought in this way merely prove that they do not recognize
the correspondence between what is discovered through
thinking and what is demanded by our drive for knowledge. The single human individual is not, in fact, cut off
from the world. The individual is a part of the world, and

has a real connection with the whole cosmos, which is broken only for our perception. At first, because we do not see the ropes and pulleys by which the fundamental powers of the cosmos turn the wheel of our own lives, we see our individual part as an entity existing by itself. Whoever remains at this standpoint sees a part of the whole as an actually independent entity, as a monad, that somehow receives information about the rest of the world from outside. The monism advocated here shows how such independence will be believed in only as long as thinking does not weave what has been perceived into the network of the conceptual world. Once this happens, the existence of separate parts is unmasked as a mere *illusion of perceiving*. Only through the experience of intuitive thinking can we can find our total, self-contained existence within the universe. Thinking destroys the illusion of perceiving and integrates our individual existence into the life of the cosmos. The unity of the conceptual world, which contains objective percepts, also includes the content of our subjective personality. Thinking gives us the true form of reality, as a unity enclosed within itself, while the multiplicity of percepts is only an illusion conditioned by our organization (cf. pp. 79 ff.). In every age, cognition of the real, as opposed to the illusion of perceiving, has constituted the goal of human thinking. Science has striven to recognize percepts as reality by discovering the lawful connections among them. But wherever it has been believed that the connections transmitted by human thinking have merely subjective significance, the actual ground of unity has been sought in an object set beyond our world of experience (an inferred God, Will, absolute Spirit, etc.). And, based on this opinion, attempts were then made to achieve—in addition to knowledge of connections recognizable through experience—a second kind of knowledge, based not on experience but on metaphysical inference. This kind of knowledge went beyond experience and revealed a connection between experience and entities that are no longer directly available to us. On this basis, then, it was believed that we can understand the coherence of the world through orderly thinking because a primal Being built the world according to logical laws. The reason for our actions was also seen in the will of this Being. Yet it was not recognized that thinking simultaneously encompasses the subjective and the objective, and that full reality is conveyed in the union of percept with concept. Only as long as we regard the laws that permeate and determine percepts in the form of abstract concepts are we dealing with something purely subjective. The content of a concept, joined to a percept by thinking, is not subjective. For the content of this concept is taken not from the subject, but from reality. It is the part of reality that perceiving cannot reach. It is experience, but not experience transmitted by perceiving. Those who cannot imagine that a concept is something real are thinking only of the abstract form in which they hold concepts in their mind. But concepts, like percepts, are present only in this separated form because of our organization. The tree that we see has likewise no separate existence by itself. The tree is only a part in the great system of nature, and is only possible in real connection with nature. An abstract concept, by itself, has just as little reality as a percept by itself. Percepts are the part of reality that is given objectively, concepts are the part that is given subjectively (through intuition, see page 89 ff.). Our mental organization tears reality into these two factors. One factor is apparent to perceiving; the other to intuition. Only the union of the two—the percept integrating itself lawfully into the universe—is full reality. If we consider mere perception alone, we do not have reality, only disconnected chaos; if, on the other hand, we consider only the lawfulness of percepts, we are dealing merely with abstract concepts. Abstract concepts contain no reality. Reality lies in thinking observation that does not one-sidedly examine either concepts or percepts by themselves, but rather considers the union of both.

[2]   Not even the most orthodox subjective idealist denies that we live in reality and are rooted in it by our real existence. Such idealists only deny that our cognition—our ideas—can reach that real life. Monism, in contrast, shows that thinking is neither subjective nor objective, but a principle that spans both sides of reality. When we observe with thinking, we execute a process that itself belongs to the order of real events. Through thinking, we overcome, in experience itself, the one-sidedness of mere perceiving. We cannot piece together the essence of reality with abstract, conceptual hypotheses (purely conceptual reflections); we *live* in reality by finding ideas to match our percepts. Monism does not seek to add anything to experience that is not experienceable (transcendental), but it sees the Real in concepts and percepts.

Monism spins no metaphysics from merely abstract concepts. For, in the concepts by themselves, it recognizes only *one* side of reality, which remains hidden to perceiving and makes sense only in connection with the percept. Monism evokes the conviction in us that we live in the world of reality, and that we need not seek outside our world for a higher reality that we cannot experience. Because it recognizes the content of experience itself as reality, it seeks absolute reality nowhere but in experience. It is satisfied by that reality, because it knows that thinking has the power to guarantee it. What the dualist looks for only behind the observable world, a monist finds within this world itself. Monism shows that, in cognizing, we grasp reality in its true form, not in a subjective picture that interposes itself between ourselves and reality. For monism, the conceptual content of the world is the same for all human individuals (cf. p. 82 ff.). According to monistic principles, one human individual considers another human individual to be of the same kind, because the same world content expresses itself in both. In the unitary world of concepts, there are not, for example, as many concepts of the lion as there are individuals who think about a lion; there is only *one* concept. The concept that A adds to the percept of the lion is the same as that of B, only it is grasped by means of a different perceptual subject (cf. p. 84). Thinking leads all perceptual subjects to the common conceptual unity within all multiplicity. The unitary world of ideas expresses itself in them as in a multiplicity of individuals. As long as we understand ourselves merely through self-perception, we see ourselves as the separate human beings that we are; as soon as we notice the world of ideas that lights up in us, embracing everything separate, we see what is absolutely real light up livingly within us. Dualism fixes on the divine, primordial Being as that which permeates all humans and lives within them all. Monism finds this universal divine life in reality itself. The conceptual content of another human being is also my own conceptual content, and I see the other *as* other only as long as I am perceiving, and not once I am thinking. Each person's thinking embraces only a part of the total world of ideas and, to that extent, individuals also differ through the actual content of their thinking. But the contents exist within a self-enclosed whole that contains the thought contents of all human beings. The universal, primordial Being permeating all humanity thus takes hold of us through our thinking. Life within reality, filled with thought content, is at the same time life in God. The merely inferred, not-to-be-experienced transcendent realm is based on a misunderstanding by those who believe that what is manifest does not bear within itself the reason for its existence. They do not realize that, through thinking, they can find the explanation for perception that they seek. This is why no speculation has ever brought to light a content that was not borrowed from the reality given to us. The God derived through abstract inference is only the human being displaced to the Beyond. Schopenhauer's "Will" is human willpower made absolute. Von Hartmann's "unconscious primordial Being," composed of Idea and Will, is a combination of two abstractions of our experience. Exactly the same can be said of all transcendent principles based on thinking that has not been experienced.

In truth, the human spirit never moves beyond the reality in which we live. Nor does it need to, for everything needed to explain the world lies within it. If philosophers declare themselves content in the end with the derivation of the world from principles borrowed from experience and displaced into a hypothetical Beyond, then such satisfaction should also be possible if the same content is left *here*, where it must be for the kind of thinking that we can experience. Every transcendence beyond this world is only apparent; and the principles transposed outside the world explain the world no better than those lying within it. Nor does thinking that understands itself demand any such transcendence, since it is only within the world, not outside it, that a thought content must seek a perceptual content together with which it can form something real. The objects of imagination, too, are merely contents; they find their justification only in becoming mental pictures that point to a perceptual content. Through that perceptual content, the objects of imagination integrate themselves into reality. A concept supposedly filled with a content, and lying outside the world given to us, is an abstraction and corresponds to no reality. We can think only the *concepts* of reality; to find reality itself, we also need to perceive. For thinking that understands itself, a primordial essence of the world whose content is *invented* is an impossible assumption. Monism does not deny the conceptual. On the contrary, it even regards a perceptual content lacking its conceptual counterpart as falling short of the

[3]

complete reality. Yet it finds nothing in the whole realm of thinking that could require us to step outside of the realm of its experience by denying the objective, spiritual reality of thinking. According to monism, a science that limits itself to describing percepts without penetrating to their conceptual complements is only half complete. But it also sees as incomplete all abstract concepts that find no complement in percepts and that cannot fit into the conceptual network that spans the observable world. Therefore, it recognizes no ideas that refer to something lying objectively beyond our experience and that are supposed to form the content of a merely hypothetical metaphysics. For monism, all such humanly created ideas are abstractions borrowed from experience—an act of borrowing that is simply overlooked by the borrowers.

[4]   Just as little, according to monist principles, can the goals of our actions be taken from an extra-human Beyond. To the extent they are in our thought, they must stem from human intuition. Human beings do not make the purposes of an objective (transcendent) primordial Being their own individual purposes, but follow the purposes given to them by their moral imaginations. A person detaches the idea that realizes itself in an action from the single world of ideas and sets it at the base of his or her will. Thus, our actions express not commands from the Beyond injected into our world, but human intuitions that belong to this world. Monism recognizes no world dictator, who would assign aim and direction to our acts from outside ourselves. Human beings find no such primal source of existence whose advice could be sought to learn

the goals that we must give our actions. We are returned to ourselves. We ourselves must give our actions their content. We seek in vain if we seek directives for our will outside the world in which we live. If we go beyond the satisfaction of natural drives for which Mother Nature has provided, we must seek such directives in our own moral imaginations, unless we find it easier to let ourselves be directed by the moral imagination of others. That is, we must either forego all action or act according to reasons that either we give ourselves from the world of our ideas or others give us from the same source. If we move beyond our sense-bound life of instinct and execution of the commands of other human beings, then we are determined by nothing other than ourselves. We must act out of an impulse that we set ourselves, and that is determined by nothing else. To be sure, this impulse is conceptually determined in the one world of ideas. But, in fact, it can be drawn down from this world and translated into reality only through a human being. It is only within human beings themselves that monism can find a basis for the human translation of ideas into reality. Before an idea can become an action, a human being must first *want* it. Therefore, such wanting has its source in human beings themselves. Human beings are thus the ultimate determinants of their actions. They are free.

Addenda to the new edition (1918)

1. The second part of this book has sought to esta- [1]
blish that freedom is to be found in the reality of human

action. For this, it was necessary to separate out from the whole realm of human actions those aspects about which, from unprejudiced self-observation, one can speak of freedom. These are actions that realize conceptual intuitions. Other actions, when viewed without prejudice, cannot be called free. Yet precisely through unprejudiced self-observation we should consider ourselves well equipped to progress along the path toward ethical intuitions and their realization. But *this* unprejudiced observation of human ethical nature cannot by itself offer a final decision about freedom. For, if intuitive thinking itself sprang from some other entity—if its own essence were not self-sustaining—then the consciousness of freedom flowing from morality would prove to be an illusion. The second part of this book, however, finds natural support in the first. The first presents intuitive thinking as an inner spiritual activity of the human being that is actually experienced. But to understand *this* essence of thinking *experientially*, is equivalent to knowing the *freedom* of intuitive thinking. If one knows that this thinking is free, then one also sees the region of the will to which freedom is attributable. We will consider human acts to be *free* if, on the basis of direct inner encounter, we can ascribe a self-sustaining being to the experience of intuitive thinking. Those who cannot do so will also be unable to find an incontestable path to the acceptance of freedom. The experience emphasized here finds *in consciousness* the intuitive thinking that also has reality beyond consciousness. With this, it discovers freedom to be characteristic of actions flowing from the intuitions of consciousness.

2. The content of this book is built on intuitive thinking *[2]*
that can be experienced purely spiritually, and through
which every percept is placed within reality during the act
of cognition. No more was to be presented than can be
surveyed from an experience of intuitive thinking. But we
must also emphasize what kind of thought formation the
experience of thinking demands. It demands that intuitive
thinking not be denied as a self-sustaining experience
within the process of cognition. It also demands that we
acknowledge its capacity, in conjunction with percepts, to
experience reality, instead of seeking reality only in an inferred world outside experience, in the face of which the
human activity of thinking would be merely subjective.

Here, then, thinking is characterized as the element *[3]*
through which we, as human beings, enter spiritually into
reality (and no one should confuse this world view, based
on the experience of thinking, with a mere rationalism).
But, on the other hand, it follows from the whole spirit of
this portrayal that the element of perception can be considered as real for human cognition only if it is grasped in
thinking. The characterization of something as reality
cannot occur *outside* thinking. Therefore, we should not
assume that sense perception is the only guarantee of reality. We can only *wait for* the percepts that emerge in the
course of our lives. The only question is whether we can,
from the viewpoint of intuitively experienced thinking
alone, *await perception* not only of what is sensory, but
also of what is spiritual? We can indeed wait for this. For
even if, *on one hand*, intuitively experienced thinking is
an active process performed within the human spirit, *on*

the other hand, it is also a spiritual percept grasped with no sensory organ. It is a percept in which the perceiver himself or herself is active; and it is an activity of one's self that is simultaneously perceived. In intuitive thinking, human beings are also transferred into a spiritual world as perceivers. What approaches us in that world as a percept, in the same way as the spiritual world of our own thinking, we recognize as the world of spiritual perception. *This* perceptual world would have the same relation to thinking as does the sensory perceptual world on the side of our senses. As soon as we experience it, the spiritual perceptual world cannot be anything strange to us as human beings, because we already have in intuitive thinking an experience of a purely spiritual character. A number of my later writings discuss such a world of spiritual perception. This book, *Intuitive Thinking as a Spiritual Path: The Philosophy of Freedom* is their philosophical foundation. In this book an attempt is made to show that the experience of thinking, properly understood, is already an experience of spirit. Therefore, it seems to me that whoever can adopt the point of view of this book in earnest will not stop short of entering the world of spiritual perception. To be sure, what is portrayed in my later books cannot be logically derived—inferred—from the contents of this book. But a living grasp of what is meant in this book by intuitive thinking will naturally lead onward to a living entry into the world of spiritual perception.

I

Philosophical objections, raised immediately after the *[1]*
publication of this book, call for the addition of the following brief discussion to this new edition. I can imagine
that there are readers who take an interest in the other contents of this book, but who will regard what follows as a
superfluous, remote, and abstract web of concepts. They
may leave this brief discussion unread. But problems crop
up in a philosophical contemplation of the world that have
their origin more in certain thinkers' prejudices than in the
natural course of human thinking itself. Other issues treat-
ed in this book seem to me to present a task that concerns
every human being who strives for clarity in regard to the
essential nature of human beings and their relationship to
the world. What follows, however, rather involves a problem some treatment of which is called for by certain philosophers in any discussion of the things portrayed in this
book. This is because those philosophers have created for
themselves certain difficulties that do not otherwise exist.
If we bypass such problems completely, some people will

be quick to make accusations of dilettantism and the like. And the opinion would gain ground that I have not sufficiently come to terms with viewpoints I have not discussed in the book itself.

[2]   The problem to which I refer is this: there are thinkers who believe that a special difficulty arises when one seeks to understand how the soul life of another human being can affect one's own (that of the observer). They say, "My conscious world is sealed off within me, just as any another conscious world is sealed off within itself. I cannot see into another person's world of consciousness. How, then, can I come to know that we both inhabit the same world?" Those who hold the worldview that it is possible to infer, from the conscious world, the existence of an unconscious world that can never become conscious, try to solve this difficulty by saying, "The world that I have in my consciousness is the representation in me of a real world that I cannot consciously reach. In this real world, unknown to me, lie the causes of my conscious world. My own real being, of which I have likewise only a representation in my consciousness, also lies there. But this real world also contains the essential being of my fellow human beings. Now, what another person experiences in consciousness corresponds to a reality in that person's essential being which is independent of this consciousness. The person's being is active in a realm that cannot become conscious, the realm of my own necessarily unconscious being. It is through that realm that a representation is created in my consciousness of what is present in a consciousness altogether independent of my

conscious experience." We can see that a hypothetical world, inaccessible to conscious experience, is here added to the world accessible to my consciousness. Otherwise, these philosophers believe, we would be forced to assert that all the external reality I seem to have before me is only the world of my consciousness, and this would lead to the—solipsistic—absurdity that other people also exist only within my consciousness.

This question, which has been created by some recent *[3]* epistemological trends, can be clarified if we attempt to survey the matter from the viewpoint of the spiritually oriented observation described in this book. What, then, do I have before me when I face another person? I look at what is immediately apparent. It is the sensory, bodily appearance of the other person, given to me as a percept, and perhaps also the auditory percept of what the person is saying, and so forth. I do not merely stare at all of this; rather, it sets my thinking activity in motion. By my standing before the other person and thinking, the percept proves to be, to some extent, transparent to the soul. When I grasp the percept through thinking, I am bound to say to myself that it is not at all what it appears to be to the external senses. By what it is directly, the sensory phenomenon reveals something else that it is indirectly. Its presentation before me is, at the same time, its extinguishing as a mere sense phenomenon. But what it manifests during that extinguishing compels me, as a thinking being, to extinguish my own thinking for the period of its activity and to replace it with *its* thinking. I grasp this *other* thinking in my own thinking as an experience, as I do with my own. I have really perceived the thinking of the other person. The immediate percept, extinguishing itself as a sensory appearance, is grasped by my thinking, and this is a process lying completely within my consciousness, which consists in my thinking being replaced by the other thinking. Through the self-extinguishing of the sensory appearance, the separation between the two spheres of consciousness is actually suspended. This is represented in my consciousness in that, in experiencing the content of the other person's consciousness, I experience my own consciousness just as little as I experience it in dreamless sleep. Just as my daytime consciousness is shut out in dreamless sleep, so is the content of my own consciousness when I perceive another person's. The illusion that this is not so persists because, *first*, when perceiving another person, what replaces my own content of consciousness is not unconsciousness (as in sleep) but rather the content of the other person's consciousness; and, *second*, the oscillations between the extinction and re-illumination of my consciousness of myself follow one another too rapidly to be normally noticed. The whole problem cannot be solved by artificial conceptual constructs that infer, from what is conscious, other things that can never be conscious. It must be solved through true experience of what results from a union of thinking and percepts. This applies to many questions that appear in the philosophical literature. Thinkers ought to seek the path to unprejudiced, spiritually-oriented observation, but instead they slide an artificial conceptual construction in front of reality.

In a treatise by Eduard von Hartmann, "Ultimate Ques-   *[4]*
tions in Epistemology and Metaphysics,"[1] my book is
classed with philosophical works based on "epistemological monism." Von Hartmann dismisses this standpoint as
impossible for the following reason.

According to the way of thinking he develops in his
treatise, there are only three possible epistemological positions. We can remain at the naive position that takes perceived phenomena as real things outside human
consciousness. In that case, we lack critical awareness.
We would be unaware that the content of consciousness
is, after all, only in our own consciousness. We would not
see that we are dealing not with a "table-in-itself," but
only with the object of our own consciousness. Whoever
remains at this standpoint, or after reflection returns to it,
is a naive realist. But this point of view is untenable, precisely because it fails to see that consciousness has no ac-
cess to objects outside consciousness.

Alternatively, we can survey the situation and fully acknowledge it. And, in this case, we become transcendental idealists. As such, we have to deny that anything of the
"thing-in-itself" can ever enter human consciousness. But
in this way, if we were sufficiently consistent, we would
be unable to escape absolute illusionism. The world confronting us would transform itself into a mere sum of objects of consciousness; indeed, the objects of our own
consciousness. And we would be compelled, absurdly, to

---

1. "Die letzten Fragen der Erkenntnistheorie und Metaphysik,"
Zeitschrift fuer Philosophie und philosophische Kritik, vol. 108, p. 55.

think of other human beings as also existing only in the content of our own consciousness.

Only the third position of von Hartmann's is supposed to be tenable: transcendental realism. This view assumes that there are "things-in-themselves," but that they cannot become immediate experiences of consciousness. Things-in-themselves cause the objects of consciousness to appear from beyond human consciousness, but in a way that does not enter consciousness. We can arrive at "things-in-themselves" only by inference from the content of our consciousness, which, though only mental pictures, is our only kind of experience.

Von Hartmann claims that an "epistemological monism"—which is how he describes my position—would really have to embrace one of his own three positions. He claims that such a monism fails to do so only because it does not draw the proper conclusions from its premises. He goes on to say:

> If one wants to find out to which epistemological position a supposed epistemological monist belongs, one need only present him with certain questions and compel him to answer them. For, on his own, he will not be inclined to express himself on these points, and he will also try in every way to evade answering direct questions, because every answer nullifies epistemological monism's claim to be a standpoint distinct from the three others.
>
> These questions are as follows: 1. Are things *continuous* or *intermittent* in their existence? If the answer is "continuous," then we are dealing with

some form of naive realism. If the answer is "intermittent," then it is transcendental idealism. But if the answer is that they are continuous on the one hand (as contents of absolute consciousness, or as unconscious mental pictures or as possibilities of perception), and intermittent on the other hand (as contents of limited consciousness), then transcendental realism is established. 2. If three persons are sitting at a table, *how many instances of the table* are present? Whoever answers "one" is a naive realist; whoever answers "three" is a transcendental idealist; but whoever answers "four" is a transcendental realist. Of course, this last example presupposes that we may combine under the common heading "instances of the table" such disparate things as the one table as thing-in-itself, and the three tables as perceptual objects in the three consciousnesses. If this seems to be too great a freedom, he or she will give the answer "one and three" instead of "four." 3. If two persons are alone in a room together, *how many instances of those persons* are present? Whoever answers "two" is a naive realist; whoever answers "four" (namely, an I and an Other in each of the two consciousnesses) is a transcendental idealist; but whoever answers "six" (namely, two persons as things-in-themselves and four persons as objects of mental picturing in the two consciousnesses) is a transcendental realist.

Whoever wanted to prove that epistemological monism is a standpoint different from these three would have to give a different answer to each of these three questions; but I do not know what this could be.[2]

The answers of *Intuitive Thinking as a Spiritual Path: The Philosophy of Freedom* would have to be as follows: 1. Those who grasp only the perceptual contents of things and take it for reality are naive realists. They do not realize that *those perceptual contents* can be considered as persisting only as long as they are observed, and therefore that what is before us must be thought of as intermittent. But, as soon as we are aware that reality is present only in thought-permeated percepts, we arrive at the insight that the perceptual content that appears as *intermittent*, if it is permeated by what is worked through in thinking, reveals itself to be continuous. What we must therefore consider to be continuous is the perceptual content grasped in directly experienced thinking, of which what is only perceived would have to be regarded as intermittent if (as is not the case) it were real. 2. When three people sit at a table, how many instances of the table are present? There is only *one table* present. But *as long as* the three people want to stay with their perceptual images, they have to acknowledge that *these* perceptual images are in no way a reality. As soon as they switch over to the table as grasped in their thinking, the *one reality* of the table reveals itself to them. They are united in that reality with their three contents of consciousness. 3. If two people are alone in a

---

2. Ibid.

room together, how many instances of them are present? There are most certainly not six —not even in the sense of transcendental realists—but only two. Yet initially both have only the unreal perceptual image of themselves as well as of the other person. There are four of these *images*, and through their presence in the two people's thinking, reality is grasped. In this thinking activity, each person reaches beyond his or her own sphere of consciousness; in it, both one's own and the other person's consciousness comes to life. In the moments of its coming to life, the two people are no more enclosed within their own consciousness than they are during sleep. But, at other moments, the consciousness of merging with the other reappears, so that, in the experience of thinking, the consciousness of each person grasps both itself and the other person. I know that a transcendental realist would call this a relapse into naive realism. Yet, as I have already indicated in this book, naive realism retains its validity in the case of thinking that is experienced. Transcendental realists by no means experience the true state of affairs in the cognitive process; they cut themselves off from it by a web of thoughts in which they then become entangled. Nor should the monism appearing in *Intuitive Thinking as a Spiritual Path: The Philosophy of Freedom* be called "epistemological." Rather, if an epithet is wanted, let it be called "monism of thought." All of this was misunderstood by Eduard von Hartmann. He did not engage the specifics of the presentation in my book, but claimed that I had attempted to unite Hegelian universalist panlogism with

Hume's individualistic phenomenalism.[3] In fact, *Intuitive Thinking as a Spiritual Path: The Philosophy of Freedom* has nothing to do with these two standpoints that it is supposedly attempting to unite. (This is also why I could not, for example, enter into a discussion of Johannes Remke's "epistemological monism." The viewpoint of *Intuitive Thinking as a Spiritual Path: The Philosophy of Freedom* is completely different from what von Hartmann and others call epistemological monism.)

---

3. *Zeitschrift fur Philosophie*, vol. 108, p. 71, note.

II

In the following, what stood as a kind of "Preface" to the first edition is reproduced in all essentials. I place it here as an appendix, not because it has anything immediately to do with the book's contents, but because it shows the mood of thought in which I wrote the book twenty-five years ago. Since there is a recurrent idea that I have to suppress some of my earlier writings on account of my later ones on spiritual science, I do not want to omit it altogether.[1]   *[1]*

Our age wants to draw forth *Truth* only from the depths   *[2]*
of the human being. Of Schiller's two well known paths, our present age prefers the second:

> *We both seek truth; you in outer life, I within*
> *In the heart, and thus each is sure to find it.*
> *If the eye is healthy, it meets the Creator without;*
> *If the heart is healthy, it surely mirrors the world*
> *   within.*[2]

---

1. Only the very first introductory sentences of this preface (in the first edition) have been completely omitted; today, they seem to me quite inessential. But what is said in the rest of it seems to me necessary to say even today in spite of—indeed, because of—the natural scientific thinking of our contemporaries. (Author's note)
2. Johann Christoph Friedrich von Schiller (1759–1805) Great German dramatist, aesthetic philosopher, and critic.

[3]   Truth that comes to us from without always bears about
it the stamp of uncertainty. We want to believe only what
appears to each of us inwardly as truth.

Only truth can bring us certainty in the development of
our individual powers. These powers are lamed in anyone
tormented by doubts. In a world of riddles, people cannot
find a goal for their activity.

[4]   We no longer want merely to *believe*; we want to *know*.
Belief demands the recognition of truths that we do not
quite understand. But whatever we do not completely
comprehend goes against the individual element in us that
wants to experience everything in its deepest inner core.
The only *knowing* that satisfies us is the kind that submits
to no outer norm, but springs from the inner life of the
personality.

[5]   Nor do we want the kind of knowing that has become
frozen once and for all in academic rules and preserved in
compendia valid for all time. We consider ourselves justified in proceeding from our closest experiences, our immediate life, and ascending from there to cognition of the
whole universe. We strive for certain knowledge, each of
us in his or her own way.

[6]   Nor should the teaching of science assume a form in
which its recognition is a matter of unconditional compulsion. None of us would give a scientific text the title Fichte
once did: "A Crystal Clear Report to the Greater Public on
the True Nature of the Latest Philosophy. *An Attempt to
Compel Readers to Understand.*"[3] Today, no one should
be *compelled* to understand. We demand neither recognition nor agreement from those who are not driven to a

given opinion by their own particular, individual needs. We do not want to cram knowledge into even an immature human being, a child; rather, we try to develop the child's capacities so that the child no longer needs to be *compelled* to understand, but *wants* to understand.

I am under no illusion as to this characteristic of my [7] time. I know how much automatism, devoid of individuality, prevails. But I am also just as aware that many of my contemporaries seek to orient their lives in the direction that I have suggested here. I would like to dedicate this book to them. It is not supposed to lead to the "only possible" path to truth but to *describe* the path taken by one for whom truth is central.

This text leads first through abstract regions where [8] thought must draw sharp contours so as to arrive at some secure positions. But the reader is also led from arid concepts into concrete life. I am certainly of the opinion that one must also lift oneself into the ethereal realm of concepts if one is to experience every aspect of existence. Someone who knows only how to enjoy use of the senses does not really know the most delicious part of life. Oriental sages have their students first spend years in renunciation and asceticism before they share with them what they know. The West no longer requires pious exercises or asceticism to attain knowledge, but it does demand the good will to remove oneself for a brief

---

3. *Sonnenklarer Bericht an das grössere Publikum über das eigentliche Wesen der neuesten Philosophie. Ein Versuch, die Leser zum Verstehen zu zwingen.* For Fichte, see also notes pp. 23 and 76.

time from the immediate impressions of life and enter the world of pure thought.

[9]   The realms of life are many. For each, specific sciences develop. But life itself is a unity, and the more the sciences busily immerse themselves in separate realms, the farther they move away from seeing the living wholeness of the world. There must be a kind of knowing that seeks, in the separate sciences, the elements that lead human beings back to full life again. A scientific specialist wants to become aware of the world and how it works through his or her insights. In this book, the goal is philosophical: science itself is to become organically alive. The separate sciences are preludes to the science attempted here. A similar relationship obtains in the arts. A composer works on the basis of compositional theory, which is a sum of all that one needs to know before one can compose. In composing, the laws of composition serve life, serve reality. In just the same way, philosophy is an *art*. All real philosophers have been *artists in concepts*. For them, human ideas have become artistic materials and scientific methods have become artistic technique. Thereby, abstract thinking attains concrete, individual life. Ideas become powers of life. Then we not merely know *about* things, but have made knowing into a real, self-governing organism. Our active, real consciousness has lifted itself above mere passive reception of truths.

[10]   How philosophy as an art relates to human *freedom*, what freedom is, and whether we do, or can, participate in it—this is the principal theme of my book. All other scientific discussions are included only because, in the end,

they throw light on these (in my view) most immediate human questions. These pages are meant to offer *a philosophy of freedom.*

If it were not aimed at heightening the *value of exist-* [11] *ence for the human personality*, all science would be nothing but satisfaction of idle curiosity. The sciences attain their true value only by showing the human significance of their results. The ultimate goal of an individual cannot be ennoblement of only a single capacity of the soul. Rather, it must be the development of all the capacities dormant within us. Knowledge has value only through contributing to the *all-around* development of the *whole* of human nature.

Therefore, this book interprets the relationship of sci- [12] ence to life not in the sense that human beings must bow down before the idea and dedicate their forces to its service, but rather in the sense that we take possession of the world of ideas to use them for our *human* goals, which extend beyond those of mere science.

We must be able to confront an *idea* while experiencing [13] it; *otherwise*, we fall into its bondage.

BIBLIOGRAPHY AND FURTHER READING

BY RUDOLF STEINER:

I. Basic Anthroposophical Works

Anthroposophical Leading Thoughts. London: Rudolf Steiner Press, 1973.

Anthroposophy and the Inner Life. Bristol, England: Rudolf Steiner Press, 1994.

Christianity as Mystical Fact. London: Rudolf Steiner Press, 1972.

The Christmas Conference. Hudson, NY: Anthroposophic Press, 1990.

Cosmic Memory. Blauvelt, NY: Garber Communications, 1990.

The Four Mystery Plays. London: Rudolf Steiner Press, 1983.

The Gospel of St. John. Hudson, NY: Anthroposophic Press, 1988.

How To Know Higher Worlds. Hudson, NY: Anthroposophic Press, 1994.

An Outline of Occult Science. Hudson, NY: Anthroposophic Press, 1972.

A Road to Self-Knowledge and *The Threshold of the Spiritual World.* London: Rudolf Steiner Press, 1975.

Rudolf Steiner, An Autobiography. Blauvelt, NY: Garber Communications, 1977.

The Spiritual Guidance of the Individual and Humanity. Hudson, NY: Anthroposophic Press, 1992.

Theosophy. Hudson, NY: Anthroposophic Press, 1994.

II. Philosophy and Epistemology

The Boundaries of Natural Science. Spring Valley, NY: Anthroposophic Press, 1983.

The Case for Anthroposophy. London: Rudolf Steiner Press, 1970.

Goethean Science. Spring Valley, NY: Mercury Press, 1988.

Goethe's World View. Spring Valley, NY: Mercury Press, 1985.

Human and Cosmic Thought. London: Rudolf Steiner Press, 1991.

Individualism in Philosophy. Spring Valley, NY: Mercury Press, 1989.

Mysticism at the Dawn of the Modern Age. Blauvelt, NY: Rudolf Steiner Publications, 1960.

Philosophy and Anthroposophy. Spring Valley, NY: Mercury Press.

The Redemption of Thinking. Spring Valley, NY: Anthroposophic Press, 1983.

The Riddle of Man. Spring Valley, NY: Mercury Press, 1990.

The Riddles of Philosophy. Spring Valley, NY: Anthroposophic Press, 1973.

Truth and Knowledge. Blauvelt, NY: Rudolf Steiner Publications, 1981. Also *Truth and Science.* Spring Valley, NY: Mercury Press, 1993.

III. Anthologies of Rudolf Steiner

McDermott, Robert (ed). *The Essential Steiner.* San Fransisco: HarperSanFrancisco, 1984.

Seddon, Richard (ed). *Understanding the Human Being: Selected Writings of Rudolf Steiner.* Bristol, England: Rudolf Steiner Press, 1993.

BY OTHER AUTHORS

I. Intuitive Thinking, Philosophy, and Epistemology

Barfield, Owen. *Saving the Appearances*. NY: Harcourt Brace & World, n.d.

—*Romanticism Comes of Age*. Middletown, CT: Wesleyan University Press, 1967.

—*What Coleridge Thought*. Middletown, CT: Wesleyan University Press, 1971.

Capel, Evelyn. *Towards Freedom*. London: Temple Lodge Publishing, 1993.

Hiebel, Friedrich. *The Epistles of St. Paul and Rudolf Steiner's Philosophy of Freedom*. Spring Valley, NY: St. George Publications, 1980.

Külhewind, Georg. *Becoming Aware of the Logos*. Hudson, NY: Lindisfarne Press, 1985.

—*From Normal to Healthy*. Hudson, NY: Lindisfarne Press, 1988.

—*The Life of the Soul*. Hudson, NY: Lindisfarne Press, 1990.

—*The Logos-Structure of the World*. Hudson, NY: Lindisfarne Press, 1986.

—*Stages of Consciousness*. Hudson, NY: Lindisfarne Press, 1984.

—*Working with Anthroposophy*. Hudson, NY: Anthroposophic Press, 1992.

Palmer, Otto. *Rudolf Steiner on His Book, "The Philosophy of Freedom."* Spring Valley, NY: Anthroposophic Press, 1975.

Schwarzkopf, Friedemann. *The Metamorphosis of the Given*. New York: Peter Lang Publishing, 1995.

Smit, Jörgen. *How to Transform Thinking, Feeling, and Willing*. Stroud, England: Hawthorn Press, 1989.

Unger, Georg. *Principles of Spiritual Science*. Hudson, NY: Anthroposophic Press, 1976.

Warren, Edward. *Freedom as Spiritual Activity*. London: Temple Lodge, 1994.

II. On Rudolf Steiner and Anthroposophy

Davy, John; Adams, George, and others. *A Man Before Others, Rudolf Steiner Remembered*. Bristol, England: Rudolf Steiner Press, 1993.

Easton, Stewart. *.Man and the World in the Light of Anthroposophy*. Hudson, NY: Anthroposophic Press, 1989.

—*Rudolf Steiner, Herald of a New Epoch*. Hudson, NY: Anthroposophic Press, 1995.

Lissau, Rudi. *Rudolf Steiner: Life, Work, Inner Path and Social Initiatives*. Stroud, England: Hawthorn Press, 1987.

Nesfield-Cookson, Bernard. *Rudolf Steiner's Vision of Love*. Bristol, England: Rudolf Steiner Press, 1994.

Prokoviev, Sergei, *Rudolf Steiner and the Founding of the New Mysteries*. London: Temple Lodge Publishing, 1994.

Samweber, Anna. *Memories of Rudolf Steiner*. London: Rudolf Steiner Press, 1991.

Schmidt, Paul E. *Rudolf Steiner and Initiation*. Spring Valley, NY: Anthroposophic Press, 1981.

Shepherd, A. P. *A Scientist of the Invisible*. Rochester, Vermont: Inner Traditions International, 1983.

Turgeniev, Assya and others. *Reminiscences of Rudolf Steiner*. Ghent, NY: Adonis Press, 1987.

Wachsmuth, Guenther. *The Life and Work of Rudolf Steiner*. Blauvelt, NY: Garber Communications, 1989.

A

absolute (being)
   dualistic relation to, 165-166
   See also authority; divine
      being; God
abstraction, 85-86, 87, 124, 132,
      134
   of concept, 234, 235, 238
   of experience, 237
   See also thinking
action
   criminal action, 152, 153
   effect on of thinking, 16, 52-53
   of free spirit, 5-6, 180, 190,
      195, 222-223, 238
   individuality of, 151-152, 154
   love of, 155
   motive for, 12, 145, 172, 195
   motive power for, 143
   relation of to object, 39
   relation of to thinking, 31, 137
   in relation to consciousness, 5-
      17
   in relation to freedom, 9-11,
      15-16
   self-determination of, 28-29,
      156, 165, 173, 190
   See also causes of action;
      event
ambition
   illusory nature of, 202-204

animal desire
   elevation of, 16-17
   hunger as, 209-214
   obedience to as compulsion,
      12-13, 153, 221-222, 229
   satisfaction of, 141
   See also desire; sexual drive
animals
   as analogy for human action,
      14-15
   ideas within, 177
   suffering of, 213
Archimedes, 42
atom
   as monistic unification, 24-25
   notional world of, 106-107
Atomistics of the Will, 12-13
authority
   operation of, 145-146, 163,
      168, 181, 229
   origin of, 160-161, 225
   See also compulsion; law

B

becoming. *See* evolution
being-in-itself, 165, 166, 167
   See also divine being; God
Berkeley, George, 57-58, 61
   See also eye
body
   as concept, 114

as percept, 71
projection of soul upon, 67
in relation to I-consciousness,
138-139
in relation to thinking, 138
in relation to will, 86-87
self-perception of, 87, 97-98,
184
See also human being;
organization
boredom, 199, 201
brain
materialistic understanding of,
35-36
processes in, 28n1, 36, 65-66,
69, 135-136

C
Cabanis, Pierre-Jean Georges,
36
cause and effect
inductive inference of, 119-
120
in relation to freedom, 9-11,
15-16, 168
in relation to will, 7-9, 130
thing-in-itself as, 61
understanding of, 51, 89, 173-
174
See also action; inductive
inference
change
as affect of percept, 60-61
consistency within, 158-159
perception of, 80
See also evolution
character
in relation to free will, 11
See also personality; self

characterological disposition
discussion of, 140-144, 148
influenced by mental picture
and concepts, 141
motive power of, 144
children, 55, 213-214
Christianity, 181, 189
church authority, 163, 192, 225
and religion, 19-20
See also authority; Christianity
cognition, 3, 23, 118
cognitive concept, 149
dualistic, 109-110, 158
elements of, 68, 128, 170, 229
limits to, 104-125, 107-108,
118
naive understanding of, 112,
115-116
relation of to intuition, 123-
124
as synthesis of percept and
concept, 85, 104, 135
See also knowledge;
perception
cognizing
individual nature of, 107-108
process of, 86-87, 109, 128,
171
in relation to feeling, 129, 132
color
perception of, 36, 56-60, 63-
64, 67, 91, 121
compassion, 142
compulsion
affect of on motives, 13-14
affect of on thinking process,
28
compared to freedom, 153-
154, 156, 167, 169

of ethical commandments,
151-152
morality as, 156
in relation to necessity, 7-9
See also authority; law
concept
affect of within consciousness,
53, 112, 125
compared to idea, 49-50
connection of through
thinking, 35-36, 90, 98,
128
of free human being, 156
moral concept, 150-151
as motive, 144
origin of in thinking, 27, 28,
49, 50, 51, 52, 79-80, 84-85
relation of to mental picture,
100, 101, 119-120, 125, 140,
144, 181, 182
relation of to morality, 144
relation of to object and
process, 28-29, 32, 85
relation of to percept, 81, 87-
88, 90-92, 102, 103, 108-
109, 120, 122-123, 135-136,
143, 157-158, 173-174,
177, 181, 206, 229, 235
See also percept
conceptual process
linking of concepts within, 49-
50, 85, 100
participation of self in, 28,
128, 129
See also motive
conceptual sphere, processes
within, 27-28
conceptual thinking, 143-144
See also thinking

conscience, expression of, 146,
164, 167
consciousness
I-consciousness, 138-139
compared to science, 26
concept and observation
connected within, 52-53, 65,
170
dualistic opposition within,
19, 20, 110, 166
of freedom, 165
mental pictures within, 74-75
as mirror for world, 74-75
naive consciousness, 63, 67,
79, 84, 94, 111-112, 174-
175, 222
in relation to action, 5-17
in relation to motives, 14
in relation to thinking, 43-44,
52, 241
in relation to unconscious, 36
self-consciousness, 52
See also I; naive
consciousness; personality
contemplation, thinking
contemplation, 44
content
created through perception,
105
individual creation of, 186
revelation of through
observation, 31
within experience, 106
within idea, 50
within thinking, 88
world content, 20
See also form
cosmos
unity within, 82, 84, 232

See also unity; world process
creation
  divine motivation for, 166-167
  process of within thinking, 40
  role of human beings in, 44,
    197
  of things, 40, 41
  See also evolution; world
criminal action
  characteristic of, 153
  compared to action, 152
  See also action
critical idealism
  compared to naive realism,
    69-70
  errors of, 69-71, 73-74, 75, 89-
    92
  See also idealism

D
Darwinism
  in relation to moral
    imagination, 180-193
  See also evolution
decisions
  of free spirit, 180
  origination of within self, 14
  See also motives
Descartes, René, 37
desire
  animal desire, 12-13, 16-17,
    141, 153
  in relation to object, 213
  in relation to pain, 18, 200,
    210-215
  in relation to will, 8-9, 202,
    216-218
  See also drive; pleasure;
    will(ing)

dietetics, 184
digestion, 40-41
divine being
  naive understanding of, 113-
    114, 164
  redemption of by human
    beings, 166-167
  See also God
dream
  confused for thinking, 46,
    174-175
  as experienced event, 38
  world as, 75-76, 77
drive(s)
  as motive power, 141, 153,
    196
  in nature, 176, 215-217
  spiritual, 218-219
  See also animal desire
drunkenness, in relation to free
    will, 9, 10
dualism
  compared to monism, 20-22
  origin of within
    consciousness, 19, 20
  reality perceived as, 104-105,
    109, 235, 236
  relation of to cognition, 104,
    105, 106-107
  relation of to nature, 25, 178
  spiritual dualism, 166
  See also monism; separation
Du Bois-Reymond, Emil, 106-
    107
duty
  as antithesis of freedom, 154,
    156, 159-160, 222-223
  ethical duty, 149
  See also compulsion

E
ear
  processes within, 65, 98
  See also sense organs; sound
effect
  concept of, in relation to
    cause, 51
  See also cause and effect
egoism, 145, 198, 207
  See also individuality;
    personality
electric field, 123
  See also forces
  emotion, feeling
ethics
  of action, 154, 220
  of pessimism, 218
  in relation to characterological
    disposition, 140-144, 148
  in relation to freedom, 155,
    163, 168, 169, 240
  in relation to moral
    imagination, 180-193
  See also morality
event
  nature of, 82, 111
  in relation to conceptual
    process, 29, 130
  as series of perceptions, 38
  See also action
evil
  consideration of, 151, 195,
    196-197
  defined, 194
  See also good
evolution
  and human destiny, 173-179
  moral evolution, 146, 149,
    166, 175, 187

  self-development within, 129,
    153, 159
  theory of, 185-188, 190
  thinking as element of, 30, 45,
    79-80
  See also becoming; change
existence
  acknowledged by critical
    idealism, 75
  hypothesis about, 105, 114,
    129-132, 194-195, 197, 208
  thinking in relation to, 37-38,
    84-85
  See also life
experience
  acquisition of, 100-101, 105,
    189, 207
  compared to knowledge, 130,
    131
  compared to thought pictures,
    23
  content of, 41, 106, 133, 171,
    189
  incomplete nature of, 80, 132,
    237
  in knowledge of human
    nature, 1, 154
  observation of, 121, 192-193,
    196-197
  practical experience, 142-143
  relation of to concept and
    percept, 49, 113, 121, 136,
    140
  of thinking, 123-124
  See also action
external world, 85-86, 94, 142
  consciousness as mirror for,
    74-75
  See also world

eye
  as percept, 71
  processes within, 65, 67, 68-
    69, 82, 98, 121
  See also color

F
fact
  percept as, 69
  thinking as, 45
  See also inductive inference;
    truth
faith, 163
feeling
  experience and expression of,
    33, 83, 128, 204
  individualizing force of, 101-
    102, 103, 130-132, 142
  mental picture of, 144-145
  and morality, 144
  non-equivalence of to
    thinking, 32-33, 84
  of pain and suffering, 201-202
  in relation to concept and
    percept, 128-129, 206
  See also love; sensation
Fichte, Johann Gottlieb, 23,
  76n1
forces
  affecting things, 113, 123
  imperceptible, 174-175
form
  in combination with other
    qualities, 58, 59
  corresponding to mental
    picture, 97
  See also content
Franz, Dr. Johann Christoph
  August, 55

free spirit
  actions of, 180-182
  human being as, 156-159, 168,
    192-193, 229
  See also human being
free will
  arguments against, 6-7
  development of, 2, 191
  in relation to character, 11
  See also will(ing)
freedom
  compared to compulsion, 7-9,
    153-154, 170
  denial of, 7-15, 167-168, 191,
    226
  in human nature, 154, 193, 222
  idea of, 135-162
  illusory, 165
  in monism, 163-172
  "philosophy of freedom," 3
  relation of to desire, 8-11
  self-determination for
    achieving, 1, 154, 159, 193,
    222, 239
  See also compulsion; will(ing)

G
Genesis, 34
genus
  and individuality, 225-230
  See also individual; species
ghosts, belief in, 111
goal
  human goals, 168, 217, 221
  linked to percept, 142
  of morality, 141
  of willing, 140-141, 199-200
God, 61, 85, 112, 164, 180, 189,
  195, 208, 233, 236

See also divine being;
supernatural
Goethe, 25
good
ethical principle of, 147
transformation of action into,
151
valuation of, 194, 220-221
See also evil; happiness

H
Haeckel, Ernst Heinrich, 187,
188n4, 189
hallucination, as experienced
event, 38
Hamerling, Robert, 12-13, 176,
191
hand
as percept, 71
See also body
happiness
concrete, 214-215
illusionary, 196, 196-197, 198,
203-204, 208, 218-219
lack of, 200
See also pleasure
Hartmann, Eduard von, 11,
47n6, 63, 66, 73, 120, 139,
142n3, 166, 195-198, 201,
205, 207, 236
heart
in relation to thinking, 16-17
See also feeling
Hegel, 50
heredity
effect of, 113
inheritance of moral law, 184
History of Materialism, 24
human action. *See* action

human being
dual nature of, 20-21, 52, 84,
124, 158, 163
ethical human being, 157, 170
evolutionary role of, 44, 159,
169
as free spirit, 154-159, 169,
222, 225
individuality of, 97-103, 153
relation of to world, 20-21,
93-95, 135
as spiritual, 20-21, 197-198
See also individual; self
human destiny, 173-179
See also evolution
human essence, spiritualist
acknowledgement of, 23
human nature
cognition within, 1, 118
freedom expressed in, 154-
156, 170
thinking and feeling within,
101
will(ing) within, 207, 219-222
See also nature
human organization.
See organization
hunger
as animal need, 209-214
See also animal desire; drive

I
"I"
"I-in-itself," 92, 119
relation of to cognition, 107
relation of to nature, 25, 26,
45-46
relation of to object, 45-46,
75-76

relation of to thinking, 45-46,
47, 138
relation of to world, 19-23, 25-
26, 30, 75-76, 78, 118, 128
subjectivity of, 101
See also consciousness; self
I-consciousness
conditions affecting, 138-139
See also consciousness
idea
moral (ethical) ideas, 147,
167, 168, 170, 175, 183-
184, 234
naive understanding of, 111-
113, 177
origin of in thinking, 23, 49,
50, 170
relation of to concept, 49-50,
128, 176
relation of to motive, 11
relation of to spirit, 23
universality of, 149-150, 154
See also concept; thinking
idealism
affect of on love, 17
as goal of individual, 102
of metaphysical realism, 115,
116
moral idealism, 208
naive idealism, 109-110, 113
of spiritualism, 23, 220
illusion, 76, 78
of perceiving, 232
satisfaction as, 196, 202, 203-
205
Illusion of Free Will, The, 14-15
imagination
contents of, 237
moral imagination, 180-193,

221, 238
in production of mental
pictures, 182-183
Immanuel Kant's Epistemology,
63
immortality, belief in, 111
imperfect, concept of, 186
independent existence
and monism, 232
personal expressions of, 28
See also existence
individual
compared to genus, 224-230
compared to object, 53
subject and object as, 82
subject as, 86
See also genus; human being
individuality
of action, 151
compared to similarity of
mental pictures, 119
compared to universality, 129-
132, 148-149, 153, 155,
156, 226, 232, 235
of concept formation, 83, 100
ethical (moral) individualism,
150, 154, 184-188, 189,
190, 223-225
of feeling, 101-102, 103, 130
and genus, 225-230
human individuality, 97-103,
141, 149, 153-155, 226
of willing, 138-139, 153
See also consciousness;
personality
inductive inference
processes of, 120-121, 124
of underlying causes, 119-120
See also cause and effect

inner world
  designation of, 60
  perceptual world as, 136
  within thinking, 133
  See also world
insight, justification of through
    soul experience, 2
intuition
  conceptual, 91-92, 143-144,
    147, 152, 228
  defined, 88, 136-137
  ideals as, 220
  individuality of, 149-150, 155,
    220, 228, 230, 238
  moral, 148, 149, 193
  relation of to cognition, 123-
    124
  relation of to mental picture,
    99-101, 140
  relation of to thinking, 88-89,
    133-134, 223, 241
  in relation to will, 147, 152

K
Kant, Immanuel, 61-62, 105,
    159-160, 186
knowledge
  acquisition of, 18-26, 84-85,
    87, 94-95, 131, 183-184
  compared to experience, 130-
    131
  and inductive inference, 119-
    120
  limited to mental picture, 63
  of motives, 12
  in relation to feeling, 128-129
  in relation to mental pictures,
    62, 77
  transcendental, 77n2

  See also cognition; meaning;
    understanding
Kreyenbuehl, 143-144

L
Lange, Friedrich Albert, 24
law
  compared to freedom, 160-
    161
  of genus, 228
  moral laws (principles), 145,
    154, 164, 167, 183, 184
  natural law, 117, 175, 176,
    178, 183, 185
  universality of, 181, 232
  See also compulsion; natural
    law
Leibniz, Gottfried Wilhelm, 195
Liebmann, O., 62n5
life
  concrete qualities of, 93, 103,
    216
  factors of, 127-134, 141-144
  moral life, 146, 163, 164, 183-
    184, 189-190
  observed thinking as, 136
  as perceived reality, 128, 132-
    133
  purpose of, 173-179, 196-197
  spiritual life, 19, 33, 35, 124
  value of (pessimism and
    optimism), 194-224
  See also existence;
    individuality; nature
life principle
  permeating organic body, 113
  See also principles
light
  perception of, 64-65, 98

See also color; eye; light
limits
    of cognition, 104-125, 107-
        108, 118
    of knowledge, 63
    of materialism, 21-22, 35-36,
        164-165
    of self-perception, 83, 84, 85,
        101-102, 236
logical process.
    See conceptual process
love
    of action, 151, 155
    compassion as, 142
    experienced in thinking, 133
    as feeling, 142
    mental pictures for, 17
    See also feeling

M
magnetic field, 123
    See also forces
materialism
    expectations of, 35-36, 171-
        172
    limitations of, 20-22, 35-36,
        164-165
    percept as insight into, 74-75
    See also object; things
mathematics, 81
matter
    ancient view of, 111
    dualistic view of, 20, 21
    monistic unification of, 24-25
    See also phenomena; things;
        world
meaning
    sources of, 117
    See also knowledge; truth

memory
    of pleasure, 200
    as process in brain, 28n1
    memory-picture, 92
    See also mental picture
mental picture
    affect of on characterological
        disposition, 140, 183
    as basis for love, 17
    defined, 92-93, 99-100
    experience of within self, 60-
        62, 75-76, 93-94, 103, 141,
        142
    experience of within soul, 66
    as limitation to knowledge, 63
    as motive, 142, 144-145, 173,
        181, 191
    relation of to concept, 100,
        125, 140, 144, 181, 182
    relation of to morality, 144,
        147
    relation of to object, 60-61, 68,
        92, 93, 94
    relation of to percept, 69-70,
        73, 99-100, 140, 181
    similarity of among
        individuals, 119, 183
    world as, 70-71, 74, 77-79, 86,
        92, 93-94
    See also motive; thought
        pictures
metaphysical realism, 114-120,
    132, 136, 164, 167
    See also reality
monism
    compared to dualism, 20-22
    compared to metaphysical
        realism, 116-119
    consequences of, 231-242

creation of through cognition, 104

ethical individualism in, 189

and philosophy, 163-172

and purposefulness, 175

role of feeling in, 129

See also ethics; morality

moral autonomy, 146

moral concept

discussion of, 150-151

See also concept

moral imagination, 180-193, 182, 191, 221, 238

See also imagination

moral laws (principles), 145, 183, 184

in relation to freedom, 154, 164, 167

See also law

moral taste, transformation of, 141-142

moral technique, 183

morality

authoritarian morality, 146

as compulsion, 156, 165-166

free morality, 159-161

human beings as source of, 159-162, 170

moral concept, 149

motive of, 144

motive power of, 141

natural history of, 150

purposes of, 219-220

in relation to characterological disposition, 140-144, 148

See also ethics; good

motion

perception of process of, 99

See also action

motivation

consciousness of, 10-12, 14, 15

See also will(ing)

motive

affect of upon will(ing), 139-140, 144, 149, 165

affect on of compulsion, 13-14

conscious vs. unconscious, 10-12, 14, 15

mental picture as, 142, 144-145, 181

in relation to morality, 144, 146

See also desire; will(ing)

motive power

consideration of for act of will, 139-140

drive as, 141

of morality, 141

Müller, Johannes Peter, 64

mysticism, errors within, 120, 131-132, 133

N

naive consciousness

belief of concerning concepts, 84

belief of concerning ideas, 111-112, 222

belief of concerning object, 63, 67, 79, 94, 174-175

See also consciousness

naive realism

compared to critical idealism, 69-70, 74

compared to illusionism and transcendental realism, 76-77

worldview of, 69-70, 89-90,
94-96, 113-118, 128-130,
132, 164, 167
See also metaphysical realism;
mysticism; reality
natural law, 117, 175, 176, 178,
183, 185
See also law; moral law
natural science, 121, 172,
189, *See also* science;
supernatural
nature
evolutionary force of, 159,
169, 210, 239
examination of for
explanation of facts, 18-19
forms of knowledge of, 39-40
natural laws of, 18-19, 117,
175, 176, 178, 183, 185
in relation to I, 25
See also human nature;
world
necessity
in relation to freedom, 7-9
See also compulsion;
freedom

O
object
creation of, 40, 41, 69
dualistic, 20, 109
effect of on sense organs, 65,
111-112
effect on of thinking, 42
illusory nature of, 75-76, 202
relation of to action, 39
relation of to concept, 28-29
relation of to mental picture,
60-61, 68, 94, 182
relation of to percept, 54, 58-
59, 60, 81
relation of to self, 32, 33-34,
35, 52, 53, 82
relation of to subject, 20, 90-
91, 92, 93, 98, 109, 117
relation of to thinking, 39, 53
separate nature of, 67-68, 78, 89
See also things; world
objectivity
of percept, 70
of will, 86-87
within science, 51
within thinking, 52-53
observation
content of, 53-54
correction of, 55-56
description of, 31
direct vs. indirect, 74
directing to one's activity, 29
of experience, 121
external, 69
internal, 69-70
methods of, 38-39
object of, as percept, 54-55,
59-60, 73
reality revealed through, 104,
190, 196
relation of to concept, 50
relation of to intuition, 88-89
relation of to thinking, 29-32,
36, 49, 51, 53-55, 87, 88-89
of thinking, 31-32, 37, 39, 79,
96, 135-136, 137, 234
Old and New Belief, The, 6
optimism and pessimism, 194-
224
organization
effect of on percept

determination, 59, 61-62, 82, 233-234
relation of to perception, 57, 63, 88, 108-109, 121-122
relation of to thinking, 137-138
relation of to will, 139, 220
requirements of, 30-31
spiritual, 81, 105, 107, 137-139
organs of perception.
See sense organs; specific organs
outer world
demarcation of by senses, 65
designation of, 60
processes of affecting self, 63-64
See also world

P

pain
in relation to pleasure, 196-224
See also suffering
Pascal, Blaise, 40-41
Paulsen, Friedrich, 184n2, 185n3
percept
defined, 54, 58-59, 91-92, 124-125, 127
as "immediate object of sensation", 54
linking of through thinking, 41, 90, 99-100, 120, 128
in monism, 167-168
objective nature of, 70, 89
relation of object to, 81, 99-100, 109

relation of to concept, 81, 87-88, 90-92, 102, 103, 108-109, 122-123, 128, 135-136, 143, 157-158, 173-174, 177, 181, 206, 229, 235
relation of to idea, 178
relation of to mental picture, 69-70, 73, 99, 100, 120, 140
relation of to perceiver, 56, 58, 127
relation of to sense organs, 65, 68-69
subjectivity of, 57, 61, 98, 114, 128-129
world as, 49-72, 83, 88, 168
See also concept; mental picture
perception
as basis for reality, 110-111, 115, 125, 131-132, 232-233
as factor of individuality, 141
function of, in origin of percept, 59, 68-69, 83, 91, 135
illusion of, 232
relation of to thinking, 78-80, 82, 89
See also observation
perceptual image
compared to self-perception, 59
as indicator of reality, 122, 124
relation of to observation, 56-57
subjective nature of, 57
perceptual world, 180
See also world
perfect
concept of, 186
See also good

personality
  consciousness of, 59-60, 75-
    76, 83, 85
  individuality of, 103, 128
  relation of to things, 75
  revelation of, 32, 101, 129
  role of, in observation of
    thinking, 34
  See also character; self
pessimism and optimism, 194-
  224
  selflessness within, 207
phenomena
  relation of to experience, 50-
    51
  role of thinking in, 30, 37, 81
  transcendence of, 19-21, 165,
    170
  See also world
*Phenomenology of Moral
  Consciousness*, 11
philosophy, 60, 216
  and monism, 163-172
  of will (thelism), 131
"philosophy of freedom," 3
physics, 111, 114, 123
physiology, 28, 65
pity, in relation to thinking, 16-
  17
Plato, 111n3
pleasure
  feeling as, 101
  hunger as, 209-213
  knowledge of by I, 46
  relation of to its object, 32,
    141
  relation of to mental picture
    and motive, 140, 144, 199
  relation of to morality, 146

relation of to pain, 196-224
surplus of (eudemonism), 217
valuation of, 211-217
See also feeling; happiness
principles, 30, 43-45
  ideal principles, 110-111
  life principle, 113
  moral (ethical) principles,
    145, 147, 148, 237
  See also idea
*Principles of Physiological
  Psychology*, 28n1
process
  in creation of sensation, 67
  relation of to concept, 28-29,
    32
  relation of to percept, 90
  See also world process
progress of civilization, 146-
  148
punishment, 181
purposefulness
  defined, 177-178
  See also will(ing)

R
rationalist worldview, 206
reality
  cognitive understanding of,
    108
  concepts of, 237-238
  intuitive understanding of, 88-
    89
  in metaphysical realism, 114-
    117
  naive understanding of, 128,
    163, 164
  of percept and object, 85, 109-
    111, 122, 124, 136

revelation of, 94, 100, 101,
    104, 122, 182, 206, 232-233,
    241-242
  of will(ing), 144
  See also metaphysical realism;
    naive realism
reason
  apprehension of concept by,
    82
  obedience to as freedom, 12-
    14, 16
  practical reason, 143, 148
  as "pure" thinking, 143
  in relation to pleasure and
    pain, 205-207
  See also cognition; intuition;
    thinking
red, 65-66, 82, 90, 121
  See also color; light
Rée, Paul, 14-15
religion, 19-20
  See also church authority

S
satisfaction. *See* happiness;
    pleasure
Schelling, Friedrich Wilhelm
    von, 39-40
Schopenhauer, Arthur, 70-71,
    85, 86-87, 195, 196, 198,
    199, 236
science, 1, 30, 91, 105, 112, 121,
    131, 210, 228, 232
  compared to conscious
    experience, 26
  critical idealism view of, 76
  natural science, 121, 172, 189,
    190
  objectivity expected of, 51

purposefulness within, 174
scientific research, tasks of, 20
self
  enrichment of, 60
  mental picture perception
    within, 60-62
  rediscovery of nature within,
    25-26
  refutation of, 93
  relation of to conceptual
    sphere, 27-28
  relation of to other beings, 83,
    98
  relation of to things, 32, 33-34,
    35, 52, 53, 61, 98, 127
  relation of to world, 19, 93, 97,
    98, 127, 131, 231-232
  See also human being; I;
    individual
self-consciousness
  development of, 52, 129, 239
  of self compared to object, 59-
    60, 128
  See also consciousness
self-perception
  affect on of percept, 60, 92
  of body, 87
  compared to perceptual
    images, 59
  compared to self-definition,
    83
  as inner world, 60-61
  limits of, 83, 84, 85, 101, 236
sensations
  compared to feeling, 54-55
  creation of, 67
  experience of, 83, 84
  experienced within soul, 65-
    66, 67, 69

sense energies, 64-65
sense organs
    affect on of object, 65, 67, 68,
        74, 111
    relation of to percept, 68-69,
        117-118, 121, 124
    response of to stimuli, 64-65,
        98
    See also specific organs
sense perceptions
    relation of to material world,
        20-21, 24, 64, 114
    See also perception
sensory world
    spiritualist interpretation of,
        22
    See also world
separation
    conquest of through thinking,
        105, 109, 118, 164, 236
    subjective nature of, 82, 84-
        85, 89, 118
    See also individual; unity
sexual drive
    compared to love, 17
    as compulsion, 156, 202, 226
    See also animal desire
Shaftesbury, Earl of, 195
society
    authority of, 163
    necessity for, 161-162, 218
    See also individual
soul
    effect on of thinking, 16, 132,
        133
    of free being, 156, 193
    naive imagination of, 111,
        112, 113, 118
    perception of life experience

    by, 1-2, 78, 79-80, 124
    sensations experienced within,
        65-68, 74, 111, 193
    thinking, as action of, 45-46
sound
    perception of, 56-57, 58, 60,
        63-64, 90, 98
    See also ear; sense organs
species, 113, 185, 187, 188
    See also genus; individual
Spencer, Herbert, 7, 50-51
Spinoza, Baruch, 7-8
spirit
    awareness of through
        thinking, 16, 136
    dualistic, 20, 21
    human experience of, 20, 237
    monistic, 24-25
    in relation to idea, 23
spiritual beings, belief in, 111
spiritual life
    percept function within, 124
    as search for unity between I
        and world, 19
    thinking as element of, 33, 35
    See also life
spiritual process, in response to
    observation, 50-51
spiritual striving. *See* will(ing)
spiritual world
    human experience occurring
        within, 3, 179
    See also world
spiritualists, 22, 23
stimulus
    proceeding from object, 109
    response to of sense organs,
        64-65, 109
Strauss, David Friedrich, 6

subject
  as individual, 86
  organization of affecting
    percept, 59
  relation of to object, 20, 90-91,
    92, 93, 98, 109, 117
  See also object
subjectivity
  affect of on characterological
    disposition, 140
  defined, 92
  human experience of, 52-53,
    58, 108, 132
  of percept, 57, 61, 98, 128
  in relation to thinking, 54, 171
  See also objectivity
suffering, 196-224
  of God, 166, 197-198, 208
suicide, 207, 216
  See also happiness; life
supernatural, 188-189, 189
  See also natural science

T
tact, transformation of, 141-142
thelism, 131
thing-in-itself
  as cause of action, 61
  concrete nature of, 87, 129
  as philosophical determinate,
    30, 75
  in relation to mental picture,
    73, 75, 76, 94-95
  in relation to subject and
    object, 105, 106-107, 110,
    113, 116
things
  acted upon by outside causes,
    8-9

compared to individuals, 53
explanation and understanding
  of, 89
relation of to self, 19, 101,
  111, 129
relation of to world, 20
self-evident nature of, 38, 111
See also object
thinker
  dualistic thinkers, 105
  as object, 38
  relation of to thinking, 33, 51-
    52, 79, 84, 134, 171
thinking
  as a fact, 45
  "abstract" thinking, 85-86, 87,
    124
  beyond subject and object, 52-
    53
  conceptual thinking, 27, 143-
    144
  contemporary, 6
  dualistic, 20
  effect of on self, 83, 153
  effect of on soul, 16, 45-46
  as element of evolution, 14-
    15, 30, 45, 79-80, 153
  essence of, 33, 35, 47-48, 50,
    83-84, 122, 132, 133, 137-
    138, 240
  experience of, 123-124
  intuitive thinking, 222-224,
    241-242
  linking of subject and object
    by, 29, 89-92, 98-100, 104,
    115-117, 122-123, 128, 130,
    229
  non-equivalence of to feeling,
    32-33

observation of, 31-35, 37, 39, 79, 96, 234
as percept, 55, 78-79, 82, 115
preconscious, 42
"pure," 143, 148
relation of to consciousness, 43-44, 47, 78, 95-96
relation of to intuition, 88-89
relation of to materialism, 21
relation of to observation, 29-32, 36, 54-55, 99
relation of to organization, 137
relation of to percept, 29, 89, 90-91, 92, 98, 99-100
role of in human life, 101, 142
in the service of understanding the world, 27-48
as source of knowledge, 131
unity experienced within, 84-85, 89
as world contemplation, 42-43, 101
See also intuition
thought
expression of, 33, 168
impure thought, 192
process examination of, 35-36, 39
in relation to materialism, 20-23, 111, 133
See also thinking
thought pictures
compared to experience, 23, 93
confused for thinking, 46
See also mental picture
time, function of, in understanding of percept, 80

touch
perception of, 98, 116
See also sense organs
transcendental realism, 76-78
See also naive realism; reality
transformation.
See change; evolution
truth
process for discovering, 95
See also fact

U
unconscious
relation of to consciousness, 36
See also consciousness
understanding
role of observation and thinking in, 29-30
See also cognition; knowledge
understanding of the world, 43
unity
between the I and world, 19
among things, 110, 176
enhanced through thinking, 84-85, 89
of matter and spirit in atom, 24-25
of monism, 21, 231-232
of subject and object, 82
within ideas, 154
See also individual; separation
universal process. See world process
universality, compared to individuality, 129-132

V
Volkelt, Johannes, 63

W
wakefulness, 124
  compared to dream state, 78
  See also dream
warmth
  perception of, 63, 64, 114, 121
  See also sense organs
will(ing)
  determination of, 1, 147, 192-
    193, 197, 215-217
  essence of, 140-141, 152, 153,
    189, 219-220
  expression of, 33, 143, 144,
    198-203
  individuality of, 148, 154
  moral (ethical), 150-151, 189,
    190, 192, 221, 223-224
  and motive, 139-140, 144
  observation and thinking
    within, 29-30
  philosophy of (thelism), 131,
    196
  relation of to body, 86-87
  relation of to intuition, 147,
    152
  relation of to organization, 139
  relation of to thinking, 46, 85,
    130-131, 132
  See also action; free will
wisdom, 197
women
  and childbearing, 213-214
  generic view of, 226-227
world
  as dream, 75-76
  dualistic, 20-21

external, 74-75, 85-86, 94, 142
forces within, 116
as mental picture, 70-71, 74,
  78, 86, 92
naive view of, 116-120
in opposition to I, 19, 25, 127
as percept, 49-72, 83, 88, 168
perceptual world, 180
purpose of, 173-179
in relation to human being, 93-
  95, 135, 169
in relation to materialism, 21-
  22
spiritual, 3, 22-23, 169, 179
thinking contemplation of, 42-
  43, 101, 118
understanding through
  thinking, 27-48, 55
unitary explanation of, 231
"world of appearance," 104
  See also evolution;
    phenomena
*World as Will and Mental
  Picture, The*, 70
world content
  transformation of into thought
    content, 20
world process
  incorrect understanding of,
    129, 131, 197
  participation in through
    thinking, 41, 98, 101, 207,
    236
  self-perception of separation
    from, 82
  See also evolution

Z
Ziehen, Theodor, 28n1, 171

DURING THE LAST TWO DECADES of the nineteenth century the Austrian-born Rudolf Steiner (1861–1925) became a respected and well-published scientific, literary, and philosophical scholar, particularly known for his work on Goethe's scientific writings. After the turn of the century he began to develop his earlier philosophical principles into an approach to methodical research of psychological and spiritual phenomena.

His multifaceted genius has led to innovative and holistic approaches in medicine, science, education (Waldorf schools), special education, philosophy, religion, economics, agriculture (Biodynamic method), architecture, drama, new arts of eurythmy and speech, and other fields. In 1924 he founded the General Anthroposophical Society, which today has branches throughout the world.